CW01190335

LETTERS TO THE EDITOR

LETTERS TO THE EDITOR

1997–2014

Nagindas Khajuria

authorHOUSE

AuthorHouse™ UK Ltd.
1663 Liberty Drive
Bloomington, IN 47403 USA
www.authorhouse.co.uk
Phone: 0800.197.4150

© 2014 Nagindas Khajuria. All rights reserved.

No part of this book may be reproduced, stored in a retrieval system, or transmitted by any means without the written permission of the author.

Published by AuthorHouse 10/08/2014

ISBN: 978-1-4969-9126-3 (sc)
ISBN: 978-1-4969-9130-0 (hc)

Any people depicted in stock imagery provided by Thinkstock are models, and such images are being used for illustrative purposes only. Certain stock imagery © Thinkstock.

This book is printed on acid-free paper.

Because of the dynamic nature of the Internet, any web addresses or links contained in this book may have changed since publication and may no longer be valid. The views expressed in this work are solely those of the author and do not necessarily reflect the views of the publisher, and the publisher hereby disclaims any responsibility for them.

Preface

It is with great pride and joy, and with a little bit of heavy heart, that I write this foreword. My project to compile all my letters to the editor in a formal book and e-book was conceived a considerable time ago—only now it has come to fruition due to the considerable assistance and guidance I have received from M Revathy of V Publishing and Mark Andrews of AuthorHouse UK for which I am ever so grateful.

The tradition of writing letters to the editor have a history as long as the institution of newspapers themselves. Over the decades and centuries these letters have served not only as a place where corrections to published stories are made—these have also served as forums where intellectual debates take place, where participants interested in particular stories have argued passionately about everything ranging from politics, history, religion through to social matters and much else, and even where ideas are put forward for general discussion for the first time.

Even government policy is sometimes derived from views expressed in these letters.

Letters to the editor have also served as places where news are revealed to the world for the first time: witness the instance in mid-1980's where Private Eye published a gossip column about a Conservative cabinet minister having fathered an illegitimate child through his personal assistant, and this was revealed to be true by the personal assistant herself through a "letter to the editor" of The Times newspaper sometime later. There are numerous instances like these but I remember this particular instance since it was one of the first instances where a gossip was revealed to be true through a "letter to the editor".

Sometimes letters to the editor are meant to act as a "lobby group" (witness the instance in early 1980's when a group of prominent economists called on the Conservative government of the time that too much emphasis on monetary policy was not having the desired effect). It is even rumoured that the "Deep Throat" used to pass messages to Bob Woodward and Carl Bernstein (the two Washington Post reporters who exposed the Watergate scandal during the Nixon Administration in the USA) through anonymous comments in the letters to the editor.

The newspaper reading masses write letters to the editor to expose their grievances—some write providing their full details, yet others write using "pseudonyms" whereas others write anonymously.

There is a rich tradition in some parts of the media industry whereby editors blank out names and addresses of people writing to the editor for the sake of protecting them and saving them from future reprisals.

Before the advent of emails, social media and Twitter, letters to the editor served as a forum where contributors who do not know each other personally air their views and thereby contribute to the richness of the intellectual debates taking place on a particular subject. This would not have happened if the editors were unwilling to publish what the general public had written to them in respect of stories that the newspapers had published.

In summary, it can probably be said, without exaggeration, that letters to the editor is one of the great literary traditions which has developed "in cohort" to the newspapers—similar in a way to editorials where a newspaper or a magazine is not taken seriously unless it contains a narrative on the editor's view with respect to a particular subject or matter.

Similarly, I personally do not believe that a newspaper or magazine is complete unless it contains a section or area whereby readers' views are aired in public for the benefit of the entire readership of that newspaper or magazine.

Even in the age of digital newspapers and magazines, the digital editions still contain areas where letters to the editor are still published and where readers have an opportunity to view what other readers are saying about a story or a subject. I believe this is truly remarkable; leading to transparency on the part of newspapers generally, and also imposing a de-facto quality assurance on the work of reporters who would otherwise not be incentivised to check the accuracy of their stories before publishing.

I am quite proud (justifiably, I hope!) of the contributions that I have made towards intellectual debates that have taken place over the years when particular stories were published by some of the newspapers. In some cases I have written to the editor to get facts straight—in others I have taken an opportunity to "fill a gap" (as it were) in some of the facts that were missing from the original stories where I felt that these gaps were vital for readers to understand the context in which the debate was taking place. Yet in others I have written some letters where I felt so passionately about a subject or a matter that I felt I needed to write to the editor irrespective of the consequences.

Whatever the underlying causes, it gives me great pleasure to compile my contributions in the form of a book and an e-book, and I do hope that you enjoy going through them. And finally, I sincerely hope that the great tradition of writing to the editors continues for the next few hundred years as it has continued ever since the advent of newspapers themselves many centuries ago.

Nagindas M Khajuria
London
15 September 2014

Forward

Every stone has a story. Similarly every human being or anything present on the planet has a story. Human beings are able to articulate their thoughts, views and opinions, perhaps much more widely.

A thinking reader has his say too. Very few readers, though, have the time, energy and facility to express themselves. Asian Voice has a unique distinction in Britain's ethnic media. On average, some ten esteemed readers communicate their views weekly. Their views may sometimes be critical of each other but based upon old Indian traditions, as well as traditions and cultures of all races, a debate is always welcome.

For several years, the Letters from Nagindas Khajuria have proved to be of added value to this dialogue within the pages of Asian Voice. NK has a unique gift of original thinking on some uncommon subjects. He has scholarship and professional background to take a detached yet in-depth look at the issue.

The most important strength of Nagindas is that he can put things in the mildest way even when a little bit of aggression could be expected—this is his upbringing as a practicing Jain.

NK has expressed his views on so many topics of interest that this compilation will give its readers, through his Letters to the Editor, a feel for the changing scenario in present day Britain, and in particular from an Asian perspective.

The subject matter is vast. Some examples are fiscal policy, geopolitical conflicts, NHS, education, inequality, crime, global financial crisis, religion, energy supplies, environment and many more.

A must read for readers.

With Best Wishes
CB Patel
Publisher/Editor
Asian Voice and Gujarat Samachar
Unit 2, 12 Hoxton Market, London N1 6HW
www.abplgroup.com

Introduction

This book is a compilation of 268 letters to the editor that were published in the British mainstream and British Asian print media from 1997 to 2014.

The letters are about current affairs that became the news of the day and were widely debated in the media. Each of the 17 years had different political, economic and social events that were happening and this book catches the mood of the period and reflects upon whether we should have accepted the then conventional wisdom or whether we should have challenged it and adopted an alternative course of action. Alternatively, the letters expand on the information being circulated and puts it into a more comprehensive perspective to educate or elucidate the reader with accurate statistics and/or historical background.

The 21st century is only 14 years old as of now and still has 86 years to run when we would begin the 22nd century. However, so much has happened in such a short period at lightning speed that we need to take stock and ask ourselves where we are going.

In many fields of such as accountancy, arts, economics, education, emerging nations, energy, enterprise, environment, European Union, finance, fiscal policy, geopolitical conflicts, global financial crisis, global institutions, immigration, law, monetary policy, politics, sports, transport and wars, these letters expand the debates to a deeper level and suggest alternatives that may initially be considered least likely, but on deeper reflection could make better sense.

The next 14 years will be crucial to reflect more deeply on all above issues. This book will inspire you to think out of the box perhaps more often than you may have done in the past.

At a Glance
The **Letters in Chronological Order** is a convenient useful **SYNOPSIS OR KEY POINT** in each letter of the entire contents of the book.

INDEX at the back
This is also very useful if you are searching for a particular topic of interest, or a place, or name of a person. Although all the letters are published in a chronological order from year 1997 to year 2014, if you refer to the Index, you can easily see, for example, that over the years, say a dozen or more letters were written on the same subject such as National Health Service. That may be easy for you to follow your area or areas of interest.

Hard Cover, Soft Cover and eBook
Books are in Black and White and the eBook is in Colour. Please research all three so that you purchase what is most suitable in your circumstances.

I hope this book will serve its purpose of filling the "gaps" in your knowledge that you really always wanted to find out about, but did not have the time to carry out the necessary research.

Contents

Preface	v
Forward	vii
Introduction	ix
Letters in Chronological Order	xxiii

1997

1.	Encouraging savings	3
2.	The end of Chinese Walls	3

1999

3.	Look at the bigger picture	4
4.	All the same under the skin	4
5.	Get London Moving	5
6.	Train spotters know best	5

2000

7.	Enterprise is held back	7
8.	Branching into quality	7
9.	Are we too stubborn to move forward?	8

2001

10.	American invasion leads to a less productive workforce	9
11.	Keep cool for best results by Dr Rajesh Khajuria	9
12.	Britain and the euro: Leaders of the pack or out in the cold?	10

13. We need full euro debate by Geoff Wood, Marlow	11
14. Put an end to jingoism	12
15. Tongue firmly in his cheek by J E Francis, Loxley	13
16. Staying in control	13
17. Exchange Rate	14
18. Off the rails	14
19. Hidden costs	15
20. Shaken but not stirred: Mrs Doyle's substitute–James Bond–etc	15

2002

21. Stretching a point	16
22. Separate Ways	16
23. No government should play tax or race card	17
24. Time for a rethink	18
25. Get Real	18
26. Scary Pound	19
27. Interest dilemma	20
28. Not the time for tax rises	21
29. Fingers in too many pies	22
30. Statistics rethink	22
31. Competence of non-executive directors & planned review	23
32. Mind the gap on universities' tuition fees	23
33. Value of degrees in today's workplace	24
34. Pensions dilemma	24

2003

35. Accentuate the positive aspects of the euro	25
36. Alice in euro land	26
37. Great idea	26

38.	All too easy to feed anti-American mood	27
39.	The all new FRSSE	27
40.	Beyond our means	28
41.	Euro issue cannot be forced	29
42.	Rose-tinted view of EU by John Broughton, Ruthun	30
43.	Back Chat	31
44.	High price of euro [1-5 para by Cliff Redman, Worthng] [6th para by David Ball, Newham]	32
45.	Give Mervyn growth and unemployment too	33
46.	Trying to book an appointment with your doctor?	33
47.	Paying for GPs is not practical by Kevin Olney, Coventry	34
48.	Mortgage debt could be tied to maintenance	35
49.	Astonishing Read by James Percival	36
50.	Education	36
51.	Keep it simple	37
52.	Conflict Zone	38
53.	What a Waste	39

2004

54.	Tories need to concentrate on substance	40
55.	Tax targets	40
56.	Blind terror	41
57.	Ditch the US link	41
58.	Banking	42
59.	Too many hats: accountancy firms should restrict themselves to one or two disciplines, not many	42
60.	Nothing right	43
61.	Airbus wins	43
62.	Work-life balance	44

xiii

2005

63. New Labour does get IT right most of the time	45
64. Rover was not about numbers	46
65. Caveat emptor	47
66. Africa's real problem	48
67. All greek to me	49
68. Educating Britain	50
69. The real objective	51

2006

70. Sharing the care for mentally ill patients	52
71. Immigration red herring	53
72. A powerful message	54
73. Experience speaks for itself	54

2007

74. Are the right checks and balances in place?	55
75. Men inflicting violence is old story	56
76. Will oil result in strife?	57
77. Young Asians lack experience	58
78. HFB needs to rethink appeal to save [cow] Shambo	59
79. Facts about ethnic minorities	60
80. The Raisôn d'être of Bollywood	62
81. Is steam yoga substantial enough to warrant a patent?	63
82. Breakthrough in global warming	64
83. Why do people resort to violence?	65
84. Indo-US nuclear accord a landmark deal	66

85.	"In it ain't broke, don't fix it"	68
86.	Tension in Darfur and its relevance to oil supply security	70

2008

87.	The shorter and simpler the better	71
88.	The Rape of Tibet	71
89.	Israel at 60	75
90.	High petrol prices	76
91.	Gordon Brown–is he a Charlie?	79
92.	Ambani brothers at war again	81
93.	Nuke Deal Jitters	83
94.	Rethink merger approval	86
95.	Land of Amarnath Yatris trigges political tremors	87
96.	60 years of NHS	89
97.	Vote of confidence to decide UPA's fate	91
98.	Deal wins [Indo-American Nuclear Accord ratified by parliament]	93
99.	£1 billion package for UK housing industry	95
100.	Common thread of violent deeds and instigations	97
101.	World markets on roller coaster–India sits pretty	99
102.	Bradford & Bingley Bank nationalisation confirmed by Alistair Darling	101
103.	Obama cites Mahatma Gandhi to back his call for change	103
104.	Where do we stand? Thinking Aloud	105
105.	Bias towards India in the Western media	107
106.	Ganga gets a tag	109
107.	The Global Financial Crisis	111
108.	India-Pakistan: Hope springs eternal	113
109.	President Medvedev comes calling	115

2009

110.	Industrial Output in India dips for the first time in 15 years	117
111.	Israel continues strikes on Gaza	117
112.	India to host International Accounting meet in mid-January 2009	118
113.	Economic downturn an invitation to innovate	118
114.	Why is our NHS such a mess?	119
115.	Supreme Court asks Vodafone to respond to Tax Authorities	119
116.	The 15th General Election in India	120
117.	Gujarat ranks 5th or 6th overall	120
118.	Indian Railways under Lalu Prasad	121
119.	Angry India moves to patent yoga poses	121
120.	Does money talk in elections?	122
121.	G20 Finance Ministers Summit	122
122.	The System and Systemic Failure	123
123.	Bank of England, Treasury and Financial Services Authority	123
124.	What is Britishness?	124
125.	Asian school governors underrepresented	124
126.	How do you solve a problem like this?	125
127.	MP Pay Reform	125
128.	Rest periods for cows	126
129.	Michael Martin: a persona non-grata?	126
130.	British Afro-Asian Party Independents (BAAPI)	127
131.	Inflation, unemployment, interest rate and Sterling	127
132.	Yes (Prime) Minister	128
133.	Poor Management of London underground Upgrading	128
134.	General Motors decline	129
135.	A wolf in Sheep's Clothing?	129

136.	Are politicians opportunists?	130
137.	Afghanistan elections	130
138.	Jawaharlal Nehru and his contributions [I met him in 1957]	131
139.	Nehru and Hindi	132
140.	Multiculturalism among Afghanistan and its borders	133
141.	Vegetarianism, protein and climate change	134

2010

142.	Tackling Naxalite Violence	135
143.	Military invasions	135
144.	World Cup 2010 in South Africa	136
145.	The Political Conference "Question Time"	136
146.	National Insurance Planned Increase in 2011	137
147.	GP Visits	137
148.	Elections: an unbiased view	138
149.	Can higher taxes solve the budget deficit?	138
150.	Living beyond ones means	139
151.	If it ain't broke...	140
152.	How has NHS evolved over the years	140
153.	Is the UK taxation system fair?	141
154.	AV Voting System in Action	142
155.	India needs to pay more attention to agriculture	142
156.	Cuts–Ready Steady Go–Cart before Horse?	143
157.	Quantitative Easing	144
158.	Divide and rule policy in Sudan for Oil and Gas scramble	145
159.	"Ostrich among us" by Bhupendra Gandhi on Nagin Letter	145
160.	How to Run Hospitals successfully	146

161.	World citizen	147
162.	Corruption is India's scourge	148
163.	Improving the education system in UK	149
164.	Chickens, drugs and football	150
165.	Further and Higher Education–England	151
166.	£160,000,000 to each of 500 GP Consortiums	152

2011

167.	Inequality is unfair	153
168.	Forecast increase in both healthcare demand and supply	153
169.	Chillcot Iraq War Inquiry	154
170.	Understanding the human mind	154
171.	Female quotas would target the wrong women	155
172.	The Female Factor	156
173.	Muslims on the Move	157
174.	Family Planning	158
175.	NHS–Last family Silver Remaining	159
176.	Strategies and issues of corruption	160
177.	The Alternative Vote Referendum	161
178.	Bad Commercial decision by Royal Bank of Scotland	162
179.	Improving NHS	163
180.	The Global Food System	164
181.	Hidden economy in the UK	165
182.	Foreign Account Tax Compliance Act [FATCA]	166
183.	Giving bank of England more powers is a bad idea	167
184.	Indian saris	168
185.	Saris and today's women by Jayesh A Patel	169

186. The Metropolitan Police Service and The Metropolitan Authority	169
187. The Metropolitan Police	170
188. Time to abandon Britain's CCTV Policing	171
189. Anarchy in the Global Economy	172
190. Scheduled Castes and Scheduled Tribes	173
191. Is UK serious about economic growth?	174
192. The known unknown	175
193. Dismantling the NHS Programme for IT	176
194. Midland Voice by Dee Katwa	177
195. The Vision of Europe	178
196. The Human Body	179
197. European Union Time Line	180
198. Does practice of Yoga lead to Hinduism?	181
199. Banking Regulation	182
200. Milestones in India's recent history	183

2012

201. United Nations Organization	184
202. Marks & Spencer & HSBC link up to open retail banks	185
203. Banks are agents, not principals	186
204. International Finance is master and real economy is prisoner	187
205. Olympics in World Financial System	188
206. Olympics in Politics	189
207. Official records	190
208. Cable's war on 'shady' tax havens	191
209. Ganga now a deadly source of cancer	192

2013

210.	Special relationship with USA	193
211.	German central bank's gold reserves and Africa?	194
212.	Animal spirit of capitalism	195
213.	Non-Violence versus Military Interventions on Valentine's Day	196
214.	UK India Special Relationship	197
215.	2013-My 40th anniversary to have become a UK citizen	198
216.	The British Budget	199
217.	Public mood is changing	200
218.	Poverty in the UK	201
219.	Monarchy Parliament Civil Society Landed Gentry and Working Class	202
220.	London needs a more visionary town planner	203
221.	The New Tory Party	204
222.	Significant developments of the 20th century	205
223.	The Good Maharaja: a tale of compassion and humanity	206
224.	Asian food	207
225.	Fiscal Budget	208
226.	Does BPJ need to rethink its policy on Andhra Pradesh?	209
227.	Secularism & Politics	210
228.	Britain is no longer a country of choice for immigrants	211
229.	Help to Buy or Help to Cry?	212
230.	German traditions compared to British	213
231.	Should use of chemical weapons be a game change?	214
232.	Accountancy news	215
233.	Syria reminds me of King Asoka and Kautalya	216
234.	Evolution of the British Legal System (part one)	217
235.	Evolution of the British Legal System (part two)	218
236.	Buying a house	219

237.	Narendra Modi as a manager rather than a leader	220
238.	John Fitzgerald Kennedy's legacy	221
239.	Boris Johnson's speech By Kevin Khajuria	222
240.	A tribute to Nelson Mandela	223
241.	PM Cameroon, cap in hand, in China	224

2014

242.	Tax evasion: Sounds familiar?	225
243.	India taxes reform debate	226
244.	Sugar produces salt in the body	227
245.	Blaming the Moguls or the British	228
246.	Darfur crisis	229
247.	The heart of the matter	229
248.	Ukraine and the Crimean Region	230
249.	Pension planning	231
250.	Multiculturalism and "The Euro Debate"	232
251.	British Business is truly international	233
252.	Parties will soon publish their 2015 election manifestos	234
253.	High speed 2 project	235
254.	Being Indian	236
255.	Nandan Nilekani of Infosys joins the race	237
256.	High Speed 2 By Lord Dolar Popat Govt Spokesman for Transport House of Lords	238
257.	Arjuna's Chariot	239
258.	Indian business acumen	240
259.	Lost opportunity	241
260.	SAARC invite	242
261.	Europe	243

262. School education	244
263. Football in India	245
264. D-Day 70th Anniversary: Rejoice or Regret?	246
265. Doing things mindfully	247
266. ISIS	248
267. 'Life'–a project for the not-so-fortunate	249
268. Footpaths, pedestrian crossings, bicycle lanes and public toilets	250
About the Author	251
Index	253

Letters in Chronological Order

Letter Number	Date Published	Name of Publication	Title of the Article	Synopsis or Key Point	Page Number
1	11/6/1997	Accountancy Age	Encouraging savings	Excessive use debit/credit cards discourages savings	3
2	10/23/1997	Accountancy Age	The end of Chinese Walls	Six big accountancy firms specialise: one hat only	3
3	2/25/1999	Accountancy Age	Look at the bigger picture	Longbridge as Rover car producer	4
4	6/17/1999	Accountancy Age	All the same under the skin	Merger of Accountancy Bodies synergies	4
5	7/25/1999	The Business	Get London Moving	Use cars less; public transport more	5
6	10/28/1999	Accountancy Age	Train spotters know best	How to improve UK rail industry as a whole	6
7	10/19/2000	Accountancy Age	Enterprise is held back	IR35 tax law is stifling enterprise	7
8	11/9/2000	Accountancy Age	Branching into quality	Kite mark for accountancy bodies bad idea	7
9	11/30/2000	Accountancy Age	Are we too stubborn to move forward?	"The Budget" should be every three years	8
10	3/15/2001	Accountancy Age	American invasion leads to a less productive workforce	Long working hours is a British American habit	9
11	3/29/2001	Accountancy Age	Keep cool for best results by Dr Rajesh Khajuria	Cool mind normal mind and angry mind	9
12	6/21/2001	Accountancy Age	Britain and the euro-leaders of the pack or out in the cold?	EU concept superior to internet concept	10
13	7/12/2001	Accountancy Age	We need full euro debate by Geoff Wood, Marlow	Joining Euro means giving up sovereignty	11
14	7/26/2001	Accountancy Age	Put an end to jingoism	Currency buying and selling rate spread is fraud	12

(*Continued*)

xxiii

Letter Number	Date Published	Name of Publication	Title of the Article	Synopsis or Key Point	Page Number
15	8/16/2001	Accountancy Age	Tongue firmly in his cheek by J E Francis, Loxley	EU concept is a brilliantly conceived joke	13
16	8/30/2001	Accountancy Age	Staying in control	Interest rate is poor tool to manage economy	13
17	9/2/2001	The Sunday Times	Exchange Rate	Manipulating exchange rates destroys economy	14
18	10/14/2001	Sunday Business	Off the rails	Release rail infrastructure to 4 private cos.	14
19	10/21/2001	Sunday Business	Hidden costs	Railways spent on stations instead of tracks	15
20	11/29/2001	Accountancy Age	Shaken but not stirred: Mrs Doyle's substitute–James Bond–etc	Tax returns should be submitted w/o accts	15
21	1/17/2002	Accountancy Age	Stretching a point	Guard public money before it leaves purse	16
22	1/27/2002	The Business	Separate Ways	Split Firms: Audit OR Consultancy NOT BOTH	16
23	2/10/2002	The Business	No government should play tax or race card	Abolish allowances; introduce 5% 10% 20% 30%	17
24	4/4/2002	Accountancy Age	Time for a rethink	Award IT etc contracts on pilot project basis	18
25	4/7/2002	The Business	Get Real	Keep interest rates low for five years	18
26	4/7/2002	The Sunday Times	Scary Pound	Deficit increased by £19 billion 1995–2000	19
27	4/14/2002	The Business	Interest dilemma	Aim to depreciate Sterling by 25% by 2007	20
28	4/18/2002	Accountancy Age	Not the time for tax rises	Go back to budget deficit system 3% of GDP	21
29	5/2/2002	Accountancy Age	Fingers in too many pies	Executive directorships in too many companies	22
30	6/9/2002	The Business	Statistics rethink	Base statistics on actual data not surveys	22
31	9/1/2002	The Director	Competence of non-executive directors & planned review	NEDs must have industry sector knowledge	23
32	10/27/2002	The Business	Mind the gap on universities' tuition fees	Mass production or production by masses?	23

33	11/24/2002	The Sunday Times	Value of degrees in today's workplace	University degree is not be all end all	24
34	12/8/2002	The Business	Pensions dilemma	Value pension funds 5-yearly, not 1-yearly	24
35	1/5/2003	The Business	Accentuate the positive aspects of the euro	EU members do have different interest rates	25
36	1/12/2003	The Business	Alice in euro land	Taylor rule = inflation rate + output gap	26
37	1/16/2003	Accountancy Age	Great idea	Economics a dual system: few big many small	26
38	1/19/2003	The Business	All too easy to feed anti-American mood	Iraq was no enemy, nor was it a threat	27
39	2/20/2003	Accountancy Age	The all new FRSSE	Separate SME accounting standards bad idea	27
40	3/2/2003	The Business	Beyond our means	UK Average deficit 2.46% of GDP 1979 to 1992	28
41	3/6/2003	Accountancy Age	Euro issue cannot be forced	International trade growth is twice GDP growth	29
42	3/13/2003	Accountancy Age	Rose-tinted view of EU by John Broughton, Ruthun	Common Agricultural Policy bad for UK	30
43	3/20/2003	Accountancy Age	Back Chat	Citizen writer is loyal to UK long term interest	31
44	3/27/2003	Accountancy Age	High price of euro [1-5 para by Cliff Rednan,Worthng] [6th para by David Ball, Newham]	Cost benefit debate about joining the Euro	32
45	7/13/2003	The Business	Give Mervyn growth and unemployment too	FRB targets inflation unemployment and growth	33
46	8/21/2003	Accountancy Age	Trying to book an appointment with your doctor?	Charge for health except means tested patients	33
47	9/4/2003	Accountancy Age	Paying for GPs is not practical by Kevin Olney, Coventry	Charge £10 for every visit to GP debate	34
48	9/7/2003	The Business	Mortgage debt could be tied to maintenance	50% of British homes not well maintained	35

(*Continued*)

Letter Number	Date Published	Name of Publication	Title of the Article	Synopsis or Key Point	Page Number
49	9/25/2003	Accountancy Age	Astonishing Read by James Percival	Poverty trap re paying GPs for each visit	36
50	10/1/2003	The Director	Education	Youngsters encouraged to be employees	36
51	10/5/2003	The Business	Keep it simple	Waste and duplication could bankrupt UK in 20 years' time	37
52	10/19/2003	The Business	Conflict Zone	Reduce Big Four's world audit share 78% to 50%	38
53	11/6/2003	Accountancy Age	What a Waste	659 MPs go with whatever government proposes	39
54	2/29/2004	The Business	Tories need to concentrate on substance	Politicians are obsessed about perception	40
55	3/19/2004	Accountancy Age	Tax targets	Middle & higher earners now pay less tax	40
56	3/21/2004	The Business	Blind terror	IMF World Bank UNO exploiting small countries	41
57	5/16/2004	The Business	Ditch the US link	Israel has to withdraw to pre-1967 borders	41
58	6/1/2004	The Director	Banking	Banks have no knowledge of local trade	42
59	7/1/2004	Accountancy Age	Too many hats: accountancy firms should restrict themselves to one or two disciplines, not many	Auditing should be split from tax advice role	42
60	7/25/2004	The Business	Nothing right	UK productivity ranking gone from 6th to 23rd	43
61	8/1/2004	The Business	Airbus wins	Airbus has stronger long term vision v Boeing	43
62	9/1/2004	The Director	Work-life balance	Policy flawed encouraging both parents to work	44
63	2/5/2005	The Business	New Labour does get IT right most of the time	IT contracts given to incompetent Western cos.	45
64	4/28/2005	Accountancy Age	Rover was not about numbers	UK plc focuses too much on numbers v issues	46

xxvi

65	5/29/2005	The Business	Caveat emptor	Financial instrument like mortgage was misleading	47
66	7/3/2005	The Business	Africa's real problem	Cow in Europe has higher subsidy v African farmer	48
67	7/7/2005	Accountancy Age	All Greek to me	Amend company law "assurance" not "opinion"	49
68	9/4/2005	The Business	Educating Britain	Secretary of State for Education is needed	50
69	9/15/2005	Accounting & Business	The real objective	UK public finances oversight not healthy	51
70	6/15/2006	The Press	Sharing the care for mentally ill patients	Set up a charity for welfare of mentally ill persons	52
71	9/9/2006	Asian Voice	Immigration red herring	Examples of deep rooted long term problems in UK	53
72	9/14/2006	Accountancy Age	A powerful message	Media peddles money, instant pleasure & greed	54
73	10/14/2006	Asian Voice	Experience speaks for itself	UNO Secretary should have been Shashi Tharoor	54
74	2/24/2007	Asian Voice	Are the right checks and balances in place?	Enterprise entrepreneurial & innovation spirit gone	55
75	4/21/2007	Asian Voice	Men inflicting violence is old story	Men can be victims of domestic violence equally	56
76	5/5/2007	Asian Voice	Will oil result in strife?	Discovery rate for new oil fallen from 80% to 20%	57
77	5/12/2007	Asian Voice	Young Asians lack experience	Raising awareness of a charity called Life in India	58
78	5/26/2007	Asian Voice	HFB needs to rethink appeal to save [cow] Shambo	US eats 9 billon animals + 17 billion fish each year	59
79	6/2/2007	Asian Voice	Facts about ethnic minorities	New houses prices up 228%; old ones up 179%	60
80	6/9/2007	Asian Voice	The Raisôn d'être of Bollywood	Media paints wrong picture about Bollywood	62

(Continued)

xxvii

Letter Number	Date Published	Name of Publication	Title of the Article	Synopsis or Key Point	Page Number
81	6/16/2007	Asian Voice	Is steam Yoga substantial enough to warrant a patent?	Patent "Hot Yoga" in US steals India idea of Yoga	63
82	6/30/2007	Asian Voice	Breakthrough in global warming	Human index of 10 qualities more important v GDP	64
83	7/21/2007	Asian Voice	Why do people resort to violence?	September 11th could be a Boston led conspiracy	65
84	8/25/2007	Asian Voice	Indo-US nuclear accord a landmark deal	Nuclear option not relevant for India's needs	66
85	9/1/2007	Asian Voice	"In it ain't broke, don't fix it"	NHS was not broke, it did not need radical reform	68
86	9/5/2007	https://news.glggroup.com	Tension in Darfur and its relevance to oil supply security	West interest in Sudan was and is for oil only	70
87	1/24/2008	Financial Times	The shorter and simpler the better	Annual Accounts should narrate % change not value	71
88	5/31/2008	Asian Voice	The Rape of Tibet	Tibetans are better off with China/Human Development Index China 81st India 126th	71
89	6/7/2008	Asian Voice	Israel at 60	Indian Diaspora statistics settled overseas	75
90	6/14/2008	Asian Voice	High petrol prices	Goldman Sachs misleading markets re crude prices	76
91	6/21/2008	Asian Voice	Gordon Brown–is he a Charlie?	UK plc has been run on a divided v united basis	79
92	6/28/2008	Asian Voice	Ambani brothers at war again	Reliance masterminded mobile coverage India wide	81
93	7/5/2008	Asian Voice	Nuke Deal Jitters	USA and Indian hard and soft power comparison	83
94	7/10/2008	Accountancy Age	Rethink merger approval	EU Competition Commission wrong re PwC merger	86
95	7/12/2008	Asian Voice	Land of Amarnath Yatries triggers political tremors	Our entire life is a pilgrimage and our body temple	87

96	7/19/2008	Asian Voice	60 years of NHS	40% of £160 billion could be saved by reforms	89
97	7/26/2008	Asian Voice	Vote of confidence to decide UPA's fate	USA instrumental in Indian software supremacy	91
98	8/2/2008	Asian Voice	Deal Wins [Indo-American Nuclear Accord ratified by Parliament]	Where can society turn to replace oil, coal & gas?	93
99	9/13/2008	Asian Voice	£1 billion package for UK housing industry	Decent housing: UK plc needs a 20-year 3-party plan	95
100	9/27/2008	Asian Voice	Common thread of violent deeds and instigations	Use of ethnic or religious identity malicious	97
101	10/4/2008	Asian Voice	World markets on roller coaster-India sits pretty	1997 crisis puncture in tyre 2008 crisis engine failure	99
102	10/11/2008	Asian Voice	Bradford & Bingley Bank nationalisation confirmed by Alistair Darling	US Bank Capital One had $49.5 off Bal Sheet loans	101
103	10/18/2008	Asian Voice	Obama cites Mahatma Gandhi to back his call for change	Paper wealth is 8/24 times true underlying wealth	103
104	11/8/2008	Asian Voice	Where do we stand? Thinking Aloud	Chose skinned wife to improve children's chances	105
105	11/15/2008	Asian Voice	Bias towards India in the Western media	India's welfare system helps 224 million poor	107
106	11/22/2008	Asian Voice	Ganga gets a tag	Water, after air, most valuable world resource	109
107	11/29/2008	Asian Voice	The Global Financial Crisis	Developing countries have grown faster for 40 years	111
108	12/6/2008	Asian Voice	India-Pakistan: Hope springs eternal	Turkey, Iran, Iraq, Afghanistan and Pakistan: 5 bricks	113
109	12/20/2008	Asian Voice	President Medvedev comes calling	Indian PM and Russian President meet regularly	115
110	1/3/2009	Asian Voice	Industrial Output in India dips for the first time in 15 years	Insurance industry sector in India is in its infancy	117

(Continued)

Letter Number	Date Published	Name of Publication	Title of the Article	Synopsis or Key Point	Page Number
111	1/10/2009	Asian Voice	Israel continues strikes on Gaza	Israel is a G20 military base for 66% of world oil	117
112	1/17/2009	Asian Voice	India to host International Accounting meet in mid-January 2009	Accountancy is a very important discipline	118
113	1/24/2009	Asian Voice	Economic downturn an invitation to innovate	85m out of 213m [40%] households in India are poor	118
114	1/31/2009	Asian Voice	Why is our NHS such a mess?	Rich need to give up NHS to make room for poor	119
115	2/7/2009	Asian Voice	Supreme Court asks Vodafone to respond to Tax Authorities	Vodafone and Hutch evaded $1.7 billion tax in India	119
116	2/14/2009	Asian Voice	The 15th General Election in India	India needs to spread wealth more commonly	120
117	2/21/2009	Asian Voice	Gujarat ranks 5th or 6th overall	Gujarat lagging behind in education, health, literacy	120
118	2/28/2009	Asian Voice	Indian Railways under Lalu Prasad	Railway Minister, a genius, reduced fares by 45%	121
119	3/7/2009	Asian Voice	Angry India moves to patent yoga poses	In Yoga body is vehicle mind is driver soul is engine	121
120	3/14/2009	Asian Voice	Does money talk in elections?	Water electricity sanitation health & education key	122
121	3/21/2009	Asian Voice	G20 Finance Ministers Summit	Relocate world institutions to developing countries	122
122	3/28/2009	Asian Voice	The System and Systemic Failure	Akin to supermarkets having no free drinking water	123
123	4/4/2009	Asian Voice	Bank of England, Treasury and Financial Services Authority	Fix Base Rate to 4% pa & tax burden to 40% globally	123
124	4/11/2009	Asian Voice	What is Britishness?	Asking minorities their ethnic origin is wrong	124

xxx

125	4/18/2009	Asian Voice	Asian school governors underrepresented	Currently too many categories in 33,000 schools	124
126	4/25/2009	Asian Voice	How do you solve a problem like this?	74% GDP comes from use of labour	125
127	5/2/2009	Asian Voice	MP Pay Reform	Move parliament to Middle England	125
128	5/16/2009	Asian Voice	Rest periods for cows	Cows artificially inseminated too soon	126
129	5/23/2009	Asian Voice	Michael Martin: a persona non-grata?	Tradition of impartiality was followed	126
130	5/30/2009	Asian Voice	British Afro-Asian Party Independents [BAAPI]	Non-whites own political party BAAPI	127
131	6/6/2009	Asian Voice	Inflation, unemployment, interest rate and Sterling	Labour record on public services good	127
132	6/13/2009	Asian Voice	Yes (Prime) Minister	UK as an economic power in decline	128
133	6/20/2009	Asian Voice	Poor Management of London Underground Upgrading	PPP bankrupted London Underground	128
134	6/27/2009	Asian Voice	General Motors decline	How to save jobs at Vauxhall Plant	129
135	7/4/2009	Asian Voice	A Woolf in Sheep's Clothing?	Trade Union's own political party TUPP	129
136	7/18/2009	Asian Voice	Are politicians opportunists?	Military economic spiritual cultural social ethos	130
137	11/7/2009	Asian Voice	Afghanistan elections	Russia China and India will not allow West to gain	130
138	11/14/2009	Asian Voice	Jawaharlal Nehru and his contributions [I met him in 1957]	India should use Hindi in business to compete	131
139	11/21/2009	Asian Voice	Nehru and Hindi	Nehru: protect your grandeur and independence	132
140	11/21/2009	Asian Voice	Multiculturalism among Afghanistan and its borders	West does not respect all cultures in Afghanistan	133
141	11/28/2009	Asian Voice	Vegetarianism, protein and climate change	Americans Australians eat 20% meat they need 10%	134

(*Continued*)

Letter Number	Date Published	Name of Publication	Title of the Article	Synopsis or Key Point	Page Number
142	2/27/2010	Asian Voice	Tackling Naxalite Violence	Politicians police tax evaders judges all corrupt	135
143	3/6/2010	Asian Voice	Military invasions	Desire to go to war compared to sexual desire	135
144	3/13/2010	Asian Voice	World Cup 2010 in South Africa	MYSA Kenya [Mathare Youth Sports Associations]	136
145	4/10/2010	Asian Voice	The Political Conference "Question Time"	Britain will produce more if it joins the Euro	136
146	4/17/2010	Asian Voice	National Insurance Planned Increase in 2011	NHS can only improve if the rich leave NHS for poor	137
147	4/24/2010	Asian Voice	GP Visits	Many GP visits are for minor ailments charge £10	137
148	5/1/2010	Asian Voice	Elections: an unbiased view	Parliament members USA 535 UK 1334 India 790	138
149	5/8/2010	Asian Voice	Can higher taxes solve the budget deficit?	Tax burden 38% but tax revenue 31% of	138
150	5/22/2010	Asian Voice	Living beyond ones means	European capitalism more moderate than USA's	139
151	5/27/2010	Accountancy Age	If it ain't broke…	Personal allowances must be abolished altogether	140
152	5/29/2010	Asian Voice	How has NHS evolved over the years	Spend more on prevention; less on treatment	140
153	9/25/2010	Asian Voice	Is the UK taxation system fair?	2% earn taxable £2.4m 24% earn £44k 74% earn £16K	141
154	10/2/2010	Asian Voice	AV Voting System in Action	Alternative vote system far more representative	142
155	10/9/2010	Asian Voice	India needs to pay more attention to agriculture	75% of Indians in villages produce only 20% GDP	142
156	10/16/2010	Asian Voice	Cuts-Ready Steady Go-Cart before Horse?	Comprehensive Productivity not Spending Review!	143

157	10/23/2010	Asian Voice	Quantitative Easing	QE: hedging 50 times over underlying current value	144
158	10/30/2010	Asian Voice	Divide and rule policy in Sudan for Oil and Gas scramble	Western crocodile tears re Darfur & South Sudan	145
159	11/6/2010	Asian Voice	"Ostrich among us" by Bhupendra Gandhi on Nagin Letter	We criticize the West but would not live elsewhere	145
160	11/6/2010	Asian Voice	How to Run Hospitals successfully	Research to justify wholesale privatisation of NHS	146
161	11/20/2010	Asian Voice	World citizen	Economics for a Crowded Planet by Jeffrey D Sachs	147
162	11/27/2010	Asian Voice	Corruption is India's scourge	33% of Indian government money lost in corruption	148
163	12/4/2010	Asian Voice	Improving the education system in UK	Only one LOCAL state and one independent school	149
164	12/11/2010	Asian Voice	Chickens, drugs and football	Indian Co buys Blackburn Rovers Football Club	150
165	12/18/2010	Asian Voice	Further and Higher Education-England	£9K University fees will create a debt of £50 billion	151
166	12/25/2010	Asian Voice	£160,000,000 to each of 500 GP Consortiums	NHS Reforms are administrative not structural	152
167	1/8/2011	Asian Voice	Inequality is unfair	Being poor is a viscous circle for generations	153
168	1/29/2011	Asian Voice	Forecast increase in both healthcare demand and supply	NHS Competition cannot work as hospitals are few	153
169	2/5/2011	Asian Voice	Chillcot Iraq War Inquiry	Iraq was invaded for oil not for democracy etc	154
170	2/26/2011	Asian Voice	Understanding the human mind	Madness can be induced experimentally	154
171	3/5/2011	Asian Voice	Female quotas would target the wrong women	Board members do not act in shareholders' interest	155

(*Continued*)

Letter Number	Date Published	Name of Publication	Title of the Article	Synopsis or Key Point	Page Number
172	3/19/2011	Asian Voice	The Female Factor	Women are generally freer from corruption v men	156
173	4/2/2011	Asian Voice	Muslims on the Move	Vital statistics on 12 Muslim countries: literacy etc	157
174	4/16/2011	Asian Voice	Family Planning	Indian population rose by 181m or 20% in 10 years	158
175	4/23/2011	Asian Voice	NHS-Last Family Silver Remaining	30% of NHS costs lumped "materials & services"	159
176	4/30/2011	Asian Voice	Strategies and issues of corruption	Most corruption happens at time of delivery	160
177	5/7/2011	Asian Voice	The Alternative Vote Referendum	Alternative vote system can be a stepping stone	161
178	5/14/2011	Asian Voice	Bad Commercial decision by Royal Bank of Scotland	RBS management and auditors Deloitte were grossly negligent	162
179	6/4/2011	Asian Voice	Improving NHS	GP-week: 87 surgeries, 15 tel calls & 5 home visits	163
180	6/11/2011	Asian Voice	The Global Food System	Monsanto etc control seeds & commodities trade	164
181	6/18/2011	Asian Voice	Hidden economy in the UK	Tax evasion in UK is costing billions every year	165
182	6/25/2011	Asian Voice	Foreign Account Tax Compliance Act [FATCA]	Banks to report deposits over $50,000 to HMRC etc	166
183	7/2/2011	Asian Voice	Giving Bank of England more powers is a bad idea	Osborne wrong to abolish Financial Services Auth.	167
184	7/16/2011	Asian Voice	Indian saris	Indian sari is longest surviving garment in history	168
185	7/23/2011	Asian Voice	Saris and today's women by Jayesh A Patel	Jeans & James Dean in "A Rebel without a Cause"	169

186	7/23/2011	Asian Voice	The Metropolitan Police Service and The Metropolitan Authority	London police cost £3.2b p a and not effective	169
187	7/30/2011	Asian Voice	The Metropolitan Police	Single bobby on the beat v double is bad idea	170
188	8/20/2011	Asian Voice	Time to abandon Britain's CCTV Policing	USA has abandoned policing by car back to on beat	171
189	8/27/2011	Asian Voice	Anarchy in the Global Economy	Big business government police press all corrupt	172
190	9/10/2011	Asian Voice	Scheduled Castes and Scheduled Tribes	Lowest income group reduced from 57.2% to 20.6%	173
191	9/24/2011	Asian Voice	Is UK serious about economic growth?	Silver bullet solution for UK economy is to join Euro	174
192	10/1/2011	Asian Voice	The known unknown	Neil Kinnock: if we had joined the Euro then….	175
193	10/8/2011	Asian Voice	Dismantling the NHS Programme for IT	NHS IT connects 110,000 doctors 390,000 nurses etc	176
194	10/15/2011	Asian Voice	Midland Voice by Dee Katwa	India lacks world class football players. Very sad.	177
195	11/5/2011	Asian Voice	The Vision of Europe	Euro currency will overtake Sterling and US Dollar	178
196	11/12/2011	Asian Voice	The Human Body	Yoga breathing can nourish 100 billion human cells	179
197	12/3/2011	Asian Voice	European Union Time Line	1951–2011 Amazing progress of cooperation in EU	180
198	12/10/2011	Asian Voice	Does practice of Yoga lead to Hinduism?	Many Christians still behave like barbarians	181
199	12/17/2011	Asian Voice	Banking Regulation	David Cameroon was wrong to use his veto in EU	182
200	12/24/2011	Asian Voice	Milestones in India's recent history	1885–2000 Indian progress. India still very backward	183

(Continued)

Letter Number	Date Published	Name of Publication	Title of the Article	Synopsis or Key Point	Page Number
201	5/26/2012	Asian Voice	United Nations Organization	Break up United Nations into 5 Regional Bodies	184
202	7/7/2012	Asian Voice	Marks & Spencer & HSBC link up to open retail banks	Need new banking model solely low income group	185
203	7/14/2012	Asian Voice	Banks are agents, not principals	16th century joint stock company model has failed	186
204	7/21/2012	Asian Voice	International Finance is master and real economy is prisoner	International finance has become opaque	187
205	8/4/2012	Asian Voice	Olympics in World Financial System	MIBOR Mumbai transparent LIBOR London not so	188
206	8/11/2012	Asian Voice	Olympics in Politics	Ideologies in British political parties all muddled up	189
207	9/8/2012	Asian Voice	Official records	Ethnic origin question is discriminatory & unlawful	190
208	9/29/2012	Asian Voice	Cable's war on 'shady' tax havens	UK tax law encourages tax evasion	191
209	11/3/2012	Asian Voice	Ganga now a deadly source of cancer	India needs to concentrate on agriculture	192
210	1/19/2013	Asian Voice	Special relationship with USA	UK referendum on EU is not in national interest	193
211	1/26/2013	Asian Voice	German central bank's gold reserves and Africa?	Gold in developing countries v poverty in Africa	194
212	2/2/2013	Asian Voice	Animal spirit of capitalism	Maintain balance between pubic and private sector	195
213	2/9/2013	Asian Voice	Non-Violence versus Military Interventions on Valentine's Day	An Asian Economic Union similar to EU?	196
214	3/2/2013	Asian Voice	UK India Special Relationship	Trade gap in sports, packaging, arts, museums, etc.	197

215	3/16/2013	Asian Voice	2013-My 40th anniversary to have become a UK citizen	45 million outside London forgotten for 50 years	198
216	3/23/2013	Asian Voice	The British Budget	If I were a Finance Minister in the UK….	199
217	4/13/2013	Asian Voice	Public mood is changing	It is UK's interest to join the Eurocurrency	200
218	5/4/2013	Asian Voice	Poverty in the UK	20% of British people are below poverty line	201
219	5/18/2013	Asian Voice	Monarchy Parliament Civil Society Landed Gentry and Working Class	Britain's brief history 12th to 21st century	202
220	5/25/2013	Asian Voice	London needs a more visionary town planner	Move Parliament or Banks to North England	203
221	6/1/2013	Asian Voice	The New Tory Party	Decision to hold referendum on EU, not join Euro?	204
222	6/15/2013	Asian Voice	Significant developments of the 20th century	How EU expanded from 6 to 27 countries in 50 years	205
223	6/22/2013	Asian Voice	The Good Maharaja: a tale of compassion and humanity	Indian Maharajas commissioned a Polish artist	206
224	6/29/2013	Asian Voice	Asian food	Asian food served in NHS hospital w of poor quality	207
225	7/6/2013	Asian Voice	Fiscal Budget	QE is deceiving the world financial system	208
226	7/20/2013	Asian Voice	Does BJP need to rethink its policy on Andhra Pradesh?	IT technology, agriculture and port: why split up?	209
227	8/3/2013	Asian Voice	Secularism & Politics	Hindus depicted as fundamentalists by West	210
228	8/10/2013	Asian Voice	Britain is no longer a country of choice for immigrants	Immigrants world wide are only 200,000	211
229	8/13/2013	Asian Voice	Help to Buy or Help to Cry?	Help to buy housing scheme will inflate house prices	212
230	8/17/2013	Asian Voice	German traditions compared to British	British people need to reflect on their culture	213
231	8/31/2013	Asian Voice	Should use of chemical weapons be a game change?	Western countries violating international war laws	214

(*Continued*)

xxxvii

Letter Number	Date Published	Name of Publication	Title of the Article	Synopsis or Key Point	Page Number
232	9/7/2013	Asian Voice	Accountancy news	Two leading accountancy firms in India join hands	215
233	9/14/2013	Asian Voice	Syria reminds me of King Asoka and Kautalya	By inflicting pain on another sect, you injure yourself	216
234	9/21/2013	Asian Voice	Evolution of the British Legal System (part one)	Legislature, judiciary and executive are not working	217
235	9/28/2013	Asian Voice	Evolution of the British Legal System (part two)	Non-lawyer appointed with two hats bad idea	218
236	10/5/2013	Asian Voice	Buying a house	Introduce 5% 10%, 20%, 30%, etc income tax rates	219
237	10/12/2013	Asian Voice	Narendra Modi as a manager rather than a leader	Modi should declare his full team, work as a team	220
238	11/30/2013	Asian Voice	John Fitzgerald Kennedy's legacy	Kennedy was killed by US military probably	221
239	12/7/2013	Asian Voice	Boris Johnson's speech BY Kevin Khajuria	What you know versus who you know for jobs	222
240	12/14/2013	Asian Voice	A tribute to Nelson Mandela	The West praises his legacy but then does opposite	223
241	12/23/2013	Asian Voice	PM Cameroon, cap in hand, in China	India needs to learn from 100 other countries how to manufacture	224
242	1/4/2014	Asian Voice	Tax evasion: Sounds familiar?	Redistribution of wealth through a fairer tax system	225
243	1/18/2014	Asian Voice	India taxes reform debate	India's total tax take is only 8% of GDP v UK 38%	226
244	1/25/2014	Asian Voice	Sugar produces salt in the body	Government advisor paid by Coca Cola and Mars Bars	227
245	2/8/2014	Asian Voice	Blaming the Moguls or the British	Moguls and the British have enriched India	228
246	2/22/2014	Asian Voice	Darfur crisis	A West sponsored fabrication of facts	229

247	3/8/2014	Asian Voice	The heart of the matter	NHS reform attempts muddled and shambolic	229
248	3/15/2014	Asian Voice	Ukraine and the Crimean Region	Sanctions against Russia re gas are unworkable	230
249	3/22/2014	Asian Voice	Pension planning	Reduce tax relief on pension contributions drastically	231
250	3/29/2014	Asian Voice	Multiculturalism and "The Euro Debate"	Making sense of multiculturalism is nonsensical	232
251	4/5/2014	Asian Voice	British Business is truly international	The missing link is joining the Euro currency	233
252	4/12/2014	Asian Voice	Parties will soon publish their 2015 election manifestos	Think about others we have permitted to fail	234
253	4/19/2014	Asian Voice	High Speed 2 project	Ditch the project and improve current network	235
254	4/26/2014	Asian Voice	Being Indian	For centuries there has been communal harmony	236
255	5/3/2014	Asian Voice	Nandan Nilekani of Infosys joins the race	1.25 million electronic voting machines in India	237
256	5/10/2014	Asian Voice	High Speed 2 By Lord Dolar Popat Govt Spokesman for Transport House of Lords	We need a trasport system suitabel for 21st century	238
257	5/10/2014	Asian Voice	Arjuna's Chariot	Hindutva embodies religion, nationalism and culture	239
258	5/17/2014	Asian Voice	Indian business acumen	Multinationals could destroy creativity & innovation	240
259	5/24/2014	Asian Voice	Lost opportunity	3 decades: regulation; deregulation; re-regulation	241
260	5/31/2014	Asian Voice	SAARC invite	India can cooperate more with its 7 neighbours	242
261	6/7/2014	Asian Voice	Europe	In or out of EU has third dinmension: join Euro	243

(*Continued*)

xxxix

Letter Number	Date Published	Name of Publication	Title of the Article	Synopsis or Key Point	Page Number
262	6/21/2014	Asian Voice	School education	Concept of academies is not the solution	244
263	6/28/2014	Asian Voice	Football in India	Modi should watch world cup final game	245
264	6/14/2014	Asian Voice	D-Day 70th Anniversary: Rejoice or Regret?	For too long we have over glorified wars, war weapons and warriors	246
265	3/1/2014	Asian Voice	Doing things mindfully	This was an Indian philosophy plagiarised by West	247
266	7/5/2014	Asian Voice	ISIS	Unfair to ignore the rights to oil revenue to 40% of Iraqi population	248
267	7/12/2014	Asian Voice	'Life'-a project for the not-so-fortunate	Life a registered charity in Rajkot India doing excellent work	249
268	7/19/2014	www.abplgroup.com	Footpaths, pedestrian crossings, bicycle lanes and public toilets	Indians in urban cities hardly walk: they need to walk more often	250

PUBLISHED LETTERS TO THE EDITOR

1997 Encouraging savings

The *raison d'être* for taxation is public-sector services and the encouragement of savings.

However, the excessive use of credit and debit cards does not encourage savings. Nor does it fully give credence to the very stringent internal controls accountants aspire to maintain. For example, the manual credit vouching system gives the name of the user on the voucher which is retained by the supplier.

However, the automated credit card systems often only show the credit card number on the document signed by the customer.

Shouldn't the name of the user as well as the holder of the credit card be shown on the slip that is given to the customer to sign?

This would enable far better accounting control all round when it comes to allocating business and private expenses when accounts are prepared both from the supplier as well as the customer point of view.

1997 The end of Chinese Walls

Regarding the proposed merger between Price Waterhouse and Coopers & Lybrand, wouldn't it be more healthy and progressive if all the Big Six firms demerged and then remerged by type of activity, for example management consultancy, auditing, tax compliance and planning, bookkeeping, financial services and so on?

The rules would not allow any Chinese walls whatsoever.

Nagindas Khajuria FCCA
Simplification Made Simple, Chartered Certified Accountants, London

1999
Look at the bigger picture

I refer to your headline article last week. I was a bit disheartened to read the emphasis placed on accounting standards treatment of, I presume, depreciation when a loss of £91m can be turned into a profit of £20m for the year 1997. Surely the wider picture is that here we have a plant which is almost 100 years old and obsolescent, productivity is low, brand charisma lacklustre, product mediocre and management has no new ideas. I wonder where the £800m spent by BMW to buy Rover has gone in four years. Surely the government should not bail them out, pouring in good money after bad. Perhaps it should be scrapped and a new plant built. Longbridge could diversify away from cars into mini-buses or locomotives.

Maybe.

1999
All the same under the skin

Your report 'CIMA urges talk not fight' (25 March, page 3) was timely. Approximately 80% of the syllabuses of all the accountancy bodies are the same. They are mainly training institutions and now have continuing professional development plus standard-setting roles in the field of accountancy.

I believe all the heads of the six (indeed seven, to include the Institute of Internal Auditors) institutions should meet once a month and thrash out each area where they can 'merge' to reduce costs.

They could use an investment or merchant bank to advise them on what their synergies are. It would be a colossal step forward.

Co-operation and competition are not mutually exclusive, and the same is true of regulated and unregulated activity. Whether an entity is a sole trader, a partnership, a quoted company or a close company, the accounting standards, tax compliance and so on are all identical in substance. For the remaining 20% of the syllabus each body could have its own unique mark of excellence.

The chartered institutes are leaders in finance and auditing, ACCA in commerce and accountancy, CIMA in industry and costing, CIPFA in public sector (30% of GDP) and economics, and the IIA in systems, procedures and internal control. The UK is still a world-class leader when it comes to accountancy. Let us not give up that leadership.

Nagindas Khajuria FCCA
Simplification Made Simple, Chartered Certified Accountants, London

Get London Moving — 1999

Sir – I read the article by Lord Hanson with a lot of interest ("Prescott – enemy of the free British car owner", 18 July). With friends like him, who needs enemies? As a British car owner as well as a public transport user on a 50/50 basis for the past 32 years in London, I would like to see car usage reduced from 90% to 70% and use of trains, the Tube and buses increase from 10% to 30%.

The ideal reforms are compulsory bus lanes on all A and/or trunk roads on both sides of the road throughout Greater London.

Train spotters know best — 1999

Your leader and Anglia Polytechnic University's article on rail delays and rail finance, (14 October) deserve careful scrutiny. There are acronyms galore: SPAD, TOC, TAC, MEAV, RAB and ATP. There are also percentages galore: 5%, 23% and 61% uplift on the value of Railtrack shares. Finally, there are rail companies galore: 25 of them.

SPAD means 'signals passed at danger'. If there is sun or glare, the driver does not see the signal properly, so he cannot tell whether it is green, yellow, double yellow or red. I hope he errs on the safe side in future and stops.

TOC means 'train operating companies'. The 25-odd companies ought to merge by April 2001 into a maximum of four: South East, South West, North East and North West.

TAC means 'train access charges'. The new charges from April 2001 should be lower. They should have been based from April 2001 on operating costs, historical cost depreciation and a 5% return on factual asset base. While Railtrack's profits have been too high, the TOCs' profits have been too low.

MEAV means 'modern equivalent asset values'. Current cost accounting is a misleading system. In any one year, the maximum replacement of assets would probably be only 1/30th of the asset base rather than 100% of the asset base.

Nagindas Khajuria FCCA
Simplification Made Simple, Chartered Certified Accountants, London

1999
Train spotters know best

RAB means 'regulatory asset base'. This is to work out what Railtrack's reasonable return on capital employed should be to compensate shareholders fairly for their investment. There are so many variations in percentage uplift on market capitalisation it may be best to drop this method. A net profit before tax falling between 5% and 10% of turnover would compare favourably with historical net profits in the motor industry.

ATP means 'automatic train protection'. Computer software failure in signalling systems was blamed for the delay in completion of the Jubilee line extension. We shouldn't rely unduly on ATP.

I don't believe fines are the real answer to train delays, poor maintenance of signals and tracks, bad management, blaming one another, etc.

I have studied the causes of train delays. During the six months ended 30 September 1997, they were as follows: in 2,500,000 loaded train movements, there were 301,974 delays (12%) of 3 minutes or more; 36,726 (1.5%) due to maintenance and renewal causes; 265,248 (10.5%) due to other causes, signalman being late for work, etc.

The total number of minutes delay was 9,708,349 (3.88 minutes per train movement) during the six months; 2,547,966 delays were due to maintenance and renewal causes (1.02 minutes per train movement); delays due to other causes were 7,160,383 (2.86 minutes per train movement).

While there were sub-divisions of the former types of cause, such as track and structures, power supply, control system and acts of God/vandalism, there were no sub-divisions for other causes. Statistics for other causes should be developed into specific sub-division data rather than lumping it all under other causes. Only then can we attempt to improve the rail industry as a whole.

Nagindas Khajuria FCCA
Simplification Made Simple, Chartered Certified Accountants, London

2000: Enterprise is held back

I recently tried to work out actual tax liability of a personal company with 31 March year end. As the deemed salary assessment was after 31 March, namely 5 April, for the same year's profits, the only way was to have two corporation tax computations: one with the normal Schedule D Case I computation and second one with the deemed salary computation the next year.

When I faxed my calculations to the Inland Revenue helpline, the inspector was not able to comment on the calculations. The rules are unworkable under current legislation.

Contractors are much more enterprising and take far bigger risks than employees. The government is effectively stifling enterprise. It takes a lot of guts to be self-employed and their rewards have historically been greater than employees to compensate them for the risk they are taking.

2000: Branching into quality

Various accountancy bodies are planning or have in place a kite mark of quality assurance.

This kite mark will be valid for five years in the case of one body.

Is this not adding another layer of bureaucracy? Or is it a marvellous idea that will encourage accountants to aspire to have a kite mark?

In my humble opinion, monitoring practices and/or monitoring quality assurance is one and the same thing. Why not extend monitoring to quality assurance?

Has Accountancy Age done any readers' survey on this? I would welcome views from interested parties. Why not leave quality assurance to ISO 9000 and BSI?

Nagindas Khajuria FCCA
Simplification Made Simple, Chartered Certified Accountants, London

2000
Are we too stubborn to move forward?

I read your article (Comment, 16 November, page 2) by Sir Geoffrey Howe, ex-chancellor, with great interest.

I have been involved with UK taxes for the past 25 years. I find that we all enjoy the annual ritual of the red book (Budget) and the amusement that we get from the very complexity of tax structure and tax law, the semantics, the nuances, the case law, etc.

We have become creatures of habit. We must now reflect upon this behaviour for the past 25 years, and realise that partly because of this complexity and bureaucracy, we have lagged behind in productivity compared to USA (40%), Germany (10%) and France (20%).

Our standard of living is also below these countries. It will require many ruthless reformers to break this culture.

I believe the annual Finance Act should be changed to every three years.

So should the Budget and the Spending Review.

We shall than have less of a boom and bust scenario.

Nagindas Khajuria FCCA
Simplification Made Simple, Chartered Certified Accountants, London

American invasion leads to a less productive workforce

I have felt for a long time that the long hours syndrome is a typical British and American style of working.

Management perceives you to be more loyal when you work long hours, when in most cases you are just less productive.

We should lean more towards Europe than the US to learn more about a balanced life style.

The US has colonised us – a coca-cola-isation has taken place with McDonald's, Kentucky Fried Chicken and Dominos Pizza.

One third of Americans are obese. One fifth of British people are obese. It is all junk food with 2,500 calories per meal rather than 2,500 per day.

There is really no need for our prime ministers to rush to the US every time there is a change of government. They have no more interest in our welfare than Europe has.

Keep cool for best results
by Dr Rajesh Khajuria

Nagindas Khajuria is right about the need to reduce long working hours (Letters, 15 March, page 19).

There are several methods available to get remarkable results by working short hours. One of them is meditation.

A cool mind works a million time better than a normal mind, which works another million times better than an angry mind. Keep cool to get remarkable results.

Nagindas Khajuria FCCA
Simplification Made Simple, Chartered Certified Accountants, London

2001

Britain and the euro: Leaders of the pack or out in the cold?

The time for surveys should now be over (In brief, page 2, 7 June). It is time for action.

The benefits of joining the European single currency should be staring us in the face. Our exports to Europe and our imports from Europe are about four to five times our exports and imports from the American Free Trade area. Europe is a local close-by market with 2000-year-old cultural and civilisation background similar to us.

As an economic concept in action, the European single currency, will have about five times as much impact as the internet, as it will bind 300 million Europeans to genuinely work together in a price-transparent environment, free from exchange rate conversion costs, in a spirit of mutuality and co-operation.

In this century, it will be the European single currency that will be the most significant event surpassing the internet as the second most significant. Our pound already has two exchange rates: one for domestic sales and one for export sales.

Export sales are effectively achieved by discounting the exchange rate by 10 to 20% or quoting in US dollars. Going in at about three DM to the pound is quite reasonable even if the euro has now depreciated by about 30% in terms of US dollars.

Conversion costs at £36bn are exaggerated. With advances in computer software technology, it would be much less. There would be an instant market for British goods overnight when we change to the euro. The benefits would be in hundreds of billions of pounds.

Our economy is fundamentally stronger than many European countries and we would end up as one of the leaders in the pack.

Nagindas Khajuria FCCA
Simplification Made Simple, Chartered Certified Accountants, London

2001
We need full euro debate by Geoff Wood, Marlow

The letter from Nagindas Khajuria (Britain and the euro, page 15, 21 June) is all too typical of those who wish to railroad the voters of the UK into accepting the inevitability of increasing immersion in Europe. Far from this being the 'time for action' we still need to have a full debate about the euro, and not just on the short-term economic benefits.

His statement that Europe is a local market with a 2000-year-old cultural and civilisation background similar to us is breathtaking in its ignorance of the last 400 years of British history. We have in fact spent much of this period resolving bloody wars caused by fundamental European ethnic and political problems.

Are we really ready to surrender our sovereignty to a German superstate and set aside so casually the sacrifices made by so many? Yes, the economic arguments set out by Mr Khajuria are persuasive, but our national strengths have always been multi-faceted, open to the entire world and free of bureaucratic constraints. If we submerge our identity in a club dominated by France and Germany, the principal axis of which is moving further east, we shall become within 50 years a peripheral blob bobbing largely ignored off the coast of this vast incompetent and impenetrable mass.

Nagindas Khajuria FCCA
Simplification Made Simple, Chartered Certified Accountants, London

2001

Put an end to jingoism

I refer to the letter from Geoff Wood (letters, page 11, 12 July). One is reminded of the Cold War, Star Wars, Entente Cordial, Splendid Isolation, Sick Man of Europe, King Henry of France from 12th to 18th century, non alignment, and so on.

The euro has come about as a result of the vision of European leaders going back about 60 years. They then had just come out of two world wars.

Had it not been for their gradual efforts and achievements in terms of moves towards a tariff-free market, more stable exchange rates, common agricultural policy, common defence policy, better social conditions for workers, and so on, we would already have witnessed a third world war by now. These 60 years have not seen any cultural or national diminution of the very distinct German, French, Italian or British cultures.

What has changed is that common economic interests have increased prosperity and reduced the chances of past ethnic or political problems.

The bureaucracy in the United Kingdom, if anything, is far greater than the bureaucracy in the rest of Europe.

The living proof of that is that the standard and cost of living in the UK is much higher than in several European countries. Europe, as it stands, is not a vast incompetent and impenetrable mass, as Mr Wood says.

Europe is in fact a vibrant, fast-moving, efficient powerhouse of what is best in art, science, medicine, cuisine, fashion, technology, high-quality public sector services, and the manufacture of goods.

The euro is merely a commodity that is used for settlement of transactions. It is nothing more. There is a costly waste of about 10% just in the spread between buying rate and selling rate when you convert and then reconvert from and to the same currency.

It is a fallacy to believe that somehow the euro reduces our sovereignty and our ability to manage our own economy.

Nagindas Khajuria FCCA
Simplification Made Simple, Chartered Certified Accountants, London

2001
Tongue firmly in his cheek by J E Francis, Loxley

What a fabulous letter from Nagindas Khajuria (page 13, 26 July). There must an anagram in there to describe my feelings.

As I read it I enjoyed his selective view of European history but thought his tongue was in his cheek.

When I got to the bit where he describes the modern Europe as 'vibrant, fast moving, efficient powerhouse...' I collapsed on the floor, rolling around in agony of laughter. It was when I recovered that I realised the whole letter was a brilliantly conceived joke (rather like the EU).

Well done, Nagindas. More power to your pen.

2001
Staying in control

I refer to the letter from Nagindas Khajuria (Letters, page 13, 26 July), in which he attempts to put forward positive reasons why this country should scrap its own currency and join the euro.

Like most of the arguments that we see in favour of the euro, the vast majority of the points are subjective and thus difficult to refute. I will not, for instance, attempt to argue with the view that the advent of the common agricultural policy of the European Union has avoided a third world war. In his concluding paragraph however, Mr Khajuria states that 'it is a fallacy to believe that somehow the euro reduces our sovereignty and our ability to manage our own economy'.

The questions I would ask Mr Khajuria are: 1. Is the ability to raise or lower interest rates a tool in the management of the economy? 2. If we entered the euro, would we retain our ability to set our own interest rates?

On the assumption that Mr Khajuria would agree that the answers are 'yes' and 'no' respectively, then entering the euro would reduce our ability to manage our own economy. QED.

Attempting to control an economy without the ability to set interest rates in line with the requirements of that economy is somewhat akin to attempting to drive a car without control of the accelerator or brake pedals, as the Germans and Irish are beginning to realise.

Nagindas Khajuria FCCA
Simplification Made Simple. Chartered Certified Accountants, London

2001
Exchange Rate

Geoffrey Dick highlighted the most fundamental problem we have — how to maintain a balance between exchange rate, interest rate, inflation rate and consumer demand (Business last week).

My view is that we should do whatever it takes to bring the British real effective exchange rate back to a realistic, sustainable level.

We could allow interest rates to fall further and further, even below the EU rate. Or we could reduce our target of a 2.5% inflation rate to 1.5%.

Alternatively, we could use the harmonised index that the European Central Bank (ECB) tracks. The Treasury could introduce this in the next budget.

And to limit consumer demand, we could introduce indirect import curbs such as discouraging imports of out-of-season fresh fruits and vegetables and so on.

2001
Off the rails

Sir – The government plan to set up a not-for-profit trust in the place of Railtrack should be reconsidered. To gauge their interest in taking a stake in the new group, the government should approach all the 25 Tocs (train operating companies) for a vertically-integrated operation. Your front page story (7 October) states that it has already approached, probably, National Express for exactly such an operation.

These Tocs should be reduced to four private successful rail companies with responsibility for tracks and signals over the next 25 years. Railtrack's mistake over the past five years was that it spent too much time, money and effort in developing stations rather than tracks. The mistake of the Tocs was to create 25 companies from one (British Rail) company instead of, say, four and five. The result is a jungle of complex fare structures, lack of punctuality, fatal accidents, blaming each other, etc.

The government has neither the time, the money nor the managerial ability to run Railtrack. Why should the infrastructure not be released to the Tocs?

Nagindas Khajuria FCCA
Simplification Made Simple, Chartered Certified Accountants, London

2001
Hidden costs

Sir – I agree with Nagindas Khajuria's view that Railtrack spent too much time developing its stations rather than its tracks (Letters, 14 October). Some of our stations, such as Liverpool Street and Paddington in London, have improved immensely in appearance, but the primary role of stations is to be points of departure.

I believe the management of Railtrack became bewitched by the example of BAA, which after privatisation set about turning its airports into shopping malls. The City should carry some of the blame. After Railtrack's privatisation, we heard lots of talk from analysts about the "hidden property assets" in the company and little about hidden infrastructure costs.

2001
Shaken but not stirred:
Mrs Doyle's substitute – James Bond – etc

I wonder why the Inland Revenue is not wising up after all those past IT contract failures.

For example, why don't they consider tendering piece meal, so that each contract is worth, say, one-hundredth of £4bn? As for national security, I do not believe that is an issue here at all.

Apart from IT, they also need to change their basic procedures. One example is to insist that tax returns are submitted without any supporting accounts and schedules.

These can even be submitted only for those boxes that are applicable. What a waste of papers and UK woodlands and national resources. What a waste of storage space.

Nagindas Khajuria FCCA
Simplification Made Simple, Chartered Certified Accountants, London

2002
Stretching a point

I read your article on Lord Sharman's review of central government accounting ('Sharman fights burial' page 2, 10 January).

I wonder whether wider investigatory powers for the National Audit Office, including access to private sector bodies that receive public money, is feasible.

It would be more practical to ensure that public money is guarded better before it leaves the public purse.

The analogy I would like to draw is as follows. Suppose I want to touch my right ear lobe with my hand. I could touch it by raising my right hand. Alternatively, I could raise my left hand which would go over my head, and touch it with my left hand.

2002
Separate Ways

Sir – As an accountant for 40 years, I read your leader article (20/21 January) with great interest. The Securities & Exchange Commission study that found the Big Five earning $2.69 in consultancy for every dollar in audit is interesting, but the idea just to split the five firms two ways is not the answer.

The commonly-quoted and known consultancy, or non-audit, fees is generally further divided into tax planning, tax compliance, financial consultancy and operational, including HR, consultancy. The two divisions should be audit and tax compliance as one entity, and tax planning, financial and operational consultancy as another.

There should be no cross-ownership of these two entities.

Nagindas Khajuria FCCA
Simplification Made Simple, Chartered Certified Accountants, London

2002

No government should play tax or race card

Sir – Bill Jamieson's article (Taxing time, 3/4 February) is worthy of great scrutiny as it looks at almost every feasible type of increase in taxation the chancellor might introduce in the budget on 17 April.

Lower direct taxes encourage enterprise and the creation of wealth. Higher indirect taxes punish the poor. Whether poor or rich, we have not been able to change people's spending habits by changes in taxation.

So, the true reason for increasing the taxes must be for better public services. The election manifesto pledge in 1997 was fundamentally flawed. No government should play the tax or race card. In fact, manifestos stifle new ideas and are best used in a very limited fashion.

The chancellor will probably need £5bn to £7bn extra every year for the next few years as both consumption and growth are likely to be very low for a number of years. The markets have reached saturation point. Prime minister Tony Blair and Gordon Brown could kill two birds with one stone by introducing a new 5% lower rate and abolish personal allowances altogether.

At the same time, they could reduce the basic rate of tax of 22% to 20% and introduce a third rate and fifth rate of 30% and 50% so that Middle England at the lower earnings level would effectively pay lesser taxes at lower levels and higher taxes at higher levels more equitably.

The Treasury and IFS computer models could look into these proposals. I reckon it would bring in about £3bn extra income tax revenue.

In addition, the chancellor could introduce a new 20% Vat rate on luxury goods, such as cars. That would bring in another £3bn extra Vat income without hurting the poor.

Finally, Mr Brown should be honest about reporting on how much public money may have been wasted during the last fiscal year by giving specific examples which with hindsight may not seem to have been the best course of action.

For example, £4bn was spent on burning 4 m animals suspected of having foot-and-mouth disease. It may or may not have been a good thing to have done.

There may be other examples. By admitting their mistakes, they could win more respect for their endeavours.

Nagindas Khajuria FCCA
Simplification Made Simple, Chartered Certified Accountants, London

2002
Time for a rethink

So the Inland Revenue is about to give a £4bn contract over 18 years to one major company.

I strongly feel that it should rethink. Most Inland Revenue, Customs & Excise and benefits and contribution agency offices reflect the same input/output throughout the UK.

Why not make one UK area, say London or Birmingham, a guinea pig and give a contract for say £4 m to a small Indian or Russian company to come up with a model that can be tested and repeated throughout the country.

Why commit to £4bn when past experience with EDS and NI computer systems has not been good? Why get their fingers burnt twice?

2002
Get Real

Sir – Your article on the MPC's dilemma was very interesting. The 2.5% per annum inflation target was set in 1997, when interest rates were generally higher than now. I believe the MPC should now urgently seek new guidelines from the chancellor in his next budget, for several reasons.

Firstly, UK GDP is only about 5% of the world's GDP. Germany's is 10%, Japan's is 20% and the USA's is 30%. Historically, all these countries have lower interest rates than the UK. To compete, we also need to keep interest rates low.

Secondly, there are signs of unease in the public sector, and wage demands are now surfacing more regularly. Increasing interest rates will only fuel cost-push, rather than demand-pull, inflation.

Thirdly, your article suggest that mortgage borrowing is rising at the rate of 10% per annum. But so are house prices – at a similar rate. The increased borrowing may be partly for luxury goods and services, but it is also for durable goods and construction and the improvement of properties, and so it is good for the economy.

Fourthly, UK competitiveness in manufacturing has risen very slowly compared with the rest of the world. If we take relative export prices as 100 in 1990, the 1998 prices were 117.2. By contrast, the relative import prices in 1998 were 108.6.

Fifthly, if sterling has risen against the euro since the euro's inception, it will rise more if interest rates increase, and

Nagindas Khajuria FCCA
Simplification Made Simple, Chartered Certified Accountants, London

2002 Get Real

our competitiveness will be even worse hit. One idea could be to "aim" for 0% inflation in five years' time by reducing the inflation target of 2.5% by 0.5% each year so that we reach the goal by year five.

For all these reasons, I believe interest rates should remain consistently low for at least the next five years.

2002 Scary Pound

I disagree with David Smith (Economic Outlook, last week). The pound is scary if you look a few years ahead. The trade deficit in the past was cushioned by a surplus in net interest, dividend and investment income. This is not likely to happen in the future judging by the reductions in forecast pension-fund values, equity returns and so on.

The record current account deficit of £7.6 billion in the final quarter of 2001 should be seen in the light of the cumulative 1995–2000 trade deficit of £113 billion offset by a cumulative invisible surplus of £94 billion.

The next five years could see a similar cumulative trade deficit but a much smaller invisible surplus. The chancellor may just find a "yes" answer to the five economic tests for joining the euro rather than a "no" answer for all these reasons.

The newly industrialised countries are coming up fast and to keep up our competitiveness we shall have to act fast on long-term low interest rates, low inflation and a lower pound.

Nagindas Khajuria FCCA
Simplification Made Simple, Chartered Certified Accountants, London

2002

Interest dilemma

Sir – I found your article (31 March/2 April) very interesting which examined the monetary policy committee's dilemma when consumer demand and private borrowing is rising fast, making them inclined to raise interest rates to deflate the economy and also presented the counter arguments by Shushill Wadhwani that the increase may inflate rather than deflate the economy.

The 2½%-a-year inflation target was set in 1997 when interest rates were generally higher than now. I believe the MPC should now urgently seek new guidelines from the chancellor in his next budget for several reasons.

First, UK GDP as part of the world GDP is only about 5%, Germany's being 10%, Japan's 20% and the US's 30%. Historically, all the latter countries (except the UK) had lower interest rates. To compete with them, we also need to keep interest rates low.

Second, there are signs of unease in the public sector and wage demands are now surfacing more regularly. Increasing interest rates will only fuel cost-push rather than demand-pull inflation.

Third, your article suggests that mortgage borrowing is rising at the rate of 10% a year. But house prices are rising at a similar rate. The increased borrowing may be partly for excesses, but partly for durable goods and construction and improvement of properties. So it is good for the economy.

Fourth, UK competitiveness in trade in manufacturing has risen very poorly compared with the rest of the world. If we take relative export prices as 100 in 1990, the 1998 prices were 117.2. By contrast, the relative import prices in 1998 were 108.6.

Fifth, if sterling has risen against the euro since the euro's inception, it will rise more by an increase in interest rates and our competitiveness will be even worse.

One idea could be to "aim" for 0% inflation in five years time by reducing the inflation target of 2½% by ½% each year so that we reach the goal by year five. Long-term measures are far better than short-term measures. Whether we join the euro or not, our import-export trade with the European Union is 57% of our total international trade.

It makes sense to aim to counteract the 25% appreciation of sterling since 1996 by a 25% depreciation of sterling against the euro by 2007. For all these wider reasons, I believe interest rates should remain very low constantly for at least the next five years.

Nagindas Khajuria FCCA
Simplification Made Simple, Chartered Certified Accountants, London

2002
Not the time for tax rises

I have read a lot recently about various measures such as national insurance tax increases, credits for research and development, etc. that might or might not have been be in the Budget box.

However, I have not read, or heard, much about what the chancellor is planning to do with the public sector borrowing requirement.

I would like to take the readers back to Kenneth Clarke's debut Budget on 30 November, 1993.

The chancellor's measures at that time were meant to reduce PSBR by £5.5bn in 1994/95, £7bn in 1995/96 and £10.5bn in 1996/97. The PSBR at the time was just under £50bn. He also wanted the PSBR to decline to zero in the second half of the decade.

Mr Brown has followed his example and reduced PSBR to almost nil or a surplus in his last five Budgets.

With interest rates at their lowest for many years it may be better to go back to a deficit budget rather than increase taxes and go for a surplus budget.

Allowing the PSBR requirement to go back to 3% of GDP at £30bn may not be a bad idea. Raising taxes is definitely a bad idea until public sector reforms are actually achieved and quantified. This would only be clear from the results of the next general election.

Nagindas Khajuria FCCA
Simplification Made Simple, Chartered Certified Accountants, London

Fingers in too many pies

I am writing with regard to non-executive directors. I do not agree with comments by Lord Yough of Graffham. Many non-executive directors stay with the same company for several years.

Surely over time, NEDs can get a good feel for the direction in which a company is going and by staying aloof and reviewing the company from a distance, they do have a vital role to play.

What Lord Young of Graffham and the institute of directors should be reviewing is the practice of full-time executor directors who have executive directorships in several companies.

That is the area that the current code of corporate governance should revise so 'full-time' really means 'full-time in one company'. That would open up so many posts for new blood and new energy that is so badly lacking in UK plcs.

Statistics rethink

Sir – I agree with many of the points made in your article UK growth data points to flaws in statistics (2/5 June). However, I do not believe ONS plans to follow American statisticians' lead and introduce "chain-weighting" to measure UK output more accurately is a wise move. ONS still relies too much on survey evidence rather than actual input figures by business and government.

A much better idea would be to rely on income tax, corporation tax and Vat returns and make it mandatory that each return contains one main industrial classification. Then there would be no need to send compulsory survey forms requesting statistical information. Some companies just throw away such questionnaires.

Nagindas Khajuria FCCA
Simplification Made Simple, Chartered Certified Accountants, London

Competence of non-executive directors & planned review

Your article about the competence of NEDs and the planned review by Patricia Hewitt and Derek Higgs is timely and relevant to the urgent needs of the financial community. The planned review could perhaps include the desirability of industry sector specialisation on top of all the other skills. NEDs could then become the stuffing in the turkey rather than just parsley on the chicken.

Mind the gap on universities' tuition fees

Sir – Seventy per cent of university mega-mergers have failed, so it's best to concentrate on quality rather than quantity. According to 1997 OECD statistics, 24% of UK females and 19% of males aged 16 to 24 were inactive or unemployed. In other EU countries (apart from Italy) and the US, the percentages were much lower.

These issues should be addressed before university mergers. Mahatma Gandhi said:

"I do not want mass production, I want production by the masses."

Nagindas Khajuria FCCA
Simplification Made Simple, Chartered Certified Accountants, London

2002
Value of degrees in today's workplace

Fault: Marrin is right about the plight and funding of UK universities. Apart from the government, it is also the fault of the private-sector employers to give so much importance to degrees. I applied for about 200 senior jobs in 200 companies during 1999 and 2000. I was rejected mainly because I did not have a degree, so I enrolled in the Open University for a master's in economics. I have only a professional accountancy qualification and 40 years' experience, which were totally ignored by all the potential 200 employers. Somehow employers think that if you have a degree, you have a better way of thinking. What rubbish.

2002
Pensions dilemma

Sir – This whole idea of valuing pensions every year is fundamentally flawed. Pensions relate to new employees, old employees and employees who leave halfway. Some die young, some die old. There is no single way of knowing what future liabilities are likely to be, nor of valuing the assets that are backing these liabilities.

Various accounting standard methods were used in the past: projected-unit method, current-unit method, discontinuance method. Various actuarial methods were used in the past: aggregate method, attained-age method, entry-age method and so on. Ten years ago, trustees valued pension funds 100%-based on a discount rate. Five years ago, it was 50% discount rate and 50% market value. Now it is 100% market value. Market values are only 50% right at any given point in time.

The funds themselves are not just a simplistic split between equities and bonds. There are UK equity funds, North American funds, Euro funds, Japanese funds and so on. What is the point of valuing all these varying assets every year? It is too short-termist a view and altogether an unnecessary exercise in number-crunching.

A far better idea would be to value pensions only every five years, taking into account long-term trends in equity and interest, income potential and long-term growth prospects.

Nagindas Khajuria FCCA
Simplification Made Simple, Chartered Certified Accountants, London

2003
Accentuate the positive aspects of the euro

Sir – In your editorial (An unhappy birthday for the euro, 22/23 December), you mention that ideal interest rates for Germany would be 1.7%, for Ireland 12.5%, Portugal 9.9%, Italy 5.2%, Spain 7.8% and France 3.8% because of their differing levels of inflation and output.

Such research is ludicrous, for a number of reasons. Historically, central banks have used several methods to expand or contract the economy or aggregate demand: interest rates, open market operations and reserve ratios. National banks will continue to engage in open market operations and standing facilities on low, medium and high levels, as they have been doing for years.

Second, the governors of the 11 national central banks and the six executive board members of the European Central Bank comprise the governing council of the ECB and these 11 national banks will continue to play a vital role in monetary policies of the euro. This is quite different from the centralised control of the US Federal Reserve.

Third, prices or inflation in the above countries is only marginally higher than in the UK. Unemployment may be higher partly because of the way statistics are prepared.

Fourth, growth could be slightly lower in the Euro countries than the UK, but for decades their public sector services have been superior in quality and far cheaper in price than in the UK.

Fifth, it is nonsensical to have different interest rates applicable to countries which have the same exchange rates. Finally, there has never been one interest rate that fits all in the EU: there has always been base rate, Lombard rate, short-term rate, long-term rate, real interest rate, nominal interest rate and effective exchange rate, all different for individual EU member countries.

It is high time your paper acknowledges the positive aspects of the far-sighted vision that the euro encapsulates, rather than just lingering on its short-term difficulties. The UK media, by playing all the time the tune the reader wants to hear, is doing a great disservice to this country.

Nagindas Khajuria FCCA
Simplification Made Simple, Chartered Certified Accountants, London

2003
Alice in euro land

Sir – Nagin Khajuria (Letters, 5/6 January) refers to your editorial a fortnight earlier in which you set out the ideal interest rates for certain euroland countries. Khajuria suggests that this is a pointless exercise since each country has the same exchange rate, via the euro, with the result that there has to be one interest rate set across euroland as a whole (it currently stands at 2.75%).

Khajuria is missing the point. Where a Euroland country's actual interest rate is significantly different to the optimum interest rate for that country's economy, the country concerned will suffer economic damage – typically, either unemployment will be too high or inflation will be too high as a result of having the wrong interest rate.

I currently compute that the UK needs an interest rate of 4.4%, and euroland 2.8% – close to the actual rates of 4% and 2.75%, respectively. I use the well-respected Taylor Rule, which expounds that the current interest rate for an economy at any given point in time is a function of that economy's inflation rate and output gap. I estimate that Germany currently needs an interest rate of 0%, putting the country in broadly the same position as Japan, which apparently needs (and, indeed, has) an interest rate of around 0%.

Germany's actual current interest rate of 2.75%, therefore, is hopelessly inappropriate. The resulting economic damage being wrought – with the Germany economy barely growing at all and with soaring unemployment – must be clear for all to see.

2003
Great idea

Congratulations on introducing your excellent new Adviser section (see Services, back pages, every edition) for small practitioners.

Classical economics defines economics as a dual system: on the one side, big enterprises which are strong in public perception and sustaining them, on the other the thousands of small manufacturers, artisans, services enterprises, merchants and other entrepreneurs and the rural masses.

Nagindas Khajuria FCCA
Simplification Made Simple, Chartered Certified Accountants, London

2003
All too easy to feed anti-American mood

Sir – Your editorial suggests that the UN resolution clearly puts the onus on Iraq to make "a currently accurate, full and complete declaration of all aspects of its programmes to develop chemical, biological and nuclear weapons, ballistic missiles and other delivery systems". Yet we should consider what is also precipitating the US into war and dragging Britain with it.

First, the US has spent an average of around 5% of its GDP on military aircraft, submarines, missiles, rockets and so on for the past 50 years to counter the threat of communism. As the cold war is over now, it wants to prove that such expenditure is warranted over the next 50 years. In 1991, military equipment revenues accounted for a substantial part of US companies' turnover: Boeing (20%), General Dynamics (84%), Grumman (89%), Lockheed (50%), Martin Marietta (43%), McDonnell Douglas (48%) and Northrop (10%). A lot of this arsenal was never deployed and was wasted as technology kept changing, Germany and Japan were wiser: they spent 1% and 0% of GDP on defence during the same period.

Second, 55% of world oil reserves are concentrated in Saudi Arabia (25%), Iran (10%), Iraq (10%) and the Gulf states (10%). US oil companies are already losing influence there due to emerging non-US oil companies.

Third, homo sapiens likes the sound of warring drums. Maybe there is no enemy, no threat – we just like to fight.

2003
The all new FRSSE

Your article on international accounting standards and SMEs (Adviser, page 33, 13 February) refers to UK experience in successfully producing and selling the FRSSE to small practitioners as a success.

I believe repeating that 'success' in a new FRSSE to take into account the new IAS or the new IRS effective 2005 would be regressive rather than progressive.

Small practitioners are competent enough to read and digest the full international accounting standards just like mid-tier and the Big Four firms, and if they are not, they should be encouraged to be so.

They can easily pick up and apply the bits that are relevant to the smaller firms, with the added advantage of understanding the broader issues. They should not be spoon-fed on what is relevant and what is not relevant to them in matters of standards.

Nagindas Khajuria FCCA
Simplification Made Simple, Chartered Certified Accountants, London

2003

Beyond our means

Sir – Your article (Brown faces a tough grilling from MPs, 23/24 February) refers to chancellor Gordon Brown frequently getting his GDP growth forecasts wrong and the unpalatable choice between yet more tax hikes, spending cuts or a big rise in public borrowing over the next few years.

Between 1979 and 1992, the average government receipts as a percentage of nominal GDP were 39.68%. Government outlays were 42.14%. That is an average deficit of 2.46% of nominal GDP, or a £24.6bn average deficit for 14 years.

Comparable average figures for the US were 30.50%/33.02%: deficit 2.52%; Japan 31.14%/32.00%: deficit 0.86%; Germany 45.8%/47.32%: deficit 1.52%; France 47.84%/49.94%: deficit 2.1%.

Germany, Japan and France have closed the technology and productivity gap with the US, the UK has not. Since 1992, we are probably still suffering from the same average deficit each year.

Maybe Mr Brown should look at the bigger picture influencing this state of affairs. We cannot carry on living beyond our means, importing more than we can export.

He should concentrate on managing supply-side factors that affect output and productivity rather than demand-side management.

Nagindas Khajuria FCCA
Simplification Made Simple, Chartered Certified Accountants, London

Euro issue cannot be forced

Your two articles, FDs' euro doubts grow and FDs' lose faith in single currency (Pages 1 & 2, 27 February) are partly misleading. If we split the 20% who were neutral, we can say that 44% were in favour and 56% against in the survey of 300 FDs.

The reasons why the 56% are misguided are as follows:

International trade is growing at twice the rate of industrial growth. It follows that trade issues are twice as important as economic issues. Consumer tastes are changing fast and very often. Communications are also much faster. This means we must be at the forefront of international trade to meet changing demands.

Because of the customs union, member countries have eliminated tariffs among themselves and established a common tariff schedule on goods from outside countries. It is fundamentally flawed for Britain to be a member of this customs union that trades internationally in the euro while the UK continues to trade in sterling using the same tariff barrier against non-EU countries.

There is a strong consensus among economists that the formation of the EEC has resulted in substantially more trade creation than diversion.

International scale economies and product differentiation have been even more significant. There is now a significant increase in intra-industry trade among all members rather than an increase in inter-industrial specialisation.

For the UK, the 'four freedoms'- to trade, to migrate, to invest and to conduct business, irrespective of national borders – are vital. Again, as members, we take part in developing community regulations and policies dealing with competition, labour, industry, social affairs, energy, the environment and consumer issues.

We are part of CAP, which on balance has been beneficial to all European farmers and we take part in formulating regional policies that aid economically backward parts of the community. Not joining the euro reminds me of the proverb, you can take a horse to water, but you cannot force it to drink.

Finally, Lyndon B Johnson once said: 'The world has narrowed to a neighbourhood before it has broadened into a brotherhood.'

If the US is a superpower, the EU is a superior superpower in the making, growing gradually, sensibly and steadily, whether you look back at the past 60 years or look forward to the next 60 years.

Nagindas Khajuria FCCA
Simplification Made Simple, Chartered Certified Accountants, London

2003

Rose-tinted view of EU by John Broughton, Ruthun

I imagine Nagin Khajuria seeks to be provocative rather than constructive in his letter (letter, page 17, 6 March). To simply halve the 'don't knows' is disingenuous – a soundly based distribution gives 57.5% against and 42.5% for.

He ignores distortions produced by the perverse intervention of the Brussels Machine eg a misrepresentation (understatement) of UK exports due to the Amsterdam effect and so on.

To state that the CAP has been 'beneficial to European farmers' is an absolute untruth. Within the UK, the CAP has been a disaster for our farmers and denies them the opportunity fully to supply their home market. The CAP has added significantly to the economic plight of UK agriculture.

Joining the euro is more than just adopting a currency. It is a complete abandonment of what remains of our sovereignty. Further, there is no discernible democracy in Brussels. The euro will only work efficiently when fiscal and economic decisions are made on a pan-EU basis.

Khajuria seems to take an extremely rose-tinted view of the EU. Sadly, the reality is rather darker and unlikely to improve. The convention producing a constitution seems determined to make the whole institution even less democratic and more remote from the people it allegedly serves.

Nagindas Khajuria FCCA
Simplification Made Simple, Chartered Certified Accountants, London

Back Chat

I refer to John Broughton's letter about the EU (page 17, March 13) and his comments about my letter on the EU (page 17, March 6).

My intentions were to stimulate sensible debate about the issues involved as a British citizen, loyal to UK's long-term interests, rather than being provocative on the matter. My counter arguments are:

- Joining the euro is no more than adopting a currency. It has nothing to do with sovereignty of a nation.
- Over the years, numerous countries have shown and are still showing enthusiasm to join the EU and the euro. If you visit any of these countries, they continue to enjoy their own culture, language, television, food and people, and you hardly notice that they are part of 20 to 30 different nations. In fact, you notice only a handful of inhabitants from other member countries.
- If a cost benefit analysis was done on whether we should join the euro, the benefits would far outweigh the costs from political, economic, social, cultural and red tape. UK home-grown red tape is a costlier nature than EU red tape.

Nagindas Khajuria FCCA
Simplification Made Simple, Chartered Certified Accountants, London

2003

High price of euro [1-5 para by Cliff Redman, Worthng] [6th para by David Ball, Newham]

Nagin Khajuria says the benefit of joining the euro 'would far outweigh the costs from political, economic, social, cultural and red tape' (20 March, page 13).

The euro may make things a little easier for multinational companies and holidaymakers, but there is clear evidence that its introduction in the countries that have joined has resulted in increased costs. It has also prevented countries, such as Germany, from taking much needed steps to boost an economy in difficulty.

It is not surprising that the leaders of some countries are showing enthusiasm for joining the EU. Virtually without exception, they can expect to receive considerable financial help from the EU, which will be paid for mainly by Germany, France and the UK. We already contribute billions of pounds a year to the EU, which could be better spent alleviating NHS waiting lists, pensioner poverty and so on.

Local councils are ceding powers to EU-inspired regional government, Westminster is rapidly becoming confined to rubber-stamping legislation that can then be overruled in European courts and our fishing industry has been decimated and officers of the proposed European police force will be immune from prosecution of any wrongdoing.

One can see plenty of costs, both financial and democratic, in EU membership, but precious little benefit. The euro is simply another manifestation of the process, and if we continue down this road we can expect to lose far more than we gain, even though we may keep our Yorkshire puddings and Devon cream!

I am happy that Nagin Khajuria is so convinced about the outcome of a cost benefit analysis on the introduction of the euro that he can tell us its outcome before it has been done. Obviously all euro sceptics should give in now.

Nagindas Khajuria FCCA
Simplification Made Simple, Chartered Certified Accountants, London

Give Mervyn growth and unemployment too

Sir – Your article on what the new Bank of England governor should do in the medium and long term, "Memo to Mervyn King: UK must do better" (6/7 July), touches on growth, unemployment, etc. The Federal Reserve Bank in the US has responsibility for the latter two in addition to the inflation target. Your paper may want to consider publishing a memo to Gordon Brown asking him to transfer responsibility for the growth rate and employment to the Bank so the latter's actions could be more appropriate for the UK economy.

Also, if we join the euro, the UK economy would improve without making any effort in exports, tourism and imports.

Finally, I do not believe the UK's savings rate averaged 9% between 1972 and 1995 as your article suggests. It was much lower.

Trying to book an appointment with your doctor?

I agree with Michael Queen that the NHS should follow the German healthcare reforms and start charging for services ('FD warns of NHS rationing', 14 August, page 3). Successive governments can no longer bury their heads in the sand.

The charge system should be reformed so that only those, and their children, who are means-tested and in receipt of state benefits should be exempt. It should not be like the current prescription charge system where five out of six prescriptions are exempt for children under 16, those over 60 and so on.

This is encouraging pharmaceutical companies to continue investing heavily into new drugs that are sometimes totally unnecessary. In 1996, prescription charges accounted for 12.1% of the total NHS bill.

A charge of £10 per visit to the doctor could raise about £3bn with an average of five visits per year per patient. In addition, visits to the hospital should be charged at £25 per visit and at £50 per day for a stay in hospital.

Nagindas Khajuria FCCA
Simplification Made Simple, Chartered Certified Accountants, London

2003

Paying for GPs is not practical by Kevin Olney, Coventry

I picked up my friend's copy of *Accountancy Age* and read with absolute disbelief the letter from Nagin Khajuria regarding charging for visits to your GP (21 August, page 11).

I am quite well paid for a factory worker and bring home around £250 per week. Out of this I pay my mortgage, but due to the fact that endowments are underperforming I am having to overpay by £200 per month. I do not have a flash car, I have a ten-year-old one. I have a small loan for work on the house. I pay into a pension. My council tax has gone up, as has my motor and house insurance, but I haven't had a pay rise in three years.

I pay for my optical requirements and dental requirements but have to save in advance. I do not smoke or drink in pubs and dine out only on special occasions. I do not get paid sick leave, I lose the money.

Would Khajuria care to explain to me where I can conjure the extra money to visit my GP? Or would it be better to strip out numerous layers of underworked, overpaid beancounters from the NHS and clamp down on 'health tourism' which costs untold millions?

Nagindas Khajuria FCCA
Simplification Made Simple, Chartered Certified Accountants, London

2003

Mortgage debt could be tied to maintenance

Sir – The article by Bill Jamieson ("Debt, the anchor on Britain's hopes of economic recovery", 31 August/1 September) was very interesting. It prompted me to compare the situation with the commercial debt-to-equity ratios and income gearing ratios used by the private sector.

The current stock of 25m homes at an average of £129,258 each gives a balance sheet total of £3,231bn. Total debt of £878bn gives a ratio of 27%. By this standard, it would still mean low gearing. The interest payable annually on this debt is about £61bn; 25m household's income at £400 per week is £520bn. Interest works out at 12% of income or interest cover is 8.5 times. Again, this situation may not be considered too bad.

Probably about 50% of British houses are not in well-maintained condition. Expenditure on maintenance, repairs and decoration account for almost 13% of average weekly expenditure. That is £68bn a year.

Future advances could be tied more strictly to home improvements by making the advances to the building contractor rather than the borrower over a certain amount. Then rising mortgage debt would serve a better purpose and extend the life of residential properties by at least a third.

Nagindas Khajuria FCCA
Simplification Made Simple, Chartered Certified Accountants, London

2003 Astonishing Read by James Percival

I was astonished to read the letter from Nagin Khajuria (21 August, page 11) regarding paying for GP visits.

The real people to suffer from such income based benefits are those just above the threshold, as they can find themselves worse off than those receiving benefits, as demonstrated by Kevin Olney's response (4 September, page 13).

For an accountant to fail to recognise the consequences of his suggestion makes it clear why politicians, who don't seem to think through the consequences of their actions, spend their life dreaming up such benefits and perpetuate the poverty trap around cut-off levels.

2003 Education

While I agree that education should be geared more towards business (Editorial, September), the advent of large companies is also partly to blame for a lack of entrepreneurial spirit in our youngsters.

In almost every industry sector, five or fewer companies control 75 per cent of the UK market. For example, over the last 25 years, the five main supermarkets have increased their market share from 50 per cent to 75 per cent. Perhaps this explains why food sold in supermarkets is so bland and monotonous. Yet the Competition Commission does nothing to stop this harmful development of multinationals in all market segments.

In such circumstances, youngsters will always be encouraged to be employees rather than employers.

Nagindas Khajuria FCCA
Simplification Made Simple, Chartered Certified Accountants, London

2003
Keep it simple

Sir – Bill Jamieson's article on the jobs boom in the public sector – a 3.9% increase in two years to 2003 Q1 ("Boom time in welfare land as Brown's billions flood in", 7/8 September) – highlights waste and duplication of public funds on a massive scale that could bankrupt the UK in 20 years' time.

What the public sector needs is drastic streamlining of the entire government machinery, its systems and procedures.

For example, to claim state benefits you have to fill in numerous forms that run to more than 50 pages, which humiliates many potential applicants too proud to be means tested and who lose out on the benefits to which they are entitled. One simple annual tax return system could be used where drawings, mortgage payments, car ownership, house ownership etc could be filled in only once each year to provide realistic data on whether an individual or a household's lifestyle is consistent with income and the need for state benefits.

Currently we use thousands of tax and benefit staff to vet thousands of forms and records which are conducive to tax evasion and fraudulent benefit claims. There are also contradictions in the system. For instance, if you do not claim benefits, then you do not need to declare your partner's income but, if you do [claim benefit], you need to declare your partner's income.

The Finance Act makes a few minor changes to tax rates and tax laws, yet the UK taxation system is horrendously complex. Rates could be set for three years with one Finance Act every three years.

Such unnecessary bureaucracy and form-filling has permeated through all government departments in the past 20 years where no real work is done and everyone is checking and ticking boxes to verify one another's work. A huge amount of glossy brochures and leaflets are published that no one reads.

One can go on and on. When you spend £50 to process an order to purchase a £3 hammer, of course you are going to need ever more government staff to handle the systems and procedures. It is all waste and it is not real employment with growth potential for any country.

One final example is dividend income. Thousands of shareholders now have very few shares in privatised companies which continue to issue cheques and dividend vouchers for a few pence every six months. Surely any cheque issued for less

Nagindas Khajuria FCCA
Simplification Made Simple, Chartered Certified Accountants, London

2003
Conflict Zone

than £10 is a complete waste if you count all the processing costs involved. Again, the pence could easily be dropped from the entire country's financial accounting and reporting system without making the slightest difference in the results.

Sir – The article on the Big Four accountancy firms ("Fires that won't go out for the Big Four", 12/13 October) raises interesting issues about the need for a new business model for them. Their dominance of 78% market share in audit services, probably worldwide, should be curtailed to around 50% by giving opportunity to second-tier accountancy firms, who could bring in better and fresher ideas. Internal audit should be abolished, and all work relating to internal audit should be done by the audit firms as part of better quality external financial and operational audit procedures by the Big Four.

Tax compliance and tax planning; corporate finance; management consultancy and human resources; and external audit are mutually exclusive disciplines. The Big Four should be split again so that they would be allowed to provide only one of these. As there is so much cross-holding between large companies, the problem of conflict of interest will not go away simply by allowing the Big Four to continue offering the other services to non-audit clients.

The same audit firm is auditing the same client often for 30 to 50 years. One firm should never be allowed to audit for more than five years. What's more, too many government contracts are also given to the Big Four firms as opposed to second-tier firms. That should also change.

Attempts to issue International Accounting and Audit Standards are a dog's breakfast, and do not go to the root of the problem which is not principles, nor practice, but conflict of interest.

Nagindas Khajuria FCCA
Simplification Made Simple, Chartered Certified Accountants, London

2003
What a Waste

Anne Redston at E&Y is right about the complex tax credit system being a waste of public money (23 October, page 3). The 1% NI introduction above a certain level is another nightmare when a simpler system could have been introduced.

A further example of waste of money is pouring billions into motorway widening. The only industry to benefit is the motor industry that is owned by foreign companies.

Money could have been much better spent on railways that are falling apart after privatisation. Our 659 MPs should make a better job of preventing waste. Very often, they just go along with whatever government proposes.

Nagindas Khajuria FCCA
Simplification Made Simple, Chartered Certified Accountants, London

2004
Tories need to concentrate on substance

Sir – Your editorial (The Roar of a Tory Mouse, 22/23 February) shows your newspaper has more vision than policy drivers at the Conservative Party. Their plans to "diminish public spending as a share of national income from 41.9% of GDP in 2005–06 to 39.9% in 2011–12" is neither here nor there. There is always a margin of error of a few percentages in forecasting over so many years.

Over 36 years, I have followed and observed UK politicians' plans, policies and manifestos. Most of them have put too much emphasis on perception and too little emphasis on substance.

Sometimes developed countries should learn from underdeveloped or developing countries' experts on how to reduce public spending drastically without sacrificing the quality or quantity of public services.

2004
Tax targets

I disagree with the majority of FDs who feel a big tax rise would hurt Labour beyond repair (11 March, page 2). As a percentage of income, middle and high earners pay less tax now than they have for 30 years. It is the low-paid who are getting a raw deal.

A low-paid worker earning £9,500 a year (there are about six million of them) was almost exempt from income tax until the early 1970s but now pays about 22%. A middle-class income worker earning £37,128 paid between 32% to 35% for 15 years after 1974 and since 1990 is paying between 27% to 29%. Fat cats were historically paying 50% to 60% during 1950s to 1980s. Since 1990s they have been paying 38%. The latter two groups have never had it so good.

Labour would do much better in the next election if they raised taxes on middle and higher income groups and lowered them on lower-paid groups. Otherwise there will be no difference between themselves and the Conservatives.

That way they could achieve their target of a £4bn surplus by 2007.

Nagindas Khajuria FCCA
Simplification Made Simple, Chartered Certified Accountants, London

Blind terror `2004`

Sir – Your editorial "How to fight the new terrorism", 14/15 March, makes the same recommendations as the official UK and US government policies and actions to date. With respect, it appears more like the blind leading the blind. Surely, more energy and resources must be diverted towards making this planet a better place to live in harmony on a wider scale.

The past 60 years may have seen peace, but it has also been the period when the Group of 8 countries have done their utmost to ensure economic domination of the world's other nations by often not very fair and legitimate means.

Attitudes and institutions such as United Nations, International Monetary Fund (IMF) and the World Bank need to change and re-direct their focus, not by instilling fear and force to combat terrorism. The IMF has often charged exorbitant interest rates and insisted on wrong, unworkable policies of privatisation and market forces in countries that did not have the infrastructure or the insititutions to support such a system with the result that these countries are still where they were 60 years ago.

Ditch the US link `2004`

Sir – I agree with your editorial ("Iraq: the uncomfortable truth" 18/19 April) that the Bush administration does not understand the long-term nature of the war against terrorism and is not willing to listen to seasoned advice from the British. Perhaps it is time to abandon the special relationship with the US that was born in 1945. It does not mean much based upon 60 years' experience, and the time may be ripe now to build a special relationship with Europe. With the latter, we have shared our civilisation for 2000 years. The US has been following a unilateralist policy for over 25 years. It needs to be counter-balanced by another bloc like the EU, but without the UK on its side, the EU does not stand a chance to rise to the occasion.

It is the intelligence that is shared between Israel and US that probably brought about the Iraq war in the first place.

In the long term, unless the UN takes over and unless Resolution 242 of the United Nations is observed and implemented where Israel has to withdraw to pre-1967 borders, the situation could escalate into World War 3. The acronym MAD comes to mind: Mutually Assured Destruction. It is the Palestine issue that is the crux of the matter and the sooner this is understood the more peaceful the world will be.

Nagindas Khajuria FCCA
Simplification Made Simple, Chartered Certified Accountants, London

2004
Banking

Your article on SMEs and banks highlighted the fact that although banks make billions of pounds every year, they don't really help SMEs and sometimes overcharge them.

We should consider the help growing businesses get in Germany, where small local banks and local authorities not only lend to SMEs, but also invest in them. They therefore have intimate knowledge of the local businesses.

Here, the big banks hardly have any trading knowledge of SMEs. Local banks and local authorities working with businesses in clusters, exploiting informal networks and with strong incentives to develop the local economy cannot be achieved by the big four banks dictating from their head offices miles away.

2004
Too many hats: accountancy firms should restrict themselves to one or two disciplines, not many

Your lead article and comment on the Big Four going back into consultancy by 2005 (17 June, pages 1 and 12) runs counter to the fundamental reasons why they were asked to hive it off.

Their income broadly comes from four areas, consultancy and business advice, human resources advice, taxation compliance and planning and audit assurance, probably in equal revenue streams.

Hiving off IT consultancy is a red herring. Most large companies are so deeply computerised that business advice cannot be separated from IT.

The Big Four have wasted too many years encouraging financial engineering and short-termism, rather than reporting on the long-term strengths of a company.

They cannot give business advice, help with management selection, set up computer systems, give tax-planning advice, then help with accounts production and tax returns and finally certify that the business is run well, paying the right amount of tax and gives a true and fair view of its annual results.

I hope the Securities and Exchange Commission and/or the EU's new constitution will make sure they are never allowed to wear more than two hats – ideally, auditing and taxation – or preferably one hat only – auditing.

Nagindas Khajuria FCCA
Simplification Made Simple, Chartered Certified Accountants, London

2004
Nothing right

Sir – The article by Allister Heath ("Big Brother and the EU art of double speak, 27/28 June) raising concern by business about the European Union Charter, especially about the Charter of Fundamental Rights, is preposterous.

What is wrong with the six articles of the Charter that he mentions as of particular concern to business? Namely, the "right to work", "worker's right to information and consultation", "rights of collective bargaining and action", "protection in the event of unjustified dismissal", "fair and just working conditions" and "the right to reconcile family and professional life"?

If business does not understand that these rights go hand in hand with higher productivity and accelerated economic growth, then business does not understand the difference between being authoritarian and being democratic.

For the past 25 years, the Conservatives and now Labour have peddled the wrong policies and wrong message to the business community, bringing down UK productivity from being sixth in world league tables to 23rd.

2004
Airbus wins

Sir – Your story ("Boeing challenges Airbus with an Advanced jumbo", 25–26 July) and Focus ("The $5.4 trillion dogfight", 25/26 July) for air supremacy was fascinating reading. I believe Airbus will be the market leader with far more orders than Boeing. One has only to go back to the history of these two companies to find out why.

The Jumbo Jet and B-52 were two of the most visible expressions of American technological and military superiority. Its capacity to take technological risks and to put building planes as its number one corporate purpose was undermined by the extraordinary pressure of Wall Street for US companies to deliver high financial returns as their over-riding objective.

To design, build and develop state-of-the art civil aircraft needed shareholders to defer their returns, perhaps for decades. You had to take a 30-year, rather than a three-year, view.

The Super Jumbo Airbus A380 with its 555 to 800 seats will beat the The Dreamliner Boeing 7E7 with its 200 to 300 seats because of increasing popularity of long-haul travel, less air space congestion, lower fares and the fact that it is something as novel as the original Jumbo.

Nagindas Khajuria FCCA
Simplification Made Simple, Chartered Certified Accountants, London

2004
Work-life balance

Jane Simms's article on work-life balance ("And another thing...", July) does not go to the root of the problem. The culture of both partners needing to earn and the taxation system encouraging both partners to work could be fundamentally flawed.

Instead of childcare handouts or domestic cleaner handouts, it is high time there were house-wives' or -husbands' hand-outs. Also maternity/paternity leave should be extended to five years, as in some EU countries, so that the bond between child and parent is solid.

The workforce would be much more productive if a legal limit to working hours was imposed and if the ethos of the EU social contract was adopted wholeheartedly in our employment laws. The latter is not accepted wisdom among UK directors. The 24/7 society is making machines out of us all.

Nagindas Khajuria FCCA
Simplification Made Simple, Chartered Certified Accountants, London

2005
New Labour does get IT right most of the time

Sir – Your article on the government's disgraceful management of IT projects ("Why New Labour doesn't get IT", 29/30 January) highlights how billions of pounds have already been wasted and billions more may be wasted in the coming years. Perhaps it should look to the East rather the West for software, design and IT enabled services.

India now excels in all the above fields. The Indian educational system is one of the best in the world when it comes to the bachelor's programme. The freedom to do what you want has robbed the American (and perhaps the British) undergraduate system of its focus. The Indian school system requires you to pass an exam every year. If you do not perform, there is no welfare system to bail you out.

As a nation, historically, the analytical and mathematical skills of Indians has been inbred. The word algorithm comes from an Arabic translation of an Indian concept. That analytical skill has been coupled with the fact the competitive basis for this industry is not capital or manufacturing intensive, but primarily innovation intensive.

Some Indian global players are as competent, or even more competent than the likes of EDS, Accenture, ICL or Fujitsu. For example, Wipro, Infosys Technologies, Sasken and MindTree are among the most prominent in VLSI (very large scale integration) services designers and providers. Itiam is a 100% DSP (digital signals processing) company. DSP is the core technology driving communications. Tata consultancy services is another giant software exporter.

Unless the government severs its cosy relationships with past IT suppliers and introduces a more competitive tendering environment, the UK will continue to lose billions.

Nagindas Khajuria FCCA
Simplification Made Simple, Chartered Certified Accountants, London

2005
Rover was not about numbers

I read with interest your front page article (21 April) about negative goodwill in Rover's accounts.

Rover's holding company, Phoenix Venture Holdings, was not stupid enough to purchase a company with a negative balance sheet value of £407m for £10. Apart from possible offsets against its taxable profits, it must have carefully weighed Rover's potential to not only recover that loss but to make a handsome return.

It also failed miserably in its tie-up in India where the automotive industry sector grew by 38% across the whole country in 2003–04.

It failed miserably in the management of Rover. It is not the accounts but management that should be investigated. Often UK plc focuses too much on numbers and too little into operations and people.

Nagindas Khajuria FCCA
Simplification Made Simple, Chartered Certified Accountants, London

2005
Caveat emptor

Sir – People must be forced to face up to the consequences of their actions, says Allister Heath ("A mishmash of tinkering, tokenism and paternalism", 22/23 May) when writing about the lacklustre opening of Parliament with 45 proposed laws and five draft bills.

I agree with him that it is a mishmash of tinkering, tokenism and paternalism in the main. As he says, prime minister Blair fails to address the credit culture and blames the wrong people, eg: lenders, while he should emphasise the caveat emptor, let the buyer beware, principle. I also agree with him that the borrower should better inform himself.

However, Mr Heath misses the deep rooted trend in the UK where accountants, lawyers and barristers are more respected and are in abundance compared to Germany or France. In those countries, engineers are more respected and rightly so. This has resulted in the typical borrower unduly relying on accountants and solicitors.

Lenders are not always straightforward and complaining to the Financial Services Authority or the Banking Ombudsman is useless, as I have found. I re-mortgaged my property in December 2003. It was clearly marketed by an independent financial advisor as a two-year fixed interest rate re-mortgage. In March 2005, I was advised that the so-called offer was from April 2003 to March 2005, so in the middle of two years, I had to go to a variable exchange rate.

Now I am re-mortgaging somewhere else and I got another letter from the lender that if I broke the agreement during the first two years from December 2003, I had to pay a 2% penalty. On the terms and conditions, the lender is right and in Annex A, after page 19, all this is spelled out. But the way the mortgage is sold, I, even as a qualified accountant, got diddled. Your paper should do some investigative journalism on lenders.

Nagindas Khajuria FCCA
Simplification Made Simple, Chartered Certified Accountants, London

2005
Africa's real problem

Sir – Your statistics on aid to poor countries and economic performance ("How not to make poverty history", 5/6 June) does not take into account the wider forces operating in these nations.

Firstly, corruption does not exist to the degree your article implies. Sometimes, the discovery of oil suddenly focuses the attention of the media on a country as may have happened in the Sudan in the Darfur area. Some African countries do have fairly honest governments with well qualified people running them.

The General Agreement on Trade and Tariffs, (now World Trade Organisation) is partly to blame for the difficulties. Under the common agricultural policy a cow in Europe has a higher subsidy than a farmer in Africa. The protection of royalties and patent rights on drugs, computer software, etc, means that people in Africa are dying because they cannot afford patented drugs and Africans are not allowed to manufacture generic drugs. African currencies are very weak and the only way they can survive is in export led growth that is effectively stifled by these rules.

Historically, there has been a substantially far higher transfer of know-how and technology to China and other Far East Countries compared with what has been accomplished in Africa and the Indian subcontinent.

Tony Blair and Gordon Brown should also remember as they attend the G8 summit in Gleneagles that charity begins at home.

There are 12m poor people in the UK according to the last Treasury report. Their time would be better spent getting that right rather than their grandiose ideas about making poverty history in Africa.

Nagindas Khajuria FCCA
Simplification Made Simple, Chartered Certified Accountants, London

2005
All greek to me

As a registered auditor since 1986 I was disturbed to read your lead article (2 June, page 1) expressing concern by leaders in our profession and institutions like the ACCA on the wording 'knowingly and recklessly give an audit opinion' in the company law reform bill.

The wording, if read as a whole, makes a lot of sense and is long overdue. Even if you break it down to its parts, I do not find any particular word out of place.

Knowingly is synonymous with consciously and intentionally; recklessly come from the 'reck' to heed to something' and reckless is synonymous with careless, heedless, rash, thoughtless; audit comes from Latin audire 'to hear', an audit was originally presented orally, to be heard; an audience is a group of assembled listeners: shareholders are accountants' audience; opinion has dual meaning: one is 'a view or judgement not necessarily based upon fact or knowledge' and two, 'a formal statement of advice by an expert or professional.

Surely the word 'opinion' should be replaced by a more definitive word like 'assurance', which comes from 'assure', to tell someone something positively to dispel doubts'. There is still time to amend the company law reform white paper to do so.

Nagindas Khajuria FCCA
Simplification Made Simple, Chartered Certified Accountants, London

2005
Educating Britain

Sir – I fully agree with your excellent article on the dire state of UK education system ("The all-party *trahison des clercs*" 21/22 August) and Professor Colin Coulson-Thomas' letter to you, (28/29 August) giving a perfect synopsis.

The UK education system has been a shambles for over 20 years. It has not got the dedication and attention it deserves compared to other areas like foreign policy, health, immigration, national security, etc. by successive governments. Education is fundamental to the UK's long-term well being. There should be two cabinet ministers, one for education and one for employment. Both areas are crucial to UK economy.

We should remind ourselves of the maxim on the first comprehensive systems of education and vocational selection written in The Republic by Plato, Socrates' pupil. He believed men (and women) essentially have different and unequal abilities. This was further expanded by educationalists in modern times such as Johann Pestalozzi of Switzerland (1746–1827).

The funding and control structure of England's 31,000 schools is muddled, over prescribed from the centre, with very little private-sector input.

Published figures of the expected levels of accomplishment in English, mathematics and science at Key Stage 1 (seven-year-olds), Key Stage 2 (11-year-olds) and Key Stage 3 (14-year olds) by the Annual National Training and Teachers' Assessments, in 1999, showed that they went down from 80%, 86% and 87% at Key Stage 1 to 68%, 69% and 76% at Key Stage 2 and 63%, 63% and 57% at Key Stage 3 respectively.

In the case of higher education, it was fundamentally flawed to call 38 polytechnics universities and to transfer their control from local authorities to central government. By calling something by a different name, it does not become different.

Nagindas Khajuria FCCA
Simplification Made Simple, Chartered Certified Accountants, London

2005
The real objective

Your article on the proposed merger between the ICAEW, CIPFA and CIMA (*accounting & business*, July/August) is interesting. Competition can of course work in tandem with co-operation. I think the key question is: what is *the* objective? Is it UK aspirations or global aspirations? The public sector accounts for 50% of UK GDP: the CIPFA membership of 15,000 versus ICAEW membership of 120,000 (half of whom are in business and not working as accountants at all) is not healthy for the long term future of financial controls in the UK.

Let us invite comments on, or research on, what we are given to understand is their real objective. Only then, we can go deeper into such issues. My suggestion would be to standardise examinations for qualified accountants as the first stepping stone, maybe even at just the Intermediate level.

At the beginning of 2005, I was invited to attend a talk and buffet at the Gherkin [Swiss Re Bank's London HQ]. The talk was by Anatoly Kaletsky, economics editor of *The Times*, on forecast for 2005. All the CEOs of all UK Plcs were there, and so was the ICAEW. ACCA, it appears, was not invited. This type of discrimination in official or semi-official circles is very unfair. Maybe this is why the Scots do not want to join the English. The ideal logical merger of course would best be between the English, Irish and Scottish institutes. If we want to win the next football World Cup, a similar merger between the best English, Welsh, Scottish and Irish football players could do the trick.

Nagindas Khajuria FCCA
Simplification Made Simple, Chartered Certified Accountants, London

2006

Sharing the care for mentally ill patients

I read with great interest your article on the 3,000 mentally ill patients, who will in future be transferred to the care of their GPs to save the NHS £1.8 million (The Press, June 8).

That is £600 per patient. The NHS pays £600 per day to major consultancy firms to give them such advice.

The opposite view in your article is that it may be a realistic decision and patients may be better off coming back into the community and given more confidence to look after themselves.

Your editorial states that "we can only hope that, a few years down the line, it is a decision which will not come back to haunt those who made it".

My own view is that some will be better off, some the same, and some worse off.

Why not set up a new charity with people from different backgrounds who feel strongly about the welfare of these mental health patients?

I would certainly be a volunteer as someone who has grass-roots experience and knowledge about mental health issues.

Such a charity could monitor and fill the gap left between primary and secondary care groups.

Nagindas Khajuria FCCA
Simplification Made Simple, Chartered Certified Accountants, London

2006
Immigration red herring

The debate created by Asian Voice's front page story "Immigrants should earn £27,000 or not settle in Britain" (2nd September 2006) is a red herring. "Immigrants" I imagine includes "UK citizens" who were initially immigrants. If we take both sides of the story, what do we get? The indigenous population is about, say 90 percent and the immigrant population is, say 10 percent. One argument is that they contribute less than 10 percent of GDP, so that in total they contribute a net of 7 percent to 8 percent. On the other side, we could say that they contribute more than 10 percent of GDP, say 12 percent to 13 percent. The true figure, let us say, is somewhere in between, so that 10 percent of the population contributes 10 percent GDP. So where is the drain on infrastructure, schools and hospitals? We are all paying through our nose for these services.

The UK media and UK politicians have been pushing down our throats at least for the past 50 years, two issues only: race and taxation. The 30 percent or so who vote at the general election and those who do not vote, have never got even an inkling of the deeply seated problems this country has had during the past 50 years. These problems have resulted in 20 percent to 40 percent loss in GDP every year.

Some of these are corruption, bureaucracy, laziness inherited from the British Empire days, incompetence, lack of numeracy skills, lack of literacy skills, politicians acting in their own interests rather than the interests of the nation, dithering between EU type of milder capitalism and the US type of greed capitalism. These are the country's real problems and have been for 50 years.

Members of Parliament behave as if they are superior beings, who are unapproachable unless they have many cronies protecting them in case they may say something that is not politically correct. Most of the time they have to "tow the line". What sort of democracy is this? All MPs should be in direct contact with their constituents and should continually discuss, reflect and formulate long lasting policies in the interests of the nation, rather than waste time in setting up utterly meaningless commissions and publishing numerous "White Papers". Stop all these words and get on with the deeds.

Nagindas Khajuria FCCA
Simplification Made Simple, Chartered Certified Accountants, London

2006
A powerful message

I would like to congratulate Diana Pringle on her wonderfully well-written article on work life balance (31 August, page 18).

I hope all your readers will take some time to read and digest it. Her message is very powerful.

I would also wish that the media and politicians would stop peddling money, materialism, instant pleasure and greed as the most coveted pursuits of modern life.

2006
Experience speaks for itself

I was extremely disappointed to read that Shashi Tharoor, 50, lost to South Korea's Foreign Minister Ban Ki-Moon who is 62 in the bid to become the next UN Secretary General. Historically, black and Asian people have remained closer to the have nots, compared to White and Oriental people.

It is a fact that the US, Europe and Japan has relentlessly pursued technology transfer and collaboration with the Oriental race in manufacturing over the past 50 years to the detriment of the other two races.

Electing a South Korean UN Secretary General, by the 15-member Security Council is yet another example of ensuring the great divide continues over the next 50 years. This Council is dominated by the five permanent members, China, Russia, UK, France and USA, who each have a power of veto on any resolution: the remaining ten are elected for two-year periods. So these 10 are neither here nor there. Indeed, South Korea, was an official observer, not holding UN membership until recently.

I am somewhat sceptical that such appointments are made based upon core competency of the incumbent. A younger Secretary General, representing a far bigger nation than South Korea, could have changed the course of history by creating a more equitable distribution of know how and consequent economic prosperity.

Nagindas Khajuria FCCA
Simplification Made Simple, Chartered Certified Accountants, London

2007
Are the right checks and balances in place?

I read the interesting article published by you on the Competition Commission planning to investigate as to whether consumers are getting a fair deal in the grocery trade when the UK supermarket scene is being dominated up to 75% by just 4 major supermarkets: Tesco, ASDA, Sainsbury and Morrisons.

If past history on this issue is anything to go by, the Commission has not been effective and "economics" has been the master of that "history". Should it still be the same?

The Commission has to take into account several other factors that are now becoming crucial to redress the balance between "small is beautiful" and "big is beautiful".

First and formost, the enterprise spirit, the entrepreneurial spirit and the innovation spirit, has been stifled in the sense that any school or college leaver will opt to have an easy life by working for these majors rather than set up shop. At one time Britain used to be the trader or "grower" of the world; now it has become a pen pusher.

Secondly, intensive farming, has produced tasteless, bland fruits and vegetables; meat and dairy products that contain a huge amount of chemicals, additives, preservatives, etc. Only about 30% of the wealthy can afford to purchase organic products. A large majority continue to eat junk food which is sometimes frozen for months, or transported from round the world which takes a week or two before it reaches the gas cooker.

Thirdly, the local community area in each town in England ends up with the same boring stores and the same long alleys of shelves. You cannot even tell in which town you are. They are also so impersonal.

Forthly, these giant firms are now entering in a big way, markets like China and India, and are luring small farmers to enter into long term contracts with them. They use massive refrigeration systems to make sure that products do not get damaged. Refrigeration emits the same amount of carbon dioxide that cars emit round the world. Shipments of drinks in heavy container loads from all over the world again use vast amounts of energy and damage the environment.

Fifthly, the dominance is not only of supermarkets in advanced economies, it is in almost every industry sector or every product.

Mergers and acquisitions and consolidations and the use of hedge funds, etc. has reached an uncontrollable stage which can only harm the world financial community, or keep the control in a handful of players without any checks and balances.

Nagindas Khajuria FCCA
Simplification Made Simple, Chartered Certified Accountants, London

2007
Men inflicting violence is old story

Nandita Das' comment that "domestic violence is a very prevalent phenomena and needs to be in the public domain, so that stigma attached to it goes away" was based upon 10 years' of physical violence that Mrs Kirantjit Ahluwalia suffered from her husband before she set him on fire. He is not there to tell his side of the story.

While historically it has been true that the aggressor has been a male in the majority of cases, recent trends have brought to light many instances where it is almost equal in both directions. The violence of many years can also be psychological and mental rather than physical. This is specially true in developed countries as opposed to developing countries.

In these countries, matters are made worse by disproportionate media attention and over zealous government policies in favour of single mothers, gay and lesbian partnerships, with hardly any attention to the fundamentally sacred relationship between a man and a woman joined in matrimony.

A lot of research papers, books, now film, etc. have highlighted the former. There is hardly any published research on say "battered husbands". May be it time to do some research of domestic violence in reverse. I am sure one would find many factual cases of murder, suicide, attempted suicide, leaving home, etc. by men as a result of domestic violence by women.

Nagindas Khajuria FCCA
Simplification Made Simple, Chartered Certified Accountants, London

2007
Will oil result in strife?

Your article on oil reserves and discovery of oil in Gujarat is interesting (Asian Voice 28 April to 4 May, 2007). My belief is that the Gujarat/Mumbai quantities would be quite small by world standards to result in strife, war, etc. like elsewhere.

The latest available statistics for 2000–01 on India are: Oil reserves: 674, on-shore production 11.7 and off-shore production 16.6 Mn. tonnes respectively. India's energy use (oil equivalent) for that year was 531.5 Mn tons. The entire world's energy use for that year was 10,009.6 Mn tons. India thus used 5.3% of world energy produced. USA used 2,281 Mn tonnes (23%) and China 1,139 Mn tonnes (11.4%).

Worldwide oil reserves 2005, according to BP statistical review of world energy, were: Africa: 8%; Middle East 57%; US and Canada: 15.5%; Latin America: 9%; Former USSR: 6%; Asia Pacific: 3% and Europe: 1.5%.

World conflicts arise principally because the ratios of what is already produced to what still is remaining underground and what is yet to find are so different. E.g. US reserves were just over 28 billion tonnes, but 26 billion have already been produced. Iran's reserves were just over 18 billion tonnes and only 7 billion have been produced to date. Saudi Arabia has 40 billion tonnes out of which 12 billion has already been produced. What is yet to find is very little by comparison to what has already been found.

Exploration activity is becoming very expensive in the sense that companies are desparately trying to find the last trace of oil trapped underneath as the discovery rate is falling much faster then the production rate. Over the past 20 years, the discovery rate has fallen from about 80% of production rate to about 20% according to Dr Mamdouh G Salameh, an international oil economist (1999 OPEC review).

Nagindas Khajuria FCCA
Simplification Made Simple, Chartered Certified Accountants, London

2007
Young Asians lack experience

Your article, Charity begins at home, (page 12, 5 May) highlighted how our young Asians mainly donate through major charities like Oxfam, Barnados, The Drum, Cancer Research, etc. Although there are over 90,000 charities, 85% of the billions raised are by just 7 or 8 of them.

My view is that our young Asians lack, relatively speaking compared to their white counterparts, the expertise in setting up, and/or growing/running more professionally and/or consolidating and/or merging hundreds of little Asian charities to make a wider mark, within UK and internationally.

Apart from money, donating precious time and energy for new ideas on fund raising, etc. is also of equal if not more value.

I have been in the process for over 18 months to register and set up or join up with a UK charity on behalf of a Rajkot, Gujarat, based Indian charity called Life that has been going on since 1978. I have now registered a website called Life-UK.orgYo as one further step.

As an honorary and a professional auditor of charities I have been involved in this sector for 10 years and am very keen to hear from young Asians to join me make this a success.

They have built about 35 schools in villages in Gujarat in partnership with individual village Panchayat and with state aid funds. They are planning 20 more. Primary education both in India and in the UK is poor in many schools and we could raise funds and time and energy to develop numeracy and literacy skills in both countries through this Like UK charity. I have visited them twice in Rajkot and surrounding villages and spoken at length to the young children. They need help urgently in so many areas. They are also physically very weak and could do with say soccer coaching.

Nagindas Khajuria FCCA
Simplification Made Simple, Chartered Certified Accountants, London

2007
HFB needs to rethink appeal to save [cow] Shambo

The Hindu Forum of Britain needs to re-think about its appeal to save the sacred bull called Shambo at Skandavale Temple in Wales. Bovine Tuberculosis' medical name is Mycobacterium Bovis or Mycobacterium Africanum. It occurs where milk is unpasteurized and is very rare in the UK. The ileocaecal area is most commonly affected, but the colon, and rarely other parts of the gastrointestinal tract can be involved. Even if Shambo is saved, he will have a miserable life and he could infect other cattle and even visitors to the temple in Wales.

This brings me to the wider picture about being cruel to be kind. India's livestock population, estimated at more than 500 million, is world's largest. More than half is cows, buffaloes and bulls, once they become unproductive, they are often illegally transported to cow slaughter houses, permitted just in two states, West Bengal and Kerala.

Even from global warming angle, methane from cattle accelerates the global warming and the ozone layer depletion. PETA's (People for the Ethical Treatment of Animals) research shows that 26 billion animals are killed for food in the US alone each year (9 billion land based, 17 billion aquatic). Finally, cows are treated very cruelly in dairy farming all over the world including India: they are almost constantly kept pregnant by artificial insemination when mating with the bull is not possible, their calf's are taken away for veal within one or two days from them (they feel immense pain when the see that), they normally live 15 years, but are disposed off for meat after about 5 to 7 years. The slaughter is also done very cruelly with clinical precision on assembly lines.

Some of the sorrow, the anger, the violence in these dumbs animals, could be passing on to us humans in our own actions against fellow human beings when we consume their milk or their meat.

May be it is time for all milk and dairy product eaters, as well as meat eaters, to cut down on the usage of these products for health, environment, peace, kindness, etc. Or may be set up innovative dairy farms where cows produce the same amount of milk but over a longer period without the use of continuous artificial insemination for longer lactation periods.

Nagindas Khajuria FCCA
Simplification Made Simple, Chartered Certified Accountants, London

Facts about ethnic minorities

I read your lead article (pp. 1, 15) and editorial comment (pp. 3), 26 May to 1 June Issue 3, Vol. 36, with great interest.

Sadly, it is still commonplace in this country to refer to "non-whites" in the same breath as terrorists, criminals and other socially destructive elements. Furthermore, it is still customary to group together completely different races via phrases that basically mean "non-white". Unconvinced? What do everyday terms in the media and among politicians such as "blacks and ethnic minorities" really mean? Why aggregate policy issues such as "crime and immigration", or "terrorism and immigration"?

Mrs Margaret Hodge, MP for Barking in East London is barking on the wrong tree. I would like to disseminate some factual data to our readers on some of the deeper issues at play in the shortage of affordable homes by ordinary British citizens and British households whose median income is between £20,000 to £30,000 per year. There are millions of white people in this category.

- In London, housing stock went up from 2,928,000 in 1991 to 3,040,000 in 1998: 1%. Owner-occupied went down from 57% to 56%. Properties rented from local authority went down from 24% to 20%. Properties rented from private owners went up from 13% to 17%. Propertied rented from registered social landlords from 5% to 7%. It is the wealthy citizens who own several houses and social housing associations who may be causing the shortage, rather than those in lower income groups.
- The average price change in Greater London New Dwellings went up from £78,084 to £178,274 between 1993 and 1999: increase of 228%. Similar averages for second hand dwellings were £80,707 to £140,347: increase of 179%. Thus new dwellings profit margins could be partly responsible for lack of available housing.
- The population of Greater London by ethnic group in percentages in 1998–99 was: 25.1% black and ethnic and 74.9% white. In Great Britain as a whole: 6.6% black and ethnic and 93.4% white. The breakdown in Greater

Nagindas Khajuria FCCA
Simplification Made Simple, Chartered Certified Accountants, London

2007
Facts about ethnic minorities

London is 4% Black Caribbean, 4.3% Black African, 2.3% Black other, 5.4% Indian, 1.6% Pakistani, 2% Bangladeshi, 0.7% Chinese, 1.8% Other Asian and 3% Other. The majority of this group are likely to be hard working in menial jobs paying rent for donkeys years to private landlords.

- The number of households in Greater London was 3,061,000 (1998). The population was 7,122,000 (1997). That is 2.32 persons per household. However, the types of households were: 38% married couples, 9% Cohabiting, 8% Lone parents, 34% one-person and 12% other multi-persons. Most of the ethnic minorities groups probably fall into the first, lone-parent and last group. It is the one-person group that could be part of the problem.

2007

The Raisôn d'être of Bollywood

I beg to differ in several respects with The Guardian's Edward Marriot book review: "Bollyood: A History by Mihir Bose" (p.36, AV, 2 June 2007).

Mr Marriott writes "that while the Indian film industry began in 1896, the genuine cross-over success did not happen until Lagaan was produced in 2001". This is not true. While a greater number of Indian films may have been average or mediocre, Bollywood has indeed produced umpteen number of outstanding master pieces throughtout the decades from 1900 onwards. These have long been popular not only in India, but also all over the world, especially Russia, former Union of Soviet Socialist Republics, the entire Middle East, North, East and South Africa, etc. Western media had just chosen to ignore this success until of late.

The book review says "the Indian film industry is rich in irony ... Kama Sutra and the erotic statutes of Khajuraho". There is no irony or hypocrisy in that at all. Not only on the screen, but in real life, both in cities and villages, kissing in public by lovers is considered indecent. Kama Sutra describes the pursuit of love or pleasure, both sensual and aesthetic, as necessary for life, but only if restrained by considerations of dharma according to Hinduism. That is why Khajuraho is a group of 20 Hindu temples, constructed mainly of sandstones, in 950–1050, where the internal and external wall structures are embellished with masterpieces of erotic art. It is also why it is considered a world heritage site.

Again, the article says "to Western eyes, the peculiarity of Bollywood is surely its eclecticism." Eclectic merely means diverse, general, broad, varied, comprehensive, extensive, wide-ranging, selective, diversified, manifold, heterogeneous, catholic, all-embracing, liberal, many sided, multifarious and even amateurish. But not just the last meaning. So what is wrong with its eclecticism? A largenumber of Indian films encourage higher moral and religious values, normally with a happy end.

Rural income in India in 2002–03 earned by households that earn less than 90,000 rupees (or £1,058) per annum each. That is just under £3 per day. The raison d'etre of Indian movies has been escapism to the urban and rural poor historically speaking. One needs to be very careful when re-writing this history so that future generations are not mislead.

Nagindas Khajuria FCCA
Simplification Made Simple, Chartered Certified Accountants, London

2007
Is steam yoga substantial enough to warrant a patent?

Your article on the Indian Government getting upset about American entrepreneurs, including Indian-born Bikram Choudhury, applying and getting the copyright and trademark to "Hot Yoga" (26 postures in a large steam room) raises deeper issues about research and development of new ideas and new inventions.

During the past 5 to 6 decades, USA and Europe began to lose ground to competition from Japan and then from the Tiger economies. In the 20th century, US, Europe and Japan has rushed headlong into unidirectional change, dragging the rest of world unwillingly. This change is largely being driven by the interests of powerful owners with money to claim and enforce a huge and complex web of legal rights that often cover just one product.

Thus intellectual property rights have tilted in the direction of corporate rights owners rather than ordinary citizens. Yet, if you go back to history, there is ample proof that absence of patent law has created more inventions.

Switzerland resisted foreign pressure to create a patent system and built up one of the largest chemical and pharmaceutical industries by copying German products.

Philips Electronics has an impressive series of inventions to its name, such as the CD. What is not so well known is that the company was set up in 1891 to exploit somebody else's invention: Edison's and Swan's carbon filament lamp. Philips had this head start because Holland had repealed its Patent Law in 1869.

Ericsson, the Swedish company now known for mobile phones, was formed in 1876, the same year as Alexander Bell made his first phone call. After being sent some of these new devices to repair, the company soon learned how to make them itself, and then began to sell its own phones to the public. The rest is history.

In the case of Yoga, it is clear as day that no scientific or technical knowledge could have been added to the art and science of Yoga. Doing Yoga in a steam room may have improved the service, but it is doubtful whether the improvement was substantial to warrant a patent.

Nagindas Khajuria FCCA
Simplification Made Simple, Chartered Certified Accountants, London

2007
Breakthrough in global warming

I do not believe that the G8 summit held in Germany achieved much by agreeing to "consider" a 50 per cent cut in global CO_2 by 2050 (your Editorial Comment, AV, pp 5, 16 June). The United Nations Conference on Environment and Development (UNCED) was held in Rio de Janeiro in June 1992. 178 governments were represented and it brought together 114 heads of state, more than any other conference on any topic. This was followed up by Earth Summit II in 1997 in New York, attended by 185 countries. After that, the world's industrialised nations met in December 1997 in Kyoto, Japan and agreed to reduce their combined emissions by about 5 per cent between 1990 and 2012, that is in 22 years.

Exactly the opposite has happened. CO_2 per capita emissions in USA, Canada, UK, China and India went up from 18.9, 15, 10, 2.1 and 0.8 metric tons per annum in 1990 to 19.8, 17.9, 9.4, 2.1 and 1.19 metric tons per annum respectively in 2003. This is an increase of 10% in 13 years.

The solution is not in setting up such targets, nor in getting on the bandwagon and spending millions of pounds in new technology, all kinds of taxation such as Landfill Tax, Climate Change Levy, Carbon Offset market, etc. The time has come to move away from converting this issue itself into big business supported by bureaucratic governments and funded by public private initiatives. People should rely more on self help and use less energy on an individual basis rather than get into a muddle like big companies getting "carbon neutral" certificates, for example.

Apart from UK, the rest of other major EU countries like Germany, Spain, Italy, France know how to live in a better way. Their CO_2 per capita emissions is about 6 metric tons per annum. China and India are even better. Why not learn from such countries?

The long term solution is in zero or negative GDP or economic growth rate over the next 50 to 100 years. Otherwise a pint of beer will cost £400 by the end of this century. The growth could be in the Human Index rate made up of the 10 main UN indicators of quality of life, such as health, education, literacy, etc.

Finally as an example, washing one's own car and dishes by hand rather than by a car wash or dish washer respectively could be the way forward. A sea change in culture, lifestyle and habits will do the trick: throw that remote TV control in the dust bin.

Nagindas Khajuria FCCA
Simplification Made Simple, Chartered Certified Accountants, London

2007

Why do people resort to violence?

Your lead article (P1, 7 July, Vol 36, Issue 9) on two bungled car bombings in London the previous week and their link to the attack on Glasgow airport the following day when two men rammed a Jeep into the terminal reminds us once again, like the 11th September 2001 attack, that educated professional people like doctors or pilots are inclined to carry out such activities. Why?

American Airlines Flight No 11 took off from Logan International Airport in Boston at 7.59 a.m. United Airlines Flight 175 departed from Logan International Airport heading for Los Angeles at 8.14 a.m. Flight No. 11 hit the first of the World Trade Centre's twin towers at 8.46 a.m. Flight No 175 hit the second twin tower at 9.03 a.m. In both cases, the interval was exactly 47 minutes. American Airlines Flight No 77 left Washington's Dallas International Airport at 8.10 a.m. and crashed into the Pentagon at 9.43 a.m. after an interval of 1 hour and 33 minutes. United Airlines Flight No 93 left Newark and smashed into a field in Pennsylvania at 10.10 a.m. It was only after two days that US Secretary of State Colin Powell broke the news that Osama Bin Laden was the prime suspect. The pilots were all Saudi Arabian citizens: so was Osama Bin Laden.

The so called "fight against terrorism" started on 11th September 2001. Afghanistan and Iraq have borne the most significant damage since then. But several key questions still remain? Were the pilots then, or the doctors now, acting alone? Who had the power to call off or reduce the usual security precautions that may have prevented the 11th September attacks?

To me, security of long term oil and gas supplies, and its 100% mandatory trading in US Dollars worldwide by all producers, regardless of the fact that only 25% is used by the US, could be the main reason why the above has happened. When the entire world trades in US Dollars, 75% of its revenue finds its way back into US dollar deposit accounts. This enables US to continue living beyond its means. It is high time that oil and gas is freely traded in all major currencies so that there is less reason to revert to terrorist activities. US will then have to live within its means just like all other nations.

Nagindas Khajuria FCCA
Simplification Made Simple, Chartered Certified Accountants, London

2007

Indo-US nuclear accord a landmark deal

I refer to your editorial comment (P3, AV, 11 Aug 2007) on the Indo-US nuclear accord that has taken two years to negotiate and is now awaiting legislative scrutity by Congress and Parliament.

There are a number of reasons why I believe that the nuclear option to replace other sources of future energy needs in India may not be as relevant as, say the future energy needs of USA.

India is on the equator and can make better use of solar power as a source of energy. USA is the northern hemisphere with more severe winters and more severe summers. They also believe excessively in automation, mechanisation, intense farming etc. Thus they need far more energy to achieve their way of life. It is best not to follow that way of progress blindly.

Nuclear waste contains a very small amount of 'high level' waste. However, this small amount contains 95% of the radioactivity. It is so hot that it has to be cooled over a 20–50 year period. It is unapproachable for centuries and highly toxic for millennia- so corrosive that it has to be moved using robotic equipment, and transported in special flasks chained to trucks and railway carriages. There is still no proven safe method available for permanant disposal. [The New Green Consumer Guide by Julia Hailes].

New nuclear power stations would require a massive amount of public subsidy. In 2003–04, according to the Ministry of Power, the installed plant capacity in Indian was 131,400 Mega Watts. (29,500 MW Hydro, 80,500 MW from coal, gas and diesal plants for utilities. 2,700 MW nuclear and 18,700 MW for non-utilities). The 11th Five Year Plan target increase in capacity from the 10th Five Year Plan is additional 19,786 MW (8,027 MW Hydro, 8,119 MW coal, gas and diesel and 3,640 MW Nuclear).

My belief is that India has or can achieve through research and development sufficient know how in civilian nuclear technology to achieve these targets on its own two feet without any umbrella treaty with USA on nuclear technology pact.

On the other hand, if this deal is being done as some kind of 'military protection' by the USA or 'military safety' by India itself through gaining such knowledge from the USA, the Indian Congress and Parliament should tread very carefully.

Nagindas Khajuria FCCA
Simplification Made Simple, Chartered Certified Accountants, London

The country may lose its current image as an impartial, non-violent, peaceful country with a strong sense of fair play in world affairs.

USA should first help India achieve a 'permanent' seat at UNO, help Indians like Shashi Tharoor to become future Secretary General of UNO, listen more to developing countries pleas for fairer trade conditions at WTO conferences, etc. Being selective and offering a 'nuclear pact' as if that was something very significant should be seen in the light of above scenarios.

2007
Indo-US nuclear accord a landmark deal

2007

"In it ain't broke, don't fix it"

The article by Mr P K Laheri, Chairman of the Narmada project (Page 17, AV 25 Aug) reflects upon the fact that recently there have been very fast changes in all directions, some pre-planned, some unexpected, some by governments and others by management gurus, innovators, etc. It also talks about coercive changes and about resistances to changes. It argues that as long as there is some planning beforehand and all those affected by change are explained the logic of the changes, people will accept them more willingly.

In the case of UK, I have noted that businesses as well as governments continue to make changes just for the sake of changes without thinking through the long term implications of such changes where the harm done comes about 20 to 30 years later. Often, stability, or no change is also far better than any change at all. Or, unless the changes are in the right directions, changes to do not help at all.

Take the welfare system as a case in point. It began in July 1948. Since then, there has been virtually thousands of changes while in essence it has not changed at all. All it has done is that it has become one of the most complex systems in the world and created a dependency culture that may be partly to blame for our current youngsters unsocial behaviour and gun culture. One Labour Minister put it memorably in the 1960s and 1970s: "For generations this country has not earned an honest living". Nothing was then done to change the system by making it less universal and more focussed to those who were in genuine need.

Another case in point is the NHS. Again, the concept of care free at the point of delivery, has not changed since 1948 even though now 40% of so wealthy families and their members do not need it all, they continue to drain the NHS to the detriment of the remaining 60%. The market concept was introduced in the public sector NHS to stimulate it into becoming more efficient. The change was introduced to bring about a system of purchasers and sellers of medical care and GP fund holding. After about seven years, the idea did not work and was abandoned. Then the concept of waiting lists and targets were introduced. Again, this was insisted upon and relentlessly pursued for several years. Suddenly, it was realised that, that was not the core issue. Now a computer system costing billions is in the pipeline so that medical records of every citizen is on computer. This very idea is fundamentally flawed

Nagindas Khajuria FCCA
Simplification Made Simple, Chartered Certified Accountants, London

2007
"In it ain't broke, don't fix it"

because most people in the UK hardly ever move from one location to another. A central data base of such records is a white elephant of very little practical use. Here again is a case of introducing a change for the sake of change, never mind the cost or the necessity.

Finally, take the trade unions. A lot of changes in law were introduced to curb their power. Sir Keith Joseph summed up 20 years of anti-union criticism in his speech in 1979:"Solving the trade union problem is the key to Britain's economic recovery". 20 years later now, it is the weak management in most organisations than strong unions that are the source of a lack of relative productivity. So were the changes to labour laws for good? Perhaps for a short term only.

So let us tread with far more care when we consider change. The adage "If it ain't broke, don't fix it" still rings true more often than not.

Nagindas Khajuria FCCA
Simplification Made Simple, Chartered Certified Accountants, London

2007
Tension in Darfur and its relevance to oil supply security

Implications: There is some truth in the fact that the Arab North in Sudan looked down upon the Black South in the 50s and 60s when I grew up in Sudan. Then there was civil war and thousands of lives were lost and there were thousands of refugees. But then US, Europe or UN were not all that concerned. Now there is oil in Sudan. Now China is in Sudan. Partly there is a perception that the current media and European leaders hyper concern about the plight of Darfurians is "crocodile tears". Where were these leaders when the same atrocities happened in the 50s and 60s? Were Black Africans not important then? The efforts to secure oil supplies should not tarnish the West's image of fair play by harping too much on the crisis in Darful. Yes there is some crisis. But it is not brought about by deliberate wrong doing: it is mainly brought about by scarcity of land and resources and poor people fighting with each other for share of a small pie, lack of rain and draught, poor cultivation skills.

Analysis: If US and Europe are not extremely truthful in the words and deeds in Darful, then their efforts will be discredited and they will not achieve the objectives they are hoping to achieve. It will be another iraq and will bring further discredit to US and Europe.

Nagindas Khajuria FCCA
Simplification Made Simple, Chartered Certified Accountants, London

The shorter and simpler the better

Sir, The letter from D.R. Myddelton, emeritus professor of finance and accounting (January 21), calling for much shorter annual accounts and reports makes a lot of sense. Apart from making them shorter and including only historical data, companies should use percentages instead of absolute numbers so that ordinary shareholders understand them better.

The Rape of Tibet

The invasion of Tibet by China in 1950. Was it really "the Rape of Tibet?". I am referring to the article by Mr Gandhi to you (AV, 17 May, P4) on the plight of Tibetans. I do not think so at all.

World Bank economists, Shaohua Chen and Martin Ravallion, estimated that roughly 1.1 billion people were living in extreme poverty in 2001, down from 1.5 billion in 1981. United Nations has long used a complicated statistical standard-income of $1 per day per person, measured at purchasing power parity to define extreme poverty.

China and East Asia accounted for 800 million of those in extreme poverty in 1981. This group, mainly China, managed to reduce this figure to 260 million by 2001. Surely Tibetans would have benefited along with all other Chinese in this area as well as in all it progress and prosperity in every direction: e.g. average GDP growth rate of 6–8% every year for 50 years.

By comparison, India and South Asia accounted for 470 million in extreme poverty in 1981. This group, mainly India, managed to reduce this figure to a still a very high 415 million in extreme poverty by 2001.

Which ideology is better? Capitalism or Communism? In the former, man exploits man, In the latter, it is the other way round: man exploits man. Recent history has proved that none of the two systems are superior to the other. Let us not forget that Russia until recently was the second most powerful country in the world. Now China has proved with their "system of communism" that in many ways they are the most successful country in the world, but only to a certain level.

Nagindas Khajuria FCCA
Simplification Made Simple, Chartered Certified Accountants, London

2008
The Rape of Tibet

In the Human Development Index (HDI) prepared by the UN Development Programme on a scale of 0–1, measured by three key components-longevity, knowledge and income, each measured by several parameters, China still comes 81st and India 126th in descending order among 177 countries. Recent events are beginning to prove that the entire world financial system, as the backbone of capitalism, could be fundamentally flawed.

China's and India's population growth will hamper their progress for generations to come and there is no way they can catch up with the West unless they work together with the West and ensure that the West also progresses and continues to buy their goods and services. In a sense the world is flat now and either everyone grow or every one fall behind. After all, China would not have been given a permanent seat at the Security Council of the UN, if that were not the case.

While it may be true that some Tibetans who want autonomy or independence may be suppressed, the Chinese culture, values and beliefs are as strong, if not stronger, that the Tibetans or the Indians. That is why they have outpaced both the Tibetans as well as the Indians. That is why they are not likely to ethnically cleanse the Tibetans nor invade neighbouring countries because they are wiser than that and also because in any case, the other countries all protected by the Himalayan mountain range thick impenetrable border. Again, China has a separate Minister in charge of Ethnic Affairs. Which other country has such a minister?

Some of the factors that has enabled China to succeed so well and so fast are:

1. The Chinese culture: "the key factor is actually a country's cultural endowments, particularly the degree to which it has internalised the values of hard work, thrift, honesty, patience and tenacity, as well as the degree to which is open to change, new technology and equality for women" according to economist David Landes, in his book The Wealth and Poverty of Nations". In UN Gender Empowerment Index, the Chinese rank 0.5 in

Nagindas Khajuria FCCA
Simplification Made Simple, Chartered Certified Accountants, London

the range of 0–1 while India does not even feature in this Index.
2. The Chinese values and beliefs: the Chinese believe in the fusion of three great religions: Confucianism, Buddhism and Taoism. They account for over 700 million people worldwide. They have believed in this for the past two and half thousand years. In that sense, they are no inferior to the Buddhists of Tibet. Confucianism, rather than a religion, is a set of moral and social values designed to bring the ways of the citizen and governments into harmony with each other.
3. The five Confucian virtues are benevolence, righteousness, propriety, wisdom and trustworthiness. Instead of God, it has five hierarchical relationships as the prerequisites in a well educated society: ruler to the ruled, son to father, younger brother to elder brother, wife to husband and the only relationship which is equal—friend to friend. The Government may be atheist, but the people are not.
4. Tao literally translates as the "Way". It implies the Way of Nature whose underlying principle and source of all being is the bond that unites man and nature.
Its message is to take no action that runs against nature.
5. The Chinese economic policy: under the vision of Deng Ziaoping, vice chairman of the CCP, the Chinese Communist Party, from 1976 and again in 1992, China followed an "open door policy" for foreign investment and collaboration as opposed to Tibet that had historically closed its doors to outsiders all along until the Chinese came along and conquered them. The latter opened up the country to the whole wide world and has definitely improved the lives of the Hans, who represent 92% of the Chinese population, as well as all ethnic minorities who represent the remaining 8% including the Tibetans.

One should not forget that the massive Tibetan plateau at an average height of 4500 metres above the sea level, is guarded on all sides by towering mountain ranges: the Himalayas separate Tibet from India, Nepal and Bhutan to the south,

2008
The Rape of Tibet

2008
The Rape of Tibet

the Karakoram from Pakistan to the west and the Kunlun from Xinjiang to the north. The plateau is the birthplace not only of the Indus, Brahmaputra and Sutlej rivers, but also the Yangzi, Mekong Yellow and Salween rivers in the east. Mr Gandhi's article fails to mention the Chinese rivers.

Finally, let us not follow the war mongering language or the divide and rule policy of splitting communities and countries which have shown that working together they could achieve far more than working as two independent countries entangled into an imaginary battle of ideology. The Tibetans are better off within China rather than without China. India also better make best use of the huge market potential of Chinese middle class so close to it by healthy cooperation and competition rather than taking a confrontational attitude without due reflection on its long term objectives, values and beliefs.

Nagindas Khajuria FCCA
Simplification Made Simple, Chartered Certified Accountants, London

Israel at 60

I refer to your editorial on Israel at 60 (AV 24 May p3). While I agree that India should foster stronger ties with Israel in all areas, one cannot put the blame on stalemate in Jewish Palestinian relations more on the Arabs. Both group are equally to blame and Israel has often been ruthless in its treatment of Palestinians during those 60 years. It has also ignored many UN resolutions simply because of their strategic presence near all the oil rich Arab countries and have got away with it because of West's geopolitical interests in that region.

I beg to disagree that the "Arabs repaid India with indifference laced with contempt" in return for India delaying the exchange of diplomatic missions with Israel until January 1992, even though India recognised Israel 58 years ago as a sovereign state.

Currently there are virtually thousands of Indian citizens and/or persons of Indian origin (PIOs) who work, do business and live in Arab states: Indian citizens:Kuwait 294,000; Oman 311,000; Qatar 130,000; Saudi Arabia 1,500,000, UAE 900,000 compared to 300 in Israel.

In addition, PIOs or Persons of Indian origin who work, do business and live in Arab or Muslim states are: Malaysia 1,600,000; UAE 50,000, Yemen 100,000 compared to 45,000 in Israel.

Private remittances to India in 2004–05 were 14,494,000,000 US Dollars. Some of this was surely from Arab countries. In Sudan, India has invested just under US $1 billion in equity in oil exploration and production activities. India imported petroleum, oil and lubricants to the value of 29,844,000,000 US Dollars in 2004–05. Some of it is surely again from Arab states. Current imports from U.A.E in 2004–05 were 4,582,000,000 US Dollars and exports to U.A.E. were 7,098,000,000 US Dollars.

In these hundreds of thousands who go abroad to work for India, there will be Muslims as well as Hindus and others. While a minority may be terrorists, the silent majority could be decent law abiding citizens or PIOs loyal to their Indian homeland.

Israel is not the only democracy in that region. Most Arab states treat their national and foreign workers fairly, have central and local governments, municipalities, rule of law, etc. and not despotic or autocratic as Western media like us to believe. I worked and lived in Libya for four years in oil exploration and production company and me and my family were treated with utmost respect as Hindus.

Nagindas Khajuria FCCA
Simplification Made Simple, Chartered Certified Accountants, London

2008
High petrol prices

I refer to your article "British motorists warned of high petrol prices" (AV 31 May, p18) in the Financial Voice section. There are a number of reasons why I do not agree at all with Godman Sachs view that there will a major shortage of oil over the next years which could see prices soar to $200 a barrel. The petroleum industry has been with us for about 300 years. Middle East oil was only discovered 75 years ago. During the past 50 years, crude oil prices have averaged US$20 per barrel of 42 galons from 1947 to 1973, about US$40 (1973 to 1978), fluctuating between $40 to $60 (1978 to 1987), went down to an average of $20 per barrel (1987 to 2003), and then fluctuated between $20 to $60 (2003 to 2006) and is now fluctuating between $60 and $120 per barrel only during the last two years. These are just headline spot prices: the real world prices are much lower.

Globally, nothing has changed so drastically in the demand for oil to warrant the entire quantity of crude oil produced of around 90 million barrels per day at an average price of $140 per barrel or upto $200 per barrel. The demand is likely to fall over the next 10 years because of the following reasons. The supply is likely to rise because oil reservoirs are being managed more professionally, wells that were shut are being reopened in US as higher prices make them viable, secondary recovery rates are getting better, Russia and Kazaksthan are likely to increase their production rates at a much faster pace, and some producers are likely to get higher cash now then lower cash in the future when renewable energy sources may dampen the demand for their products.

Car manufacturers are switching over to more fuel efficient and/or hybrid or bio-fuel or electric smaller cars.

Consumers are doing the same.

Air pollution in the cities is mainly caused by CO_2 emmissions from cars: future air pollution is likely to be more strictly controlled.

It is likely that public transport systems, including trains, trams, buses and underground metro lines will gain further momentum.

While oil and gas reserves may still have another 100 years to run, coal is coming back into fashion. There is still about few centuries worth of coal underground and new electricity generating plants using the latest clean coal technology are already being commissioned in UK and elsewhere.

Nagindas Khajuria FCCA
Simplification Made Simple, Chartered Certified Accountants, London

2008

High petrol prices

Crude oil is useless until it is transported, refined, stored, marketed and delivered to industrial units or consumers.

Apart from the major 4 multinational companies operating in 40 to 80 countries and all the major nationalised oil country producing companies, there are hundreds of smaller businesses involved all over the world in geologic surveys, exploration, drilling, bulk transport, storage depots, pipelines, tankers, etc. and all are working in their own national interests rather than global interests. Thus a particular country, if it is in severe cashflow needs, would sell its oil at a lower price than another one. Again, those companies that are well run can sell at lower prices than those which are poorly run.

There may not be another Iraq war over the next 10 years. The strategy used in the past of perpetual war for perpetual peace may give way to a more constructive dialogue in trouble spots like Nigeria, Sudan, Iran, Iraq, Afghanistan, Pakistan, Shri Lanka, Zimbabewe, Tibet, Congo, etc. and then less oil will be needed to fund all these trouble areas, while these countries themselves would produce more oil.

As food prices are going up, countries will decide to rejuvenate their own organic agricultural production rather than importing fresh fruits, vegetables and meat from the other side of the globe. In the that case less oil will be needed for shipping costs.

Again, hypermarkets are downsizing to supermarkets and supermarkets to smaller metro shops. That may save on fuel bills of jaggernauts and ships transporting goods between nations and on sea waters.

Fuel duty is currently 62P, VAT is 17P, making a total of 79P taxes on a litre of unleaded petrol costing 119P per litre. The other 40P covers exploration costs to find the oil, production cost to lift the oil out of the ground, pipeline and/or tanker transport to refinery costs, refining costs, storage costs in bulk terminals and finally petrol stations marketing and selling costs. At every stage there is also a profit element. Thus this 40P could be divided into 3P each cost and 3P each profit element of these six stages before the gasoline reaches your tank.

Most of these costs and profits are incurred and enjoyed in the country that uses the crude oil ultimately rather than the producer and yet we keep on feeding misinformation about the relationship between high crude oil prices and final gasoline

Nagindas Khajuria FCCA
Simplification Made Simple, Chartered Certified Accountants, London

2008
High petrol prices

prices. It is comparing apples with pears. When they are incurred within the oil producing country, they are recovered from the national oil companies by the private oil companies directly or indirectly through long term production sharing agreements.

Crude oil itself is half of what comes out of the ground. The other half is gas. Media does not quote the price of gas on a daily basis like oil. The former is quoted in BTUs, and can range from 1000 to 1500 BTUs with varying prices.

From half of the crude, only half ends up in gasoline. The other half is heating oil, LPG, Naphta, Bitumen, etc.

The US Dollar is only half of the world currency and yet it is used to measure the entire world's oil production. The US Dollar has gone down in value compared to EURO, Sterling, Japanese Yen significantly. That makes a mockery of forecast oil prices in US Dollars and futures market in US Dollars.

Nagindas Khajuria FCCA
Simplification Made Simple, Chartered Certified Accountants, London

2008
Gordon Brown—is he a Charlie?

I refer to "Gordon Brown – is he a Charlie? Article (Kapil's Khichadi, AV 24 May p11) and Arun Vaidyanathan reply (AV 7 June p 4) on the 10P fiasco and proportional representation versus first past the post system of voting.

It is my firm belief that reform of the electoral system is urgent now. The predominance of two parties over the past 40 years has meant that the country is run on a divided rather that a united basis on all key public sector areas without any long term jointly agreed investment plans.

The recent 10P tax rate abolition was not a fiasco at all. It was a very clever use of hype, hyperbole and obfuscation to swing public opinion. The ethos of "service" has gone from public sector and the lure of "financial gain" has crept in public life.

The true situation was that actual tax on 18 million earning £17,000 was £2,364 in 2006/07 compared to £2,400 in 2007/08 without the 10P rate but with a reduced to 20P rate.

In 1983, votes cast were 43.5% Conservatives, 28.3% Labour and 26.1% Lib-SDP. Seats won: Conservatives 397, Labour 209 and Lib-SDP 23. 67% of those eligible to vote voted. Thus, conservatives formed a majority Conservative government based on 29% of UK population over 18.

The following voting systems should be urgently debated:

First past the post system (FPTP): whoever gets the most votes in a constituency wins, even if they secure a minority of all votes cast.

Alternative Vote (AV): candidates are ranked by electors and redistributed until a candidate with 50% support emerges.

AV plus (AV+): this is what Lord Jenkins recommended in May 1997. Here a small top-up list of MPs with no specific constituencies would be elected according to their share of vote in different areas.

Single Transferrable Vote (STV): multi-member seats elected by proportional representation—favoured by Liberal Democrats.

The case against proportional representation is that it does not produce a majority government, but unstable coalitions and breaks the bond between MPs and their constituencies.

I do not believe that is the case. Coalitions can be sensible and stable and can act in the long term interest of the country. India is a prime example currently with 85 political parties. Minority parties can bring in fresh ideas, diversity and

Nagindas Khajuria FCCA
Simplification Made Simple, Chartered Certified Accountants, London

2008
Gordon Brown—is he a Charlie?

challenge decisions that are taken so often for political gain, reversed when the next party comes, and again reversed back when the first party comes back in power. Such activities waste billions of pounds which the public would otherwise see in fairer wealth, jobs and income distribution.

Finally, there is hardly any bond between the members of a constituency and an MP. They are normally too high headed and almost impossible to meet up informally. All you can do is to communicate with them in an impersonal way by letters. Most citizens' experience is going once every five year to vote and then all is forgotten until next 5 years elapse.

2008
Ambani brothers at war again

I read your article on "Ambani brothers at war again" (AV 21 June) with great interest. The war is about RCOM (Reliance Communications), part of ADA (Anil Dhirubhai Ambani) Group wishing to merge with MTN, South Africa's largest mobile operator. Combined group would mean 115 million subscribers according to FT.

Mukesh Ambani, part of RIL (Reliance Industries Limited) has challenged this merger claiming he has first right of refusal.

Now that India is a global player, both brothers should consider what outcome would benefit the country as a whole. To my knowledge, their father and the two brothers' combined ingenuity, technical know how and foresight was instrumental in making ICT industry sector an outstanding success.

Their telecommunications success story began long before 2006 when they split up. Reliance's diversification from manufacturing into information technology and communications (ICT) sector was in three areas: laying a broadband network in the entire country, offering a GSM mobile phone service in several states, and most ambitiously covering the entire country with a CDMA mobile service.

The GSM mobile services that began in 2001 covered 15 states by 2002–03 and accounted for over 400,000 subscribers. Through Reliance Infocomm jointly owned by the two brothers, Reliance connected 115 cities through 60,000 km of broadband cable network. It also held licenses for national and international long distance call services.

In year ending 2002, Reliance slashed it CDMA mobile service rates by half compared to others and managed to cover 673 cities. It also threw in free incoming calls and low STD rates. Long distance calls were reduced to the cost of a paan. This was achieved in two ways—the enterprise software of CDMA mobile technology was developed in house and a decision was made to offer roaming facilities allowing for only limited mobility.

Thus in my opinion, both brothers are now entitled to share equally the success of RComm which superseded RInfocomm.

The other interesting aspect of this war, or rather "battle", is the Bombay Stock Exchange (BSE) Sensitive Index and how it is computed. The Stock Exchange Sensitive Index of Equity Prices or "Sensex" as is popularly called is based upon equity

Nagindas Khajuria FCCA
Simplification Made Simple, Chartered Certified Accountants, London

2008

Ambani brothers at war again

shares of 30 companies in different industry sectors. The financial year 1978–79 was chosen as the base year.

The index was based upon the "Full Market Capitalization Method" until 31 August 2003. Effective 1 September 2003, index construction was changed to the "Free-float Market Capitalization Method. The latter is regarded as an industry best practice globally.

In the free-float method, shareholdings held by investors, that would not, in the normal course come into the open market are treated as 'controlling/strategic holdings' and hence are not included in free-float BSE Sensex Index movement which is calculated every 15 seconds. Free-float factual data has to be submitted to BSE every quarter.

On 21 January 2004, the free-float adjustment factor for RIL was 0.55. That meant that 45% of the shares were owned by controlling/strategic owners at that time. Anil Ambani is proposing to exchange most of his 66% shareholding in RComm for 40% share in MTL. RComm would then be a subsidiary but with almost controlling interest. According to FT, the other big shareholders in MTL are Newshelf (13%) on behalf of employees, Public Investment Corporation (13%) on behalf of public sector pension fund and Ml (10%) on behalf of Lebanon's Mikati family.

Above consideration could save battling out in Indian courts and/or compliance with South African laws obliging Anil Ambani to buy out the other shareholders if his offer went above 34.9% stake in MTN.

Nagindas Khajuria FCCA
Simplification Made Simple, Chartered Certified Accountants, London

2008

Nuke Deal Jitters

Your leader article "Nuke Deal Jitters" (AV p1 28 June) advises that the Left-UPA (United Progressive Alliance) Joint Committee will meet on Wednesday 2 July 2008 to discuss the United States-India Peaceful Atomic Energy Cooperation Agreement. The world community will perceive it to be both a peaceful and military cooperation agreement. A hundred years later, historians will be able to condemn or praise their vision.

USA's military or 'hard' power is strongest in the world. In addition, its "soft" power is Hollywood, McDonalds, Microsoft, American universities, Boeing, Intel, MTV, Coca Cola, Kodak, etc. With the help of its European and Far East allies, it has become widely accepted as a way of life among the developed world.

India's military or hard power is enough to defend itself against any aggression without the need to become a US protégé such as Israel. India's soft power is its rich heritage since 3012 BC, Bollywood, pluralism, democracy, cuisine, fashion, vegetarianism, non-violence, scriptures, pluralism, yoga, meditation, spirituality, etc.

Currently it has a Roman Catholic ruling political party President, a Sikh Prime Minister and until recently a Muslim Head of State.

USA and Europeans belong to developed, wealthier 50 or so nations with some degree of inner superiority complex. India belongs to the developing or under developed group of 150 or so nations representing the less fortunate group as a whole. The latter group's way of life is superior in maintaining the biodiversity and beauty of this planet and is more sustainable and sensible all way round.

When you watch Wimbledon tennis, or the European League Football Championships, you cannot fail to realize the overrepresentation from the former 50 countries and the under-representation from the latter 150 countries.

Although the latter group belong to a body called "The Commonwealth", the wealth is more common among some nations and less common among other nations.

At this time in the history of India, members should remember and reflect upon the following:

OECD (Organisation for Economic Cooperation and Development) was formed in 1961 to assist member states to develop economic and social policies aimed at high sustained

Nagindas Khajuria FCCA
Simplification Made Simple, Chartered Certified Accountants, London

2008
Nuke Deal Jitters

economic growth with financial stability. Its 29 members are Canada, European Union members, Japan, Luxembourg, Mexico, New Zealand, Switzerland, Turkey, Korea and USA. It has helped these countries become so successful in 50 years. It is based in Paris.

- OECD started as OEEC (Organisation for European Economic Cooperation) in 1948 after World War II. Its name was changed to OECD when non-Europeans were allowed to become members from 1961.
- NSG (Nuclear Suppliers Group) was founded in 1975 after India carried out a nuclear test in 1974. Its 45-member nuclear supplier group includes Argentina, Australia, Brazil, Canada, China, Cyprus, Japan, Kazakhstan, Malta, New Zealand, Russia, South Africa, South Korea, Switzerland, Turkey, Ukraine, all European Union members and USA.

The protest rally in Mumbai last Tuesday by Jammat-E-Islam against India's possible civilian nuclear deal and the Communist Party members are right to throw this baby out of the water. The main parties should be grateful to them to open their eyes. Why should Israel have nuclear weapons and not Iran?

USA and European foreign policies have been misguided for the past 50 years. They have concentrated more on the weapons of mass destruction and less on the weapons of mass salvation.

According to Jeffrey D Sach, he says on page 287 of his book called "Economics for a Crowded Planet – Common Wealth":

"The Middle East has experienced a century of Western imperial meddling. Britain and the United States toppled governments (Iran in 1953, Iraq in 1968), supported wars (Iran-Iraq in 1980–87), tolerated tyrants when convenient (Saddam Hussein in the 1970s and 1980s), and toppled them when inconvenient (Saddam Hussein in 2003). The United States supported Osama bin Laden and his mujahedeen in the Afghan civil war (against Soviet Union) only to help create Al-Qaeda".

Nagindas Khajuria FCCA
Simplification Made Simple, Chartered Certified Accountants, London

2008
Nuke Deal Jitters

I have worked with Americans for 19 years. I believe their people are good. For the time being, they are the best we have as world leaders.

Only their policies now need to change. Their military and overseas spending in 2007 was US $572 billion in military, 11 billion on international security, 14 billion in overseas development aid and 11 billion for diplomatic functions. Can they explain the rationale behind such behaviour?

In the 21st century, the country that spends more on development aid will steal the march from US to be the next world leader.

Nagindas Khajuria FCCA
Simplification Made Simple, Chartered Certified Accountants, London

2008
Rethink merger approval

I fully agree that the 10th anniversary of the merger between Price Waterhouse and Coopers and Lybrand should make us rethink how such mergers are approved (26 June, page 1).

At that time, I felt very strongly that those from smaller audit firms should be allowed to also review the 700-page justification document sent to the EU Competition Commission and that Financial Reporting Standards were not fully in place to address global issues and should be addressed before mergers could be considered.

The recent credit crunch where banks have written off more than US$400 billion on long term loans in the past six months indicates that the Big Four, because of their size, have not been able to discover all these weaknesses over the past ten years.

It is not a healthy audit environment. We need about ten big audit firms, especially as the Big Four audits 97% of the world's major companies.

Nagindas Khajuria FCCA
Simplification Made Simple, Chartered Certified Accountants, London

2008
Land of Amarnath Yatris trigges political tremors

I feel very sad about the events described in your article "Land of Amarnath Yatris triggers political tremors" (P1 & 30, also P4, AV 5 July). While holy places have spiritual energy, our entire life is a pilgrimage and the real temple is a place of inner worship.

The tit for tat subsidy dispute between the Amarnath Cave Shrine for Hindu pilgrims and Haj flights for Muslims in Kashmir is a symptom, not the disease. The immense potential in the state will continue to remain unutilised until a permanent solution is reached.

The disease is the inability of both countries peoples to resolve the issue while their leaders continue to bury their heads into the sand.

Pakistan invaded the state on 22 October 1947 and secured 78,114 sq. km (35%). China invaded the Aksai Chin part of Ladakh and managed to secure 42,839 sq.km (19%) and India has ended up keeping 101,283 sq.km (46%) out of the original 222,236 sq. km (100%), Maharaja Hari Singh had signed the instrument of Accession to India on 26 October 1947 and that should have been honoured by Pakistan and China.

The population facts are: Pakistan 150 million Muslims (12%), Bangladesh 138 million Muslims (11%) and India has 138 million Muslims (11%) and 828 million Hindus (66%). Total subcontinent population is 1,254 million excluding Sri Lanka. Overall about 34% Muslims and about 66% Hindus live side by side. All are originally "Indians" over 2000 years.

The ethnic, religious and linguistic conflicts of 10 million people in Jammu and Kashmir have had most damaging repercussions on the welfare of 1,254 million people over the past 60 years.

In the 2004 general elections, in Jammu and Kashmir, of a total of 87 seats, Jammu and Kashmir National Conference won 28, Indian National Congress 20, Peoples Democratic Party 16 and Independent Party 13.

Across India, in 2004 Congress and its allies won 218 seats; National Democratic Alliance won 187 seats, Left and its allies 60 and others 64.

It is incomprehensible why these political parties are fighting among each other on religious, ethnic and linguistic grounds while they should be fighting on social justice issues such as literacy skills, education, health, equal opportunity,

Nagindas Khajuria FCCA
Simplification Made Simple, Chartered Certified Accountants, London

2008

Land of Amarnath Yatris trigges political tremors

clean drinking water, shelter, etc. Surely the latter should be the battleground for the coming general elections in 2009.

Punjab-Haryana-Delhi (PHD) Chamber of Commerce based in Delhi now covers 10 states and one union territory, namely Chhatisgarh, Delhi, Haryana, Himachal Pradesh, Jammu & Kashmir, Madya Pradesh, Punjab, Rajasthan, Uttar Pradesh, Uttaranchal and the Union territory of Chandigarh. It is known as PHDCCI. It was formed in 1905. These states together account for 40% to 45% of India's GDP. "PDH" became an accronym for Progress-Harmony-Development since 1981 when other states joined the Chamber.

It has compiled important data on Jammu and Kashmir and how it compares with other Indian states. Please visit www.phdcci.in. Its per capita income in 2005–06 was Rs 17,463 compared to the national average of Rs 21,005. Its urban population is 25%. Its literacy rate 55%. It has 75 towns and 6,653 villages.

The principal crops are rice, barley, apples, and saffron. Major industries are handicrafts, sericulture, horticulture and tourism. I flew to Srinagar from Delhi in 1976. The view below from the aircraft was like heaven on earth: Switzerland multiplied by 1000 times.

My message is: stop dithering on the Heaven on Earth piece of land and get cracking on attracting tourists after a permanent solution is implemented by mutual long lasting agreement.

2008
60 years of NHS

The entire page 15 of your newspaper (AV 12 July p15) is full of praise by the Health Minister and others on 60 years of the National Health Service in the UK.

I believe the National Health Service itself is aging and needs a fundamental change in its ethos, its systems and procedures and its future strategies.

The hypothesis was "to receive health care on the basis of clinical need, regardless of ability to pay". However, the antithesis of this has been "regardless of the ability of NHS body as a whole to pay". NHS has been wrongly managed in the latter way.

Rationing is now very urgent. Otherwise its funding is not sustainable. The time has come to think and hive off perhaps a third of NHS to the private sector lock stock and barrel so that the remaining two thirds get decent medical care.

Health promotion should have been at the core of this system. Resources, money and powerful lobbies have evolved only on the cure side as it was more profitable to do so.

Queuing and waiting for treatment has become the norm in NHS. Vested interested are not allowing fundamental reform which could dilute their share of the cake.

Some examples of what has gone badly wrong are given below:

Rates of treatment per 100,000 residents can be a minimum of 36 hip replacements in one area to a maximum of 152 hip replacements in another area. Similar situation arose in coronary artery bypass graft, knee replacement, etc.

10% of patients contract an infection while in hospital.

NHS standards of service state that patients be seen within 30 minutes. It is normally one hour in a GP surgery, two hours in an outpatient department and three hours in A & E while not one second of consultant's time is wasted.

Scarcity in NHS is managed by rationing of medical care and those who shout loudest manage to get the maximum attention.

In personal injury claims, patient's claimant solicitors take about 40%, NHS defendant solicitors take about another 40% and the injured patient ends up with a meagrely sum of about 20%.

Waiting lists to go into hospitals continue to range from half million to one million throughout the 60 years.

Nagindas Khajuria FCCA
Simplification Made Simple, Chartered Certified Accountants, London

2008
60 years of NHS

The planned expenditure for NHS is £104 billion in 2008–09, Personal Social Services £24 billion and Social Protection £161 billion including tax credits, a total of £289 billion. Social services and care for the elderly and community health form part of health care so the true NHS total is more likely to be £160 billion spread between central government and local authorities. 40% of this could be saved by more rigid financial controls and drastic restructuring.

The state of the mind and emotional health can damage our body parts immensely. Feelings such as anger, frustration, anxiety, fear, etc are stresses of modern living. More needs to be done tackle this paradigm.

Desirable body weight tables with heights including 2.5 cm heels shoes, and weights including indoor clothing for small, medium and large frame men and women aged over 25 should be readily available in all GP surgeries and hospitals so that people learn more about sensible life style etc. They hardly ever are.

Nutritionists give advice on healthy eating to healthy people while dieticians give advice to ill people. The former are severely underrepresented in NHS.

British adults with no natural teeth fell from 17% in 1983 to 10% by 1995 in Greater London, while in Yorkshire and Humberside it fell from 33% to 21% of the adult population.

There have been several very costly attempts to reform the NHS over the past few decades which wasted billions of pounds. Some reforms were reversed.

Enoch Powell, The Conservative Health Minister was right when he said "There is virtually no limit to the amount of medical care an individual is capable of absorbing.........."

Why not introduce a charge every time you wish to see a GP? This was recommended by John Willman in his book "A Better State of Health" – "A Prescription for the NHS". I agree with his ideas wholeheartedly.

The current plan to computerise patients' medical records is fundamentally flawed and will not serve any purpose at all. It is a waste of £12 billion pounds initial investment and £3 to £4 billion pounds annual running costs of the system.

Nagindas Khajuria FCCA
Simplification Made Simple, Chartered Certified Accountants, London

2008

Vote of confidence to decide UPA's fate

I refer to your editorial comment article "Vote of confidence to decide UPA's fate" (AV 19 July p3) on the decisive vote in the Indian Parliament as regards the Indo-US civilian nuclear accord.

What is the better option for India?

In the eighties, Rata Tata, Jamshyd Godrej, Rahul Bajaj and Tarun Das, the Head of Confederation of Indian Industries used to go every year to the USA and try to meet CEOs there to get business. It took them one year to meet Jack Welch, CEO of General Electric who initially said he was not interested in India. India was corrupt. He did not want to do business with India.

It turned out that GE was one of the first American companies that started outsourcing work to India and now India is a world leader in information technology, business processes and knowledge processes outsourcing. A lot of credit goes to USA Inc.

This time the US has come to India to export their nuclear fuel processing technology. Should India say no? Or should it say yes and pay billions of dollars only recently saved up in dollar reserves? Is it a luxury or a necessity? I believe it is a luxury India does not need at this stage of its industrial development.

What if the next Albert Einstein is an Indian scientist? India could then export civilian nuclear fuel processing technology rather than import it, or at least do both.

Will this accord also help Indian national security and its borders from invasion?

The Indian government's Kirit Parikh report on integrated energy policy for India has forecast that even if a 20-fold increase takes place in India's nuclear power supply by 2031–32, the contribution to India's energy mix is at best expected to be 4–6%.

Should India put all its eggs in one basket? Apart from US, France, Sweden and Finland currently have the latest technology in civilian nuclear fuel technology. Why not join the European Organization for Nuclear Research (CERN) based in Switzerland whose members include USA, most EU members, Israel, Japan, Russia and Turkey in lieu of a bilateral agreement with USA and the International Atomic Energy Agency?

The West has been wasteful in the use of energy for 50 years. Western habits at home, in modes of travel by car, train and plane, consumerism, over zealous production of manufac-

---

Nagindas Khajuria FCCA
Simplification Made Simple, Chartered Certified Accountants, London

2008
Vote of confidence to decide UPA's fate

tured goods are likely to change drastically as society becomes more caring towards the planet earth. The savings in the West may cushion the increased energy demand in the East.

Let India not hurry or be pushed into an agreement where its Parliament appears to be split in the middle. This is non-partisan issue and all MPs should vote in India's long term national interest when they meet to ratify or reject this accord.

2008
Deal wins [Indo-American Nuclear Accord ratified by parliament]

I refer to your lead article (AV, p1, 26 July) on 'Deal wins' and 'Bizarre drama after bribery allegations' on the Indo-US Nuclear Accord.

I am really glad that the United Progress Alliance under Manmohan Singh has won over the Bhartiya Janata Party and Communist Party Alliance to get the Indo-US Nuclear Accord ratified by the Indian Parliament.

Originally I was against this Accord. On reflection, I am now in favour. My reasons are as follows:

- India has never been part of the Club of powerful nations. It can now use its influence by being an insider rather than an outsider.
- There are 8 to 9 countries that have nuclear weapons. Other 20 nations could develop such weapons if they wanted to. By agreeing to have India's nuclear facilities to be inspected by the international community, India is effectively discouraging nuclear weapons proliferation, which is a good thing.
- India knows the damage it can inflict upon itself if it does not realise that there will always be nations who will try to break it by the well known method of divide and rule. Recent bombings in Ahmadabad and Banglore remind us of that. May be we should have a few states in India where meat is prohibited a) to encourage other nations to follow India and b) to discourage violence to animals in addition to humans.
- That is ALSO why the inquiry into vote rigging, bribery of MPs, bullying tactics, should be dropped otherwise those who may have tried to divide and rule India may have succeed sooner than later.
- The bribery charges against MPs in this voting reminds me of the joke that when other countries complained to God why He had bestowed so much upon India, God responded and told them: "Do not worry; I shall put more corrupt people there."
- All parties should now stand united about this historic decision and make the most it by expanding its power generation capacity through nuclear reactors.
- The important aspect they should remember is health and safety. The explosion in Chernobyl story is not over yet. Currently they are building a huge aircraft hanger

Nagindas Khajuria FCCA
Simplification Made Simple, Chartered Certified Accountants, London

2008
Deal wins [Indo-American Nuclear Accord ratified by parliament]

like construction costing 800 million dollars to cover reactor number 4 remains that had exploded 20 years ago. No 1, 2 and 3 were decommissioned in year 2000.
- India must now also concentrate on all other sources of power generation.
- It should get on with power generation through more advanced capture of biomass (plant and animal waste).
- Sea based and lands based wind farms can generate a fair amount of electric power. In Denmark, wind generates about 20% of all its electricity.
- Panels covered with photovoltaic cell capture the sun at a solar park near Leipzig, Germany. With 33,500 panels, it is one of the planet's largest arrays.
- Solar energy costs have gone down a lot over the past 30 years and further reductions are likely. Some countries have laws requiring new building to have solar energy.
- When we drove extensively in Andalucía, Spain, a couple of years ago, we so hundreds of wind mills generating electricity for people and/or mass production of tomatoes in hundreds of small green houses, one after another for miles and miles.
- Readers of Asian Voice need to study three very interesting articles I recently came across that argue some of the above points in more depth that I can do here.
- "Powering the Future: where on earth our energy-hungry society can turn to replace oil, coal, and natural gas? By Michael Parfit; and
- "Living with the Bomb: it has been 60 years since Hiroshima and Nagasaki. Today nuclear weapons stoke nations' dreams of power and give their citizens nightmares" by Richard Rhodes; (National Geographic August 2005).
- "Inside Chernobyl plus Nuclear Power Reconsidered" by Richard Stone (National Geographic April 2006).
- They all make a lot of sense and we should learn form them.

Nagindas Khajuria FCCA
Simplification Made Simple, Chartered Certified Accountants, London

2008
£1 billion package for UK housing industry

I refer to the Chancellor's two recent announcements to help lower income groups buy their own homes: increasing the exempt band of Stamp Duty from £125,000 to £175,000 and to provide "free" loans up to 30% of the value of new built properties for first time buyers (your article "£1 billion package for UK housing industry" in AV, 6 Sept, p18). The Stamp Duty announcement is apparently for one year only. I do smell "power politics" when such announcements are made.

If you study the laws, the changes, the reforms, the political battles fought between the Conservatives and the Labour parties over the past 50 years on housing policies, you will find that both parties went into different directions all these years.

Some examples are: the move away from Local Authorities to Housing Associations, Sale of Council Homes, public spending on housing going down in real terms by 54.6%, rent and landlord controls v relaxations, tenants voting labour and owner occupiers voting conservatives, etc.

Surely, on such vital issues as housing, food, energy costs, all the three parties must work and decide a long term, say 20 year plan, on housing rather than tinker at the edges as above. The above announcement should have been discussed with the other two parties.

If 67% of the home ownership is already owner occupied, why should we aim at increasing this type of ownership? Surely in Germany and other more efficient economies, people are encouraged to rent so that people move where jobs are all the time.

The current mortgage debt on housing is 173% of total annual income. Retail Price Index was 100 on 13th January 1987. In February 2008 it was 211.4. This is an inflation increase of 111.4% in 21 years, or an annual average increase of 5.31%. On the other hand, the Housing Price Index was 100 in January 1983. In February 2008 it was 626.1%. This is an increase of 526.1% over 25 years, or an annual average increase of a staggering 21.05%.

While the RPI is made up of some 160 items price movements and weighting each month, what is shambolic is the fact that the Housing Price Index has been kept out of it altogether. About 50% of housing costs are land costs, while the other 50% are building costs. With population growth, one would expect increases in land prices. The other 50% relates to building costs: why have they gone up by so much in both categories? Surely some it is due to greed, speculation and the

Nagindas Khajuria FCCA
Simplification Made Simple, Chartered Certified Accountants, London

2008
£1 billion package for UK housing industry

wrong culture of relying on housing to boost the economy, rather than its use as decent accommodation for the many.

When I worked and lived in Libya for 4 years between 1974 and 1978, suddenly one day the authorities came in and advised me that as my landlord had another house where he was living. My villa was nationalised and I was to pay future rents to the government.

The US Treasury today nationalised two biggest mortgage lending banks. What can UK Treasury do?

In the last Asian Voice issue (20 Sept), I read several articles that had a common thread of violent behaviour in thought word or deed on the basis of religious identity:

- Christians or Maoists killing Swami Laxmananda and his four disciples on the holy day of Janmastami on 23 August 2008 (p11);
- Indian Mujahideen claiming responsibility of 5 Delhi serial bomb blasts killing 30 innocent people last Saturday during holy Ramadan (p1);
- Fatwa issued against Salman Khan's family for celebrating Ganeshotsav at their home (p29);
- Yorkshire Coast College changing their college calendar from the terminology "Christmas and Easter breaks" to "End of Term breaks" ostensibly in a bid to avoid offending students from other religions (p7).

2008
Common thread of violent deeds and instigations

All of us tend to identify ourselves by the society we live in, our culture, our religious and other values and beliefs, our civilisation, etc. There is nothing wrong with that. However, when good relations among different human beings are identified in this singular way to the exclusion of other ways, human beings are deeply miniaturized and deposited into little boxes.

We must realise that all of us have multiple or plural identities. For example, I was born into a Hindu/Jain family in Sudan, a Muslim country. I was educated there by Italian Catholic missionaries (age of 8 to 18). Then I worked up to age 25 at the US Embassy in Khartoum under Jewish or Protestant bosses. For interests, I went to the British cultural centre to learn Scottish country dancing and to the British Council to watch or take part in plays, such as Dial M for Murder, Importance of Being Ernest, etc.

My best ACCA studies friend was El Hadi El Gibriel who worked at the Ministry of Finance and we studied accountancy together in the evenings. After 40 years, I visited Khartoum in February 2007 and looked him up. He still remembered me and invited me to go to his six two-bedroom block of flats residence on the Tuti Island.

He took out a photograph of mine I had gifted to him 40 years ago within 15 minutes of our meeting from about 100 photos he had kept in a Cadburys chocolate round tin box. There were tears in our eyes and we embraced each other.

Nagindas Khajuria FCCA
Simplification Made Simple, Chartered Certified Accountants, London

2008

Common thread of violent deeds and instigations

This photograph, with my own handwriting signed 14 September 1967 on the back, is attached as a living proof of this encounter. I had left for UK in that same month of September 1967.

We now live a global village. All of us have plural identities. Should we not see other human beings in different ways according to the circumstances?

Oscar Wilde once made the enigmatic claim "Most people are other people".

With suitable instigation, a fostered sense of identity with one group of people can be made into a powerful weapon to brutalise another. Actively promoted sectarian hatreds can spread like wildfire.

All people involved in the above four incidents should read economist and Nobel Prize Laureate Amartya Sen's recent book called "Identity and Violence – The Illusion of Destiny": they may stop their violent actions in thought, word and deed and embrace other people.

Nagindas Khajuria FCCA
Simplification Made Simple, Chartered Certified Accountants, London

2008

World markets on roller coaster – India sits pretty

I do not agree with your headline article "World markets on roller coaster, India sits pretty" (AV, Vol. 37, Issue 21, 27 Sept, p1). Indian banks and Indian business have followed herd of G8 nations for too long. They now need to expand deeper into non G8 nations economies, learn other key foreign languages and their business models. The demand from G8 nations is likely to go down for Indian exports. That happened during the Asian crisis in 1997. That was a puncture in the tyre. This is engine failure. Current events remind me of the proverb: "You can fool some of the people all of the time, all of the people some of the time, but you cannot fool all of the people all of the time."

Some examples are:

The word "opinion" in Audit Report is fundamentally flawed. It should be "assurance". Annual reports run into 300+ pages and are impossible to understand by shareholders. It turns out they were useless.

During the quarter ended 30 June 2008, 120 Indian companies set aside RS 8,900 crore for currency fluctuations, exotic derivative products and mark-to-market losses to hedge their exports. Surely, historical accounting is the way forward with any changes in market values (that move up and down 100% every year) to be stated by way of a note only. IFRSs need to be restructured.

By changing interest rates too frequently, central banks and their political masters have knowingly or unknowingly given wrong signals to the market economy. A culture of minute-by-minute speculation in all these products is being nurtured all the time through advanced information technology and communications.

The world financial crisis is blamed on sub-prime mortgages and very little has been said about the hyper activity of mergers and acquisitions, re-invented by private investment banks during the past 25 years with disproportionate level of debt finance as opposed to equity finance as publicly quoted company board of directors became poorer managers.

All these years a belief has been rammed down our throats that private sector is "efficient" and public sector is "inefficient".

As a shareholder of Vodafone plc, I was able to get into their official website two years before Arun Sarin became CEO. The Balance Sheet had an asset value of £100 billion pounds that included goodwill value of £30 billion.

Nagindas Khajuria FCCA
Simplification Made Simple, Chartered Certified Accountants, London

2008
World markets on roller coaster—India sits pretty

Based upon my understanding from the accounts, of the company's future prospects, I sent an email to the Vodafone and the Accountancy Age Letter to the Editor, stating that the Auditor was wrong in signing off the Balance Sheet and justifying keeping the goodwill value on the Balance Sheet based on the next 10 years revenue stream forecast in Note 1.

My letter was not published. Arun Sarin became the CEO two years later and wrote off £28 billion goodwill in the following year.

Finally, as a policy holder in Standard Life, I was strongly opposed to the concept of demutualisation. Mutual building society concept is a business model India should adopt for India's housing boom.

2008

Bradford & Bingley Bank nationalisation confirmed by Alistair Darling

I refer to your article "Bradford & Bingley bank nationalisation confirmed by Alistair Darling" (AV, 4 Oct 2008, p22). When banks fail, or when confidence in the banking system fails, should Governments take "quick, decisive action"?

How do you value a sinking bank with 2.7 million customers and a £21 billion deposit book? How was £612 million value worked out so quickly? What is the net present value of the mortgage debt book the government took over in addition to the £612 million it received?

Is it right that both Management and Government decide within hours of panic that shareholders get nothing? £21 billion deposits could make 1% net in banking activities and £21 billion of loans in non-banking activities could make 2%. Total income could be 3% on £21 billion that is £630 million every year. So has the bank been sold off at one year's net income?

A temporary moratorium of three to six months could be imposed during which time the government could guarantee all deposits without any limit only for that particular bank to enable extraction of maximum value while a right price private buyer is sought. Government can also compete with the private sector in a final auction for disposal at a suitable date.

Commercial banks have ventured too far into non-banking activities. Should not there be a cap on value of non-banking business? Say 25% instead of the current 50%+?

I reviewed this week the 2007 Annual Report of Capital One Financial Corporation, 8th largest commercial bank in the USA. The segmental Managed Loans, related net income/(loss) and net margins respectively were: Credit Cards US$ 52.1 billion, (US$ 2,116m), 4.06%; Auto Finance 25.1 billion, (33.8 m), -0.12%; and Global Financial Services 29.3 billion, (299.4m), 1.02%. Total loans 106.5b, total net income 2,381.9m, and net margin 2.24%. Whereas bank deposits book 73.3 billion, net income 574.2 m, a low net margin 0.78%.

The Balance Sheet did not balance. On top of the 106.5 billion Managed Loans, there were additional Managed Loans of 49.5 billion dollars that were described as "Off-Balance Sheet Securitizations". These involve transfer of pools of loans receivables to one or more third-party trusts and accounted for as sales, although they are not fully sales.

International finance involves global trade, Foreign Direct Investments and Foreign Institutional Investments. It

---

Nagindas Khajuria FCCA
Simplification Made Simple, Chartered Certified Accountants, London

2008
Bradford & Bingley Bank nationalisation confirmed by Alistair Darling

is very complex. There are 77000 Multinational Companies, 770,000 affiliates, which employ 62 million people and generate US$4.5 trillion in value added.

Both Congress and the House of Representatives should not have approved the 850 billion dollar bail out. US Government should have guaranteed bank deposits without limit but only in those institutions which approach them for help while assessing their true potential over a six months moratorium period.

Strict accounting rules have been developed under Basel II, instigated by Bank of International Settlements (BIS) in Switzerland, the central bank of all central banks of key 100 countries. Under US accounting rules, they were not mandatory for Capital One Bank.

2008
Obama cites Mahatma Gandhi to back his call for change

Your article "Obama cites Mahatma Gandhi to back his call for change" (AV 11 Oct p35) is interesting in the sense the he appeals to the American nation as a whole "to rededicate themselves every day from 2 October 2008, Mahatma Gandhi's birthday, to 4 November 2008, US election day."

For sure, these 33 days are becoming very painful days all over the globe. It was always believed that banks, at least, those which were known to be "first class banks" never, or hardly ever, fail. May be all nations should reflect deeply on change as current system is too costly for 60 to 70% of the world population.

Obama also had two other men he most admired: Abraham Lincoln and Martin Luther King Jr. He took a lot of inspiration from the civil rights movement and the way the movement brought ordinary people in extraordinary positions of leadership. It struck him that lasting change came from the bottom up and not from the top down according to "From Promise to Power" by David Mendel, pages 200-01.

On one hand, we have individuals, businesses and governments who have surplus cash and want to find suitable assets where they can invest their surpluses and make some return for a rainy day. On the other hand, there are individuals, businesses and governments who want to borrow money so that they can make better use of it because of their ability to create real wealth. Financial intermediaries connect these two groups.

Currently, because paper wealth is probably anything between 8 to 24 times the underlying asset and value of a business, an individual, a government, or a country as a whole, it is impossible to figure out where the weaknesses are and where the strengths are.

One solution could be if competition reform laws were passed where no business could have a larger than 10% share of the market, both in the public sector and the private sector, so that at least there are 20 players competing each other. Banks should be either fully private or fully public owned.

The cost of credit needs to be reduced drastically. This cost is not only the interest rate differential but all the hidden charges and commissions that are paid to financial intermediaries to broker between the savers and the borrowers when big money is raised.

A country's exchange rate strength is the supply of or the demand for its currency. When exports are more than imports,

Nagindas Khajuria FCCA
Simplification Made Simple, Chartered Certified Accountants, London

2008
Obama cites Mahatma Gandhi to back his call for change

the demand is higher than supply. When imports are more than exports, the supply is higher than demand. In the former case, the currency becomes stronger. In the latter case, the currency becomes weaker. However, when speculators start hedging on foreign currency rates, the fundamentals are changed. Why not settle imports and exports in the currencies your countries live in rather than use a third country's currency to avoid the need for hedging in the first place?

Nagindas Khajuria FCCA
Simplification Made Simple, Chartered Certified Accountants, London

2008
Where do we stand? Thinking Aloud

I welcome this new article in the Asian Voice. I hope it becomes a regular weekly feature where many more ordinary migrants speak of their real life experiences. In that effort, I like to be one of the first ones.

I was very young when I did not really understand worldly adult matters like marriage, children, wealth, opportunities, etc. But one thing I noticed in Sudan was that fair Europeans where generally more successful. I decided to marry a fair person when I became older so that my children would not suffer.

At that time, I also read that there were four races in the world: white, yellow, brown and black. Their wealth and job and education opportunities are skewed in that order to this day, 55+ years later.

Obama's skin colour and how he could not really be trusted to be the President of the US, and by implication, of the world is being put forward in the current US election. People forget that even 8 years ago, the US election was only won by 2%. That 2% was the subject of Florida vote dispute. It was decided in favour of Republicans by a jury of 9 people, 5 Republicans and 4 Democrats without recount and without voting second time. The motion was carried by a vote of 5 to 4.

Then and now, the US elections are about two different ideologies, values and beliefs held by two different political parties, not just two Presidents.

One ideology difference could be in management bonuses. In Europe, take Volkswagen, Nokia and Michelin. Compare them with General Motors, Motorola and Good Year Tyre Co. The three US CEOs can earn up to $500 million pa compared to the three EU CEOs who earn $50 million pa.

As an official Labour Party Member, as a shareholder and as a policy holder I had sent letters to John Prescott, Reuters, and Standard Life on 23 October 1997, 8 January 1998 and 15 January 1999 respectively. I still have copies.

To Mr Prescott, I suggested that there was a phrase about Property: Location, Location, and Location; and to adopt similar phrase for Education: education, education, education.

To Mr Rob Rowley, the Finance Director of Reuters PLC, I recommended not to return hundreds of millions of

Nagindas Khajuria FCCA
Simplification Made Simple, Chartered Certified Accountants, London

2008
Where do we stand? Thinking Aloud

pounds cash back to shareholders as Reuter's capital would be too thin and I would challenge him in the AGM.

To Mr A S Bell, M D of Standard Life, I suggested that the increase in "unrealized gain on investments had gone up in his annual 1997 accounts from £1,189.7m in 1996 to £3,330.4m in 1997. This inflated the revenues in the accounts by £2.1 billion in one year. I suggested to him that market values should best be kept in the notes to the accounts rather than body of the accounts.

It is clear that races of different colours do not see eye to eye.

Bias towards India in the Western media

Your Media Watch last week (AV 8 Nov 08 pl6) was very interesting about India sending a spacecraft outside the earth's orbit for the first time in its history and how The Times (23 Oct 08), the Financial Times (29 Oct 08) and Wall Street Journal (24 Oct 08) commentary on this mammoth achievement was reported.

I agree with the thrust of your arguments that there is still some bias towards India in the Western media to promote a political cause or a particular point of view.

The Times talk about the poor in India implying that the space money of US Dollars 80 million could have been spent on the poor. The welfare system in India differs in practice and concept to the UK system as it delivers grains and fuel (rice, wheat, sugar, kerosene) instead of cash.

With about 476,000 retail outlets catering to about 224 million households and distributing about 24 million tons of food grains, the Public Distribution System (PDS) is one of the biggest distribution networks in the world. Ration cards are issued to poor families which buy from government sponsored "Fair Price" shops.

It is true that there is corruption: diversion of about 30% of grains earmarked for PDS issue to open market sector; usage of bogus cards; overstocking by central government (60 million tonnes instead of optimum 20 million); consequent unnecessary use of food grain bank credit that could be diverted elsewhere; and finally price and take up disparity between states.

In 2003, the average Tamil Nadu State Open Price of rice in Rupees per kilogram was 11.79; Central Government Issue Price to those "Below Poverty Level" (BPL) 5.65; to "Above Poverty Level" (APL) 8.30; and finally State PDS Issue Price: 3.50. Subsidies in Tamil Nadu alone have reached 15 billion Rupees or 275 million US Dollars as opposed to 80 million dollars spent on the moon venture for entire India.

Major reform of the Public Distribution System is highly desirable ASAP. Population below poverty line in India went down to 19.1% (Urban 15.1%; Rural 21.1%). in 2007 from 54.9% in 1974. In the UK, the population below poverty line has gone up during the same period from about 20% to 25%.

Nagindas Khajuria FCCA
Simplification Made Simple, Chartered Certified Accountants, London

2008
Bias towards India in the Western media

As for Asean (Association of South East Asian States), it is now most urgent they work on a common Asean currency to replace the 20 odd currencies currently at play. Hedging on foreign exchange contracts has been part of the reason for current global financial crisis.

Finally, the "brain gain" in the Western economies is ten times the "brain drain" in Western economies by Asian students going to Western universities and then returning to their homeland. 9 out of 10 remain in Western economies getting middle management pay doing top management work, while perhaps one in ten goes back: this is opposite of what Wall Street Journal implies in their article.

2008
Ganga gets a tag

Your article" Ganga gets a tag: national river" (AV, 15 Nov 2008, p32) suggests that the final blueprint is expected to be placed on the table within two months. I sincerely hope that this idea is dropped: it goes against the very grain of secularism where India has outshone all other nations of the entire world.

All rivers in India are very important. Historically all cities and villages over the past 2000 years grew along their banks.

All these rivers, not just Ganga, suffer from the problem of sub-standard urban liquid waste removal and treatment and supply of clean drinking water. This problem has now become worse because of increasing use of pesticides, herbicides and fertilizers in Indian agriculture.

Like Ganga, many of the rivers cross through several states. The almost 50 years history of the Narmada Dam controversy and how excellent laws and procedures have evolved over the years to manage inter-state disputes on upstream and downstream water usage, pro-dam and anti-dam factions, misuse of issues to gain political advantage, can all be needlessly repeated by calling Ganga "the National River".

Indeed, three factors have increased water scarcity in India: growing population; increasing consumption due to rapid industrialization and rising consumerism; and thirdly, depletion of water resources through environmental degradation.

India's total precipitation averages approximately 400 million hectare meters (mhm) annually (97% rain and 3% snow) over a land-mass of 329 million hectares (mha). About 17.5% immediately evaporates, another 41.25% transpires through forests and vegetation (including crops), 12.5% goes underground and recharges ground water supplies and 28.7% joins the existing surface flow.

Rain bearing monsoon winds, which travel from southwest to the north-east from June to September and then reverse and sweep southward during September to December are unpredictable and in some parts of India periodically fail altogether. Most of the country receives rain for only about 100 hours per year; and half of that total is received in less than about 20 hours.

For all these reasons, all Indian rivers are national rivers and vital for its citizens and its industry and its agriculture. Realpolitik suggests that there may be an ulterior motive behind calling Ganga the "national river": first time this is

Nagindas Khajuria FCCA
Simplification Made Simple, Chartered Certified Accountants, London

2008
Ganga gets a tag

happening in the history of India and it should be nipped in the bud.

Water, after air, is the most valuable resource we have globally. In the UK, when I go for a swim in my local club and a shave afterwards, I see my fellow club members shaving next to me: they all leave the tap running all the time while shaving: contrast that with one bucket of water for one bath in India. Let us not waste this valuable resource.

Nagindas Khajuria FCCA
Simplification Made Simple, Chartered Certified Accountants, London

2008 The Global Financial Crisis

The Global Financial Crisis? Really? by C H Makanji (AV 22 Nov p23) raises some interesting questions.

The latest attempt to reform the GFA (Global Financial Architecture) is the new FSF Financial Stability Forum set up in February 1999. Its members are from the finance ministries, central banks and regulatory authorities of the G-7 countries, as well as the IMF, World Bank, Basle Committee, IOSCO (International Organisation of Securities Commission), International Association of Insurance Supervisors, BIS (Bank of International Settlements), OECD, Committee on Global Financial System and Committee on Payment and Settlement System.

President Nixon declared unilaterally on 15 August 1971 that the US Dollar was no longer convertible into gold: this was the beginning of the current crisis by a gradual process. Real economies are supposed to lead and shape the GFA; instead it has become a prisoner of GFA.

It is one of the ironies of the last forty years that although developing countries, as a group, have grown much faster in real GDP terms than developed countries over this entire period, their representation and their voting power in all above organisations has declined.

The equal strength of public and private sector banks in India is the right business model for the G-7 to adopt urgently.

The US Dollar needs be replaced urgently by the Euro (with Sterling agreeing to join the Euro) as the Western world currency. An Eastern world currency needs to emerge urgently to counter balance the Euro in the 21st century.

For example, the international foreign exchange market is a 24-market in which foreign currencies are bought and sold by central banks, commercial banks, businesses, investors, governments and speculators.

In 2004, the most traded currency pair was euro/US dollar (28%), followed by US Dollar/yen (17%) and the US Dollar/£ Sterling (14%). The first pair is quoted to the fourth decimal point and the last two pairs to two decimal points.

If the domestic currency remains the same and the foreign currency changes, it is called a direct quote. If the foreign currency changes, it is called an indirect quote. If the AD (Authorised Dealer) is willing to buy and sell a currency, then it is called a two-way quote. The buying rate is called the bid rate and the selling rate is called the ask rate.

Nagindas Khajuria FCCA
Simplification Made Simple, Chartered Certified Accountants, London

2008
The Global Financial Crisis

Recently I changed £200 Sterling into Euros at Post Office. Within one minute, I deliberately changed the Euros back into Sterling. I lost 10% in the process. Iceland is now considering joining the Euro: some UK experts believe UK should join. I have long campaigned for UK to join the Euro. Last 50 years has seen severe volatility and daily speculation in foreign currencies.

Finally, governments need independent and different knowledge and skills vis-à-vis the private sector. The current US treasurer's previous job was CEO of Goldman Sachs: the firm recently forecast oil prices rise to $200 per barrel from $140: it fell to $50. Train civil servants with a different mindset.

Nagindas Khajuria FCCA
Simplification Made Simple, Chartered Certified Accountants, London

India-Pakistan: Hope springs eternal

India-Pakistan: Hope springs eternal (AV, 29 Nov, p3). No sooner I read this article we all witnessed what happened in Mumbai and how the Deccan Mujahedeen are being linked in some way to Pakistan. In the same issue, there are some articles about Hindu majority being marginalised by Muslim minority (Ramesh Jhalla p4) and Hinduism awareness (Alpesh Patel pl7).

I am really surprised that we continue to live in the past and harp on this Hindu-Muslim divide when there is more that binds us than divides us. Both countries should have matured after 60 years and realized that they can no longer be fooled by the "Great Game" that bigger powers may be playing over them, again and again.

AV readers should read "The Shadow of the Great Game – The Untold Story of India's Partition" by Narendra Singh Sarila (2005). It is clear from that book that the Big Powers and politicians were responsible and not the general public for the Partition of India.

Let me quote to you the unsigned memorandum dated 19 May 1948, entitled "The Strategic and Political Importance of Pakistan in the Event of War with the USSR" (Mountbatten Papers, Hartley Library, Southampton) from this book:

"The Indus Valley, western Punjab and Baluchistan (the northwest) are vital to any strategic plans for the defence of (the) all important Muslim belt...the oil supplies of the Middle East. If one looks upon this wall as a strategic c wall (against Soviet expansion), the five important bricks in the wall are: Turkey, Iran, Iraq, Afghanistan and Pakistan.

Only through the open port of Karachi could the opponents of the Soviet Union take immediate and effective countermeasures. The sea approaches to all other countries will entail navigation in enclosed waters directly menaced by Russian air fleets...not only of the sea lanes of approach, but also the port of disembarkation.

If the British Commonwealth and the United States of America are to be in a position to defend their vital interest in the Middle East, then the best and most stable area from which to conduct this defence is from Pakistan territory.

Pakistan is the keystone of the strategic arch of the wide and vulnerable waters of the Indian Ocean."

Second extract from Winston Churchill, Memories of the Second World War, Vol. 6, War Comes to America (Cassel & Co, London, 1950).

Nagindas Khajuria FCCA
Simplification Made Simple, Chartered Certified Accountants, London

2008
India–Pakistan: Hope springs eternal

"We (British) do not think that logic and clear-cut principles are necessarily the sole key to what ought to be done in swiftly changing and indefinable situations....We assign a larger importance to opportunism and improvisation, seeking rather to live and conquer in accordance with the unfolding events than to aspire to dominate them by fundamental decisions."

Hindus, Muslims, Sikhs, Christians, Jews, Parsees, Jains, Buddhists all have contributed to this great nation called India: let us not foolishly create divisions between them: outsiders are already jealous of the progress being made in India. The atrocities of Mumbai are a puzzle that needs to be solved by plural India itself.

Nagindas Khajuria FCCA
Simplification Made Simple, Chartered Certified Accountants, London

2008
President Medvedev comes calling

Russia and Russian people have always been a great nation: systematic way of both countries leaders meeting regularly each year, once in Russia and once in India, started by President Putin in 2000, is how leaders should conduct themselves.

Joint projects in science and technology, Indo-Russian designed war plane to match American F-22, agreement to build 4 Russian civilian nuclear reactors in Tamil Nadu, (although the fall in oil prices may require cost benefit reassessment), export of up to 200,000 Indian labour force a year to Russia and stronger relations with Russia is a good thing.

Two years ago, I was surprised to see about 100 Russians at a resort I was staying in Goa: they had come to study and enjoy in minute detail the face and eyes and body movements, the facial painting, the emotions being projected, the consumes and the rich colours exhibited by Kathakali dancers with full explanations in English over two hours. It was a great performance and I wondered at their interest in our culture.

Honesty and transparency in all major countries policies as far as exchange rates, interest rates, inflation rates, long term fiscal policies and long term monetary policies will be vital in the 21st century to create a level playing field as far as international trade in goods, services and technology transfer is concerned. For example, the Russian rouble was devalued recently by 1%.

The current meltdown was partly the result of lack of transparency in these areas. Over the years, it created opportunities to benefit at the expense of others, but at the same time, it created an opportunity for others to speculate and outwit the official manipulators. Ultimately, the result has been that the entire system that has evolved became so complex that those who created it no longer understand it. The global financial architecture has become an uncontrollable monster that is eating up thousands of jobs every day. No one really knows what the long term answers are.

Just one recent example is the pound Sterling. Historically, after Breton Woods, the subsequent attempts to reform the IMF were the Smithsonian Agreement (1971 to 1973), Snake in the Tunnel (EU countries); the Jamaica Accord (IMF accepting flexible exchange rates); Plaza Accord (dollar fell by 35% 1985 to 1987); Louvre Accord and finally EMS (Euro).

Nagindas Khajuria FCCA
Simplification Made Simple, Chartered Certified Accountants, London

2008
President Medvedev comes calling

The main idea was that exchange rates should be "managed responsibly within reasonable bands between major currencies (1.25%, 2.5%, 5% but no more). Recently the pound Sterling was allowed to depreciate by 25%.

UK is bound to lose its reputation as a great country to trade with or invest in or to continue to be a world financial centre for raising international equity or debt money.

It is far better to have a coordinated joint parameters policy and when there are major realignments, they are done by official announcements of devaluation or revaluation.

Kind regards and best wishes for Xmas and the New Year to all staff at Asian Voice in London and Ahmedabad.

Nagindas Khajuria FCCA
Simplification Made Simple, Chartered Certified Accountants, London

World Bank forecast has pegged India's growth at 6.3% for 2008 and 5.8% for 2009. Even in the recent previous years, India's growth has always fluctuated: 4.4% (2000–01); 4% (2002–03); 8.2% (2003–04); 6% (2004–05); 8% (2005–06).

While there may not be much to panic about, it is important to begin the year by finding gaps in the market that can genuinely stimulate the Indian economy much faster if everyone puts it mind to it.

A good way to save in the future may be by taking our life, health, unemployment, or retirement, trade, fire, theft, liability insurances through modern innovative products that combine insurance with savings.

Currently the public sector companies have the lion's share of the market: however, if they do not computerize, modernize, innovate, compete fiercely on cost and service, with the private sector, their employees are likely to be poached by these new comers.

At present, life and general insurances are available to only 22% of the population that is eligible. Much more can be done to reach esp. the middle and lower income urban and rural population.

2009
Industrial Output in India dips for the first time in 15 years

Hamas is an acronym for Harakat al-Muqawama al-Islamiyya. Muqawama means uprising: It was founded in Gaza in 1987 from a faction of the Muslim Brotherhood founded in Egypt in 1928 to counter Western domination.

Israel has been a G20 military base indirectly protecting 66% of the entire world's gas and oil reserves around its borders that belong to the Arabs and Iran, in addition to being an independent country of about 5 million Jews and 1 million Arabs.

The conflict has been going on for over 60 years. It should be the United Nations that should be reformed so that a majority vote, either in the 5-member Security Council, or in the 15-member extended Council, is sufficient to issue a two-state binding resolution. The veto system should be abolished. Ehud Barak is an army general: his problem cannot be solved by Barak Obama, a civilian.

2009
Israel continues strikes on Gaza

Nagindas Khajuria FCCA
Simplification Made Simple, Chartered Certified Accountants, London

2009
India to host International Accounting meet in mid-January 2009

India's regulators should air their views on framing of common global standards with new ideas.

The use of the word "rules" instead of "standards": a proposal I made when I attended a one-day Symposium hosted by The British Accounting Association Special Interest Group and ACCA on 9th January 2009, is one new idea.

"Rules" could inspire more respect than "standards", "principles", "practice"; "gaap = general accepted accounting practice (UK definition)'; gaap = generally accepted accounting principles (US definition)"; "historical cost", "mark-to-market" and "fair value conventions".

Accountancy is a very important discipline. Global Financial Crisis was partly due to poor record keeping and window dressing in financial reporting.

There are seven different groups whose interests must be respected when accounts are prepared: shareholders, creditors, employees, government, financial analysts, the business contacts group, and the general public. New idea: 8th group: suppliers.

2009
Economic downturn an invitation to innovate

The comment in AV about the need to concentrate on the domestic demand, but unwise on financial stimulus by reducing interest rates that destabilises exchange rates.

In urban India, there are 5 levels of income: Richest 10% of population: 6 million house-holds, next 14%: 8 million, next 24%: 15 million; next 33%: 20 million; and bottom 18%: 11 million households.

In rural India there are 4 levels of income: richest 4% of population: 6 million households, next 10% 15 million, next 35% 51 million and bottom 50% 74 million households.

Only 31.5% of level 3 urban and 8.3% of level 3 rural own two-wheelers. The GDP growth and credit growth on equated monthly payments concept will see 20%+ growth annually in durables including colour TVs, Telephones, PCs, and refrigerators.

(Source: Rama Bijapurkar in "Understanding the Logic of Consumer India").

Nagindas Khajuria FCCA
Simplification Made Simple, Chartered Certified Accountants, London

Why is our NHS such a mess?

2009

Labour Government on the whole has improved NHS by doubling spending. The hospitals and wards are in far newer buildings and more advanced equipment from this 11-year spending.

The blame put by Mr Bhupendrabhai M Gandhi on waste, bureaucracy and red tape applied equally when Conservatives were in power.

People almost "enjoy" going into hospital: it should just be a garage for body repair and not a church like a religion. A £10 charge for GP visit would force people to learn about their bodies.

Higher private versus public health spending is the long term answer. As a % of GDP UK spent 5.8% public & 1.1% private; Germany 7% & 2.5%; France 7.6% & 2.1%, Italy 5.9% and 2.4% and Spain 5.7% & 1.6% respectively in 1993.

NHS budget should be spent far more on health education. The wealthier should go private.

Supreme Court asks Vodafone to respond to Tax Authorities

2009

The Indian tax authorities are claiming Capital Gains Tax of $1.7 billion from UK's Vodafone on their purchase of 67% stake in China's Hutchison Essar in February 2007 for $11.2 billion. As both buyer and seller used offshore companies, buyer argues it is outside India's jurisdiction.

Indian mobile market, with 347 million subscribers last year paying $8.6 per subscriber and using an average of 448 minutes per month grew 48% this year and is projected to grow 35% next year, adding 10 m new subscribers per month (FT).

India does need foreign investors that bring in money, expertise, innovation and higher standards. However, Vodafone must pay the same taxes as its competitors Reliance and Bharti Airtel. Rather than a long drawn out battle, I would suggest some horse trading so that it is a win-win outcome.

Nagindas Khajuria FCCA
Simplification Made Simple, Chartered Certified Accountants, London

2009
The 15th General Election in India

The Model Code of Conduct during the elections should ensure that the ruling party does not take any advantage of its official position. The Code forbids corrupt practices, vote banks, announcements of grants, use of official buildings and transport for election campaigns.

In the last 14th election of Lok Sabha, the changes from the (13th elections) in terms of seats were: Indian National Congress: 145 (114); Bhartiya Janta Party 138 (182); Rashtriya Janta Dal: 21 (7); Janta Dal United: 8 (21); Telugu Desam Party: 5 (29); Communist Party of India-Marxist 43 (33); Communist Party of India 10 (4); Samajwadi Party 36 (26).

By closing down Guantanamo Bay system of military trials and by limiting executive pay to $500,000, Obama has shown the way forward: we need someone like him. Commonwealth of India needs to spread its wealth more commonly with organic growth and welfare insurance.

2009
Gujarat ranks 5th or 6th overall

While Gujarat State has made rapid economic progress in urban areas, it has lagged behind other States in education, health, literacy and employment.

The following compares Gujarat with states of Maharashtra, Punjab, Haryana, Tamil Nadu, Karnataka and Kerala respectively:

Male literacy rates are 80%, 86%, 75%, 78%, 82%. 76% and 94%. All India state average: 75%; Female literacy rates are 58%, 67%, 63%, 56%, 64%, 57% and 88%. All India state average: 54%.

The number of teachers in primary schools per 100 in 2003–04: 1.80; 2.70; 2.80; 2.80; 2.80; 2.60 & 3.60. All India state average: 3.30.

Total expenditure per child in age group 6–14 years on elementary education in 2003–04: Rs. 3,866; 5,311; 5,052; 3,547; 4,797; 3,914 & 8,175 respectively, All India state average: Rs. 6,175 per child.

Household access to drinking water and toilets in rural areas: 17%; 8%; 44%; 11%; 6%; 10% and 62%.

Nagindas Khajuria FCCA
Simplification Made Simple, Chartered Certified Accountants, London

2009
Indian Railways under Lalu Prasad

Indian Railways, with 1.4 million employees and 1.1 million pensioners, is one of the busiest rail networks in the world. It transports 17 million people and one million tonnes of freight daily.

Lalu Prasad, by increasing capacity of a typical long-distance train to 2000 passengers from 800, reduced unit costs by 45% and reduced fares by 45%, reduced freight train load/unload time from 7 to 5 days. Trains now have air conditioning with cushioned seats and suction toilets. He increased revenue from $200 million to $6 billion.

He plans to set up cold storage and purchase points as well as freezer containers for agricultural produce at railway stations so that farmers can avoid middlemen, get fairer prices and products move further across the country and beyond.

Privatisation is not always the answer. An organisation just needs to have honesty, vision and commitment to succeed. Well done Mr Prasad.

2009
Angry India moves to patent yoga poses

What is Yoga? Why it has become a 225 billion dollar industry? Ancient yogis developed a deep understanding of what we humans are all about.

The physical body was seen to be the vehicle. Using the modern analogy of a car, the mind is then the driver. The complex combination that gives the car its ability to travel is seen as the "soul", or the "core" of the person.

All aspects of the vehicle need to be working harmoniously for forward motion to occur. Thus, the yogis placed the mind in context with the rest of the person, NOT as the core of the person.

They also observed that physical movement and breathing techniques helped to steady the function of the mind.

Unfortunately this meaning was lost in translations as Western world has no soul concept. (Sue Lilly ISBN 1-84067-289-7).

Nagindas Khajuria FCCA
Simplification Made Simple, Chartered Certified Accountants, London

2009
Does money talk in elections?

Lok Sabha election costs estimated at US$2 billion for 543 constituency seats works out at US$3.7m per MP, 20% public and 80% private funding.

In September 2003, company and individual contributions to a political party became 100% tax deductible.

In October 2003 candidate expenditure ceiling was raised to Rs 2.5 million for a Lok Sabha election and Rs 1 million for an assembly election.

Company contributions are limited to 5% of average net profit over past three years, approved by Board and shareholders.

Election Commission requires in Form 24-A a list of donations received of over Rs 20,000, audited annual accounts and daily returns during campaign periods. Useful websites to visit are www.lawmin.nic.in and www.loksatta.org and www.eci.gov.in.

Citizens Help Centres idea to empower the ordinary citizen at Taluka Level to complain about five services to the poor: water, electricity, sanitation, health and education, is excellent.

2009
G20 Finance Ministers Summit

BBC TV's Andrew Marr missed his first chance to discuss newcomers' views: he only spoke of US, UK, Germany and France views.

The same old views about stimulus, helping the poor, etc were discussed. What should have been discussed is the reform and relocation of the headquarters of the World Bank, the IMF, United Nations with their many sub-departments like ILO, WHO, etc. where all G20 to have equal voting rights, powers and duties over many years to come.

UN could be relocated in India, IMF in Russia, World Bank in China, etc. with just one world currency or to start with six world currencies for six continents: American, European, Asian, South American, African and Middle East dollar.

Reform of institutions, markets and instruments and principles, practice and transparency: not 500 or 1000 billion dollars stimulus please. Mind not money.

Nagindas Khajuria FCCA
Simplification Made Simple, Chartered Certified Accountants, London

2009 The System and Systemic Failure

The system is institutions operating through markets via contracts.

Institutions are retail and wholesale banks, mutual societies, general and life insurance companies, pension funds, corporations, stock and commodity exchanges, independent financial advisors and unregulated lenders.

Capital market refers to new stock issues (long term); money market refers to short term lending under one year; derivatives are issued and traded: its value is based upon the underlying asset, e.g. commodity derivatives, currency derivatives, index derivatives, etc. Stock futures and stock options are traded in Stock Exchanges. Stock forwards, swaps are traded Over the Counter (OTC). Mortgage backed securities are securities with tenors of between 3 and 10 years.

Contracts are commercial paper (corporate bonds, debentures or loans); gilts are treasury or government bonds, bank notes, equity, securitised debts, preference shares, debentures, collateral transactions and counter-party guarantees.

Many reasons for systemic failures: e.g. no drinking water fountains in major supermarkets.

2009 Bank of England, Treasury and Financial Services Authority

Historically, Bank of England has managed Sterling's money supply worldwide by interest rates. Thus BoE implements UK monetary policy using macro-economic statistics at country level. Interest rate has averaged at 5% pa with minor tinkering.

The Treasury has managed the public sector annual revenue and expenditure by levying and collecting taxes and spending taxes. Thus Treasury has managed fiscal policy. Deficit has ranged from low to high over years and now stands at about 70% of GDP including off balance sheet items. Tax burden has averaged at 40% pa with minor tinkering.

Financial Services Authority is the renamed Securities and Investment Board (1998). It is the Regulator, Listing Authority, Compensation Scheme Administrator and Ombudsman. It supervises individual banks, insurance companies, investment firms and markets.

Global interest rate of 4% pa and global tax burden of 40% pa would force inflation, exchange, unemployment and speculation rates to fall in line.

2009
What is Britishness?

I heard a program this morning about Britishness. UK plc now needs all the help it could have from all British nationals.

I hope the Government will take this opportunity to abolish form filling and recording of ethnic origin data on 45 databases. Instead all forms should only ask whether one is a British national or a foreign national.

After about 20 years, there will be pride and honour about being British wherever you come from.

2009 could be the year the story began. From 2010, you could even start promoting people based upon merit rather than whether someone is British by birth or by naturalisation.

2009
Asian school governors under-represented

For 40 years, the funding of schools has been opaque. That has ruined 2/3 of 33000 schools' standards.

Categories are:
County, community or state (47%): entirely financed by Local Education Authority.

- Voluntary controlled 9%: run by voluntary organisations but LEA would nominate 2/3 of governors, pay all running costs and appoint teachers.
- Voluntary aided 14%: they receive 85% of their running costs from Secretary of State or LEA. Funder would nominate 1/3 of governors.
- Special agreement or foundation (3%): small number of Catholic or Church of England Schools.
- Direct grant schools 6%: they receive some grant aid. They were grammar schools; now called independent or private schools.

Ideally, the ratios should be 33% State, 11% each controlled, aided and foundation and 33% direct grant as the quantity of pupils and teachers would naturally fall along those lines. Moral science instead of religion should be taught. Parents should contribute 10% of costs.

Nagindas Khajuria FCCA
Simplification Made Simple, Chartered Certified Accountants, London

2009
How do you solve a problem like this?

Historically, after the industrial revolution, the ideology of the Tory Party was to support business; while the ideology of the Labour Party was to support the Labour Class.

Gradually, the UK economy moved from a mixed base of manufacturing and services to a predominantly services economy.

About 25% of GDP is exported, or re-exported after being partly imported and value added here. Another 25% is imported with a similar functional process in reverse.

The fundamental flaw in this two party system is that if 74% of business revenue comes from use of labour, as opposed to land, capital or management, then unless labour interest is served first, business interest cannot be served efficaciously.

In 1968, a fellow accountant remarked while chatting at Hendon Hall Hotel in Hendon during a lecture on the Budget: he said of course you support the Tories? I felt flabergasted: irrelevant?

2009
MP Pay Reform

MP's pay and allowances are subject to income tax and national insurance partly as employees, but partly as "office holders", like ministers, NHS consultants, JPs, auditors, secretaries, clergy, trustees, executors, LA councillors, similar positions and sub-postmasters: latter with more favourable tax treatment. Effective tax rate can be under 20%.

Average annual earnings and/or allowances £300,000: salary: £70,000; staff £70,000; office costs: £30,000; second home: £30,000; communication allowance: £10,000; other allowances and private income including speeches: £90,000.

Reform may not be needed. It may just need improved audit procedures. Private interests should be discouraged so that MPs concentrate more on their core activities.

In the long run, both Houses could be moved to middle England to make substantial savings and internal control. It would also enable the City of London to grow to a world class financial centre. Washington, Berlin and New Delhi are examples.

Nagindas Khajuria FCCA
Simplification Made Simple, Chartered Certified Accountants, London

2009
Rest periods for cows

Amul Brand of milk and dairy products began as a cooperative movement in 1965 in Anand, Gujarat. Lal Bahadur Shastri appointed Verghese Kurien as Head of National Dairy Development Board to replicate the Anand model everywhere.

Operation Flood started in 1976: Government spent Rs 100 crore per year for 20 years that is Rs 2000 crore in total. India's milk production soared from 20 million tons to 86 million tons by 1996. By then, added value was Rs 66,000 crore per annum. World Bank reported world record: "lowest input, highest output".

Today there are 175 Anands successfully competing with Hindustan Lever, Nestle and New Zealand and Australian producers in milk, margarine, yogurt, butter, (pizza) cheese, condensed milk and ice cream.

India, however, needs to treat its cows more humanely. Currently cows are artificially inseminated too quickly after calf birth to produce milk faster. Cows need a rest period between births.

2009
Michael Martin: a persona non-grata?

The tradition of impartiality in the Speakership began with Arthur Onslow for 33 years from 1728 and Michael Martin has held it well all his time. He relinquished his allegiance to a political party.

In the US, the Speaker is a leading party politician and frequently takes part in controversial political debate. In Germany and France, the President elects a senior member of the party in office as the Speaker.

The best solution is to have a revolving Speaker every six months, who must be impartial, but could be appointed by leaders of all political parties in rotation.

Josip Tito in Yugoslavia from 1945 to 1980 revolved the Presidency every six months among the seven nations: Slovenia, Croatia, Bosnia Herzegovina, Serbia, Montenegro, Kosovo and Macedonia.

Nasser, Nehru and Tito were the Trio who promulgated non-alignment, rather than being a poodle of US or Russia.

Nagindas Khajuria FCCA
Simplification Made Simple, Chartered Certified Accountants, London

2009
British Afro-Asian Party Independents (BAAPI)

There is now a movement towards selection/election of independent MPs, MEPs and Local Councillors. If a new BAAPI Political Party is born, it would have more clout for ALL INDEPENDENT CANDIDATES.

London's population of 7 million encompasses 5,257,000 white majority and 1,743,000 ethnic minorities- Black Caribbean 280,000; Black African 287,000; Black other 161,000; Indian 378,000; Pakistani 112,000; Bangladeshi 140,000; Chinese 49,000; Other Asian 126,000 and Others 210,000. Many do low jobs whites would not do.

Conservative and Unionist Party was formed in 1830s, were in power 1886–1905, 1922–1945, 1951–64 and 1979–1997. Labour Party started in 1900, overtook the Liberals as the main opposition party in 1922. Labour Party was in power 1945–51, 1964–70 and 1997 to date. Liberal Party started in 1850. Socialist Democratic Party was formed in 1980; it merged with the Liberal Party in 1987.

A BAAPI Leader is needed to lead BAAPI MPs, etc.

2009
Inflation, unemployment, interest rate and Sterling

Some people think we can choose between inflation and unemployment....but it does not work like that "(Budget broadcast, 10 March 1981, Geoffrey Howe).

"Rising unemployment and the recession have been the price we have had to pay in order to get inflation down—but that is a price well worth paying" (House of Commons, 16 May 1991, Norman Lamont).

Empirical research is required to confirm my proposed concept that all four must be given EQUAL WEIGHT when insulating the economy from boom or bust. Today I felt that I was in Heaven when I landed at Hounslow East modernised underground station. Brown, Darling and Livingstone had the guts to spend money to refurbish significantly stations, schools, hospitals and buses in 10 years. Conservatives sold all family silver in previous 20 years.

Voters in the 34 local, 72 MEPs and 3 mayoral elections must tread with caution on 4 June.

Nagindas Khajuria FCCA
Simplification Made Simple, Chartered Certified Accountants, London

2009
Yes (Prime) Minister

During my life in London for the past 40 years, I have heard the three major political parties often play the tax card and/or the race card; or, the leader says: "I do have big ideas but I shall only make them public after you elect me as Prime Minister"; for some time they debated the 5 economic tests on joining the Euro; latest is nation's tacit approval of UKIP and BNP and their isolationist policies.

40 years ago, UK was the 5th richest nation behind USA, Japan, Germany and Russia. 40 years later, it is 10th behind France, Italy, Spain, China and India.

What is a Nation? It is the aspect of a whole people as an organised power. By their moral values, culture and beliefs, European political leaders are teaching their children that a country, or an economic bloc, is greater than the ideals of humanity and self-sacrifice.

2009
Poor Management of London underground Upgrading

Management of upgrading London Underground under the £30 billion 30-year Public Private Partnership had gone wrong since Accountancy Age published its article "London Underground slams PPP groups over accounts" on 4 August 2005.

Two private firms were involved: a) Metronet owned by Balfour Betty, Thames Water, EDF, WS Atkins & Bombardier; and b) Tube Lines owned by Amey (Ferrovial-Spanish) and Bechtel (American private partnership).

Both firms did similar work but on different tube lines and used two different accounting policies: Financial Reporting Standard 5 versus Statement of Standard Accounting Practice 9 respectively.

LU was therefore unable to compare costs and value for money between the two firms.

Metronet is bankrupt now with £1.7 billion bailout, £450 million wasted, and £23 million accountancy fees.

Upgrade budget from 2010 to 2017 is £4.1 billion: Tubes Lines recommends £7.2 billion. PPP Agreement Legal drafting costs were £500 million.

Nagindas Khajuria FCCA
Simplification Made Simple, Chartered Certified Accountants, London

2009 General Motors decline

General Motors filed for Chapter 11 protection from creditors on 1 June 2009. Media placed the blame partly on having to continue paying benefits to 493,000 retired workers and union demanding higher wages than Toyota etc. as well as historical mismanagement for decades.

Their latest decision to sell to Magna International (Canadian auto-parts firm) rather than Fiat (European proper car *firm*), was *unwise*: European buyers are more likely to purchase cars from a European than a Canadian owner.

Besides, Fiat was partly responsible among 20 designers for the design of Tata's Nano. Fiat's sense of design for small cars and their technical knowhow would produce higher quality cars. Still there is time for a re-think.

The more lean new owner could also mean saving of jobs at Vauxhall in the UK.

Fiat SpA auto sales were number 1 in Italy, No 2 in Europe and No 6 in the world in 1993.

2009 A wolf in Sheep's Clothing?

The paper's revelations about MPs' expenses and income from outside jobs may mislead the public's voting intentions next year.

The future is in the Trade Union Congress severing its ties to a particular political party and forming its own political party called Trade Union Political Party (TUPP).

In Parliament, it could vote with the idea or ideas that best improve the social capital of the country.

British employers have refused to accept the basic standards of their EU counterparts. Insecurity, intensification of work, growing inequalities in rewards and exclusion from any voice in the destiny of the enterprise stand out as important trends eating into quality of life.

In 1992, membership of trade unions was: 9 unions (250,000+ members) had 5.5 million members; 11 unions (100,000 to 250,000 members) had 1.7 million members; rest of 248 unions were very small with 1.8 million members.

Second job should be illegal while serving as an MP.

Nagindas Khajuria FCCA
Simplification Made Simple, Chartered Certified Accountants, London

2009
Are politicians opportunists?

Congress Party managed to establish itself with the help of Communist parties. Once established, they got rid of them in the second term. Similarly Charan Singh defected from the BJP and helped Congress win elections before.

The signing of Nuclear Accord with USA was not a right move. India's interests are best served by being non-aligned and secular. Current Prime Minister is a good Finance Minister like Gordon Brown was.

Minorities are best served if, while their chances to progress are equal to majority's chances, should not be allowed to take over the office that is of the highest national importance, where India's military, economic, spiritual, cultural and social ethos (esp. vegetarianism, respect for environment, abstention from alcohol, openness, simplicity, etc.) are concerned.

Even in the UK, I find Asian radio and TV stations catering far more for certain groups and much less for other groups among the sub-continent Diaspora.

2009
Afghanistan elections

USA, Canada, Australia and EU countries on one side and Russia, China and India (?) on the other side are playing the Great Game in 21st century that started in the 19th century.

Daily explosions with 20 or 50 or 100 dead in Iraq, Afghanistan, and Pakistan are common place. The civilized world takes them lightly, while the brave mountain warriors of many tribes defy them all.

Surely it is not a humane way to treat these people who live in the Mountains of the Gods.

The Hindu Kush mountain range stretches 650 miles across Afghanistan with 23,000+ feet peaks. The Pamirs range in Tajikistan has 22,000+ feet peaks. The rocky and icy Karakoram Range linking Pakistan and China is home to 30 of the world's 40 highest peaks; the beautiful Himalayas stretch over the Indo-Chinese border; and finally the flat Tibetan Plateau.

Why? Why?

Nagindas Khajuria FCCA
Simplification Made Simple, Chartered Certified Accountants, London

2009
Jawaharlal Nehru and his contributions
[I met him in 1957]

As a young student, I stood only one foot away from him when Pandit Nehru visited the Omdurman Indian School in Sudan in 1957. I remember gazing at him while anger was clear on his extremely handsome, fair almost red face, while criticising the Gujarati community for not teaching Hindi.

He was Prime Minister of India for the first almost 17 years after independence.

Mr Nehru is credited with non-alignment; Hindi as the official language of India; secularism: both individual and state; Five-year Central Economic Planning system but with freedom at State Level; introduction of IITs; building of other foundations and institutions. All alive today.

Time has come for Hindi to become the official commercial language of banking, insurance and finance in India as Western English language gobbledygook in derivatives, hedging, etc. has almost destroyed the entire world's financial system. Other countries use their own languages.

Nagindas Khajuria FCCA
Simplification Made Simple, Chartered Certified Accountants, London

2009
Nehru and Hindi

The letter written by Nagindas Khajuria regarding Pandit Jawaharlal Nehru is absolutely correct in relation to the importance of Hindi as a language in India. It is fashionable amongst the young generation in India to speak in English all the time. Sonia Gandhi speaks Hindi all the time but the original Indians can't speak it. What a shame!

I wish to describe a very small incident when I was in primary school in Junagadh. A motorcade including Panditji was passing by, travelling from Junagadh to Keshod. I was standing on the road holding a rose which my late father had given me in order to welcome Panditji. The motorcade with high police officials passed and suddenly the car stopped. The window was lowered and a very handsome face with a white cap appeared; Panditji asked me in Hindi "Bacha kya Hindi bolsakte ho?" (Child, can you speak Hindi?) I replied 'haan' (yes). He asked me to come to the car and very happily accepted the flower, and told me a sentence in Hindi – "Bacha desh ki abadi aur azadi dono ka khayal rakhna" (Child, make sure you keep in mind the population and India's struggle for independence).

I took my son to the Nehru Bhavan in Delhi. I read the open will for Indians dedicated to our people written in Hindi outside the gate, which is very emotional.

Jai Hind!

Dr Pravin Kalaiya, Honchurch Essex

2009
Multi-culturalism among Afghanistan and its borders

Afghanistan has had migration from neighbouring countries and various ethnic groupings vied for power over centuries.

Afghanistan -Sunnis 84%, Shia's 15%; languages: Pashtu 35%, Afghan Persian (Dari) 50%, Turkic 11%; literacy 36%; poor 23%.

Iran -Shia's 89%, Sunnis 10%; languages: Persian 58%, Turkic 26%, Kurdish 9%; literacy 79%; poor 40%.

Turkmenistan -Muslim 89%, Eastern Orthodox 9%; languages: Turkmen 72%, Russian 12%, Uzbek 9%; literacy: 98%; poor 34%.

Uzbekistan -mostly Sunnis 88%; Eastern Orthodox 9%; languages: Uzbeck 74%, Russian 14%, Tajik 4%; literacy 99%.

Tajikistan -Sunnis 85%, Shia's 5%; languages: Tajik (official) but Russian in government and business); literacy 99%.

Pakistan -Sunnis 77%, Shia's 20%; languages: Punjabi 48%, Sindhi 12%, Siraiki (a Punjabi variant) 10%, Pashto 8%, Urdu 8%; literacy 46%; poor 35%.

From 1992 to 96 Burhanuddin Rabani, an ethnic Tajik was President of Afghanistan; in 1997 Saudi Arabia and Pakistan recognised Taliban as the legitimate rulers of Afghanistan while other countries continued to recognise Rabani. Current President Hamid Karzai is a Pashtun royalist.

The region needs techno-economic assistance, not military invasion by a Christian army that does not respect all cultures and/or ethnic mix of all peoples living there for centuries.

2009
Vegetarianism, protein and climate change

It is true that protein is the principal building material for the growth in children and maintenance of our bodies in adults. However, it comes in varying amounts from meat and fish, from cereals and pulses (dry beans, peas, broad beans, lentils and chick peas) and from nuts, oil seeds and oil containing fruit.

Milk, closely followed by eggs, is a complete food.

See below where M means Meat, F means Fish and PR means Protein Retention. Some nations by overeating meat continue to damage the environment irreversibly.

Americans North: M 19.4% F 0.8% PR: 11.9%; rest of protein is flushed in toilet;
Central: M 5.1% F 1% PR: 10.1%; rest of protein is obtained from vegetarian sources;
South: M 8.5% F 0.5% PR: 10.3%.
Europeans North: M 13.4% F 1.4% PR 11.3%;
South: M 6% F 1.3% PR 12.1%.
African N M & E: M 3.1% F 0.2% PR: 11.1%;
African tropical: M 2.3%, F 1.3%; PR: 9%.
Indian: M 0.3%; F 0.2%; PR: 10.3%.
Indonesian: M 1.1%; F 1.1%; PR: 8.9%.
Australasian: M 20.7% F 0.7 PR 11.6%.
Russian: M 9.9% F 0.5% PR: 11.4%.
Japanese: M 2.2% F 3.5% PR: 12%.
Chinese: M 6.6% F 0.7%; PR: 11.6%.

Time is running out.

Nagindas Khajuria FCCA
Simplification Made Simple, Chartered Certified Accountants, London

2010 Tackling Naxalite Violence

Your comment article (AV 20 Feb p3) suggests that India is an upworldly mobile society. My own estimate is that the official statistics that describe people living in poverty as 30% is incorrect. The likely figure is around 60%.

That can indeed flare up in guillotine type revolution that took place in France in 1789 after which equality became a very French entrenched belief.

In healthcare, India ranks 171 in the list of 175 countries on public health spending. There are 3.0 beds per 1000 population in urban areas versus 0.2 beds in rural areas, 3.4 doctors versus 0.6 doctors.

The youth is desperate to get out of India and study and settle overseas. Income and consumption inequalities are increasing. Inequalities in entitlements and opportunities are also increasing. Corrupt netas, corrupt policemen, tax evasion and black market are all flourishing. Governments, businesses and voluntary sector need to put their act together very fast.

2010 Military invasions

Military invasions serve a useful purpose of testing ever more sophisticated weaponry used in ground, sea and air battlefields. They also give practical training in real life combat situations to army, navy and air generals and their soldiers, seamen and pilots.

Terrorism, instead, is high jacking of air planes as happened on 11th September 2001. High jacking then gets connected to nuclear, chemical and biological weapons of mass destruction being planned by one country or another.

In addition, ethnic or racial grouping of one sort rise against other grouping within a country. They fight to take on the incumbent government that may be propped by military support from foreign countries. They produce suicide bombers in training camps, etc.

Your lead article "Afghanistan-Pakistan requires realism" (AV 27 Feb P3) asks for realism.

May be there is no realism.

The first writer who wrote about war 200 years ago said the desire to fight can be compared to desire to procreate by mating. It is a biological need inherent in human nature. Remember the proverb "The King is Dead, Long Live the King".

Nagindas Khajuria FCCA
Simplification Made Simple, Chartered Certified Accountants, London

2010 World Cup 2010 in South Africa

African population grew from 200 million in 1960 to 600 million in 2000. African footballers playing in professional European football teams increased from fewer than a hundred to over 1,000 by year 2000. Why none from the Indian sub-continent with 1.8 billion population?

My father had taken me to see the great footballer Ferenc Puskás' Hungarian team play a match in Sudan in the mid fifties. Puskás' life size photograph today sits in Real Madrid Stadium in Barcelona describing him as "Footballer of the Century".

3 billion people round the world will watch together for 90 minutes World Cup Final. There is no other single human activity that brings so many people together.

British Asians can help set up hundreds of youth football clubs in the Indian sub-continent perhaps with the help of organisations such as MYSA (Mathare Youth Sports Association) founded in 1987 in Kenya, Africa's largest youth organisation, running around 100 leagues for 1000 teams, including 200 girls' teams.

2010 The Political Conference "Question Time"

Your conference was timely (AV, 27 March, p7). The following questions could shape Britain's future:

1. Should UK hold a Referendum on Alternative Vote System? Historically 28% of those eligible to vote have formed majority government.
2. Tax burden. UK tax burden is 40%. USA is 30%. Germany, France, Sweden etc is 50%. Should UK move towards EU or US model?
3. In USA far more Asians are in senior posts compared to UK. When Bloomberg, the New York Mayor flew to congratulate the London Mayor, he advised Johnson to promote people on merit. Should Britain do more in this area? Quality of senior managers is broadly lacking.
4. Britain ranks 23rd in production league internationally. There is over-supply of academic university education and shortage of vocational training. Should some universities be rebranded polytechnics?
5. For better economic growth, should Britain rely less on financial and insurance services and more on manufacturing?
6. Should Britain hold a Referendum on joining the Euro? When?

Nagindas Khajuria FCCA
Simplification Made Simple, Chartered Certified Accountants, London

National Insurance Planned Increase in 2011

National Insurance is a contribution rather than a tax to pay for the National Health Service, State Pension and other Welfare benefits. It raises £100 billion a year.

When NHS was planned by Beveridge in 1943, the Tory led Assheton Committee reviewed the proposal, "it was for those who could not afford better".

The Committee recommended that those earning above £420 per annum would not be obliged to pay contributions to NHS.

The logic was that if NHS was to cover the entire nation, the role of the private sector would be narrowed so much that there would be lowering of standards in the medical professions.

This has now indeed happened. NHS is hugely over-crowded.

One quarter of UK population is capable of providing for medical care privately. However, human nature being what it is, only one-eighth of UK population actually has private medical cover and even that only partly.

GP Visits

I called for an appointment for same day GP consultation. I had to wait for 18 minutes before I was put through. I was late by 15 minutes. I was told off.

The national average is four face to face consultations per year, seven for those who are young or old. Total is about 250 million GP visits. A GP with premises and staff costs about £3,000 per week. 6 to 12 minutes consultations vary from 100 to 200 consultations per week per GP and cost £22.50 per visit by my calculations.

A substantial number of these visits are for minor ailments. They could be prevented by spending more on health promotion and/or by introducing a charge of £10 per visit.

Means testing would mean free GP visits for 100 million visits and paid 150 million GP visits benefiting from £10 charge, saving NHS £1.5 billion a year and GPs concentrating more on those in greater need.

Nagindas Khajuria FCCA
Simplification Made Simple, Chartered Certified Accountants, London

2010 Elections: an unbiased view

I had a quick review of the 3 manifestos: Conservative, Labour and Liberal Parties via Google.

The most compassionate, realistic and visionary manifesto is that of Labour. Conservatives have some good ideas such as reducing the number of MPs by 10%. Liberals manifesto is rubbish.

Compared to other countries, UK has too many MPs. When UK was "The British Empire" it was necessary. Labour's plan to half the House of Lords and Alternative Vote referendum in 18 months is still better.

UK with 60 million people has 659 MPs and 675 Lords. USA has a Senate: 100 members (6 years) and House of Representative: 435 members (2 years). India's Lok Sabha: 545 members (5 years) and Rajya Sabha: 245 members (6 years). Germany's Bundesrat: 69 members (terms vary) and Bundestag: 669 members (4 years).

Labour is in touch with the ordinary citizen more often: the other two one day every 5 years.

2010 Can higher taxes solve the budget deficit?

Yes. Tax burden means the percentage of revenue lost by private sector to finance the public sector. In the UK, it has been the same at 38% for the past 38 years based upon elasticity of supply and demand and impact of grey economy.

Tax incidence as a percentage of GDP according to HMRC 2009 accounts for the past five years was 31%. That meant that the revenue lost by private sector to finance the public sector was 31% rather than 38% based upon GDP.

Private sector creates wealth. But of recent, private sector has destroyed wealth and continues to do so. The Big Four audit quality has been shambolic.

It is time we respect Governments and civil servants and their attempts to provide public services with 20% of working force managing 30% of revenue, while 80% of work force generate 100% of revenue. By comparison, the latter may be generating 120% of revenue but declaring 100% only.

Nagindas Khajuria FCCA
Simplification Made Simple, Chartered Certified Accountants, London

2010
Living beyond ones means

Since 1945, that is 65 years ago, the Liberal Party has not been in government. Now that it is, Nick Clegg's vision of a hot seat in Europe side by side with Germany and France would mean a far better macro and micro economic management of UK plc.

The US special relationship since 1945 has meant that UK plc has been under constant political, economic, financial, social and cultural influence of USA. That relationship has taught us to be far greedier than the intrinsic nature of a true Briton.

Compare the remuneration packages of senior employees of Ford, Goodyear and Motorola with Volkswagen, Michelin and Nokia and you will find the US packages are 10 times higher than EU companies. Compare the productivity of these companies. It is 10 times the other way round.

Britain does not need to be the Policeman of the world and be a member of the Security Council any more. Let the richer nations do that. Let Britain concentrate on improving the training and skills of its own nation to improve its exports.

When the next General Election is fought in a few years' time, Nick Clegg should present himself as the future Prime Minister and promise a referendum on joining the European Monetary System. He should educate the public on its merits. His vision of being compassionate and global rather than insular like the Conservatives is the new way forward in a global village economic scenario.

Nagindas Khajuria FCCA
Simplification Made Simple, Chartered Certified Accountants, London

2010
If it ain't broke...

I understand the G4 (Osborne, Laws, Clarke and Cable) are planning to raise the personal allowance to £10,000 over the lifetime of the current parliament. I believe this will be a blunder like other tax changes blunders in the past that Gavin Hinks writes about in your article "Osborne warned over hasty tax decisions" (20 May).

As they are also planning to change the welfare tax credit system, I recommend they go the other way and abolish personal allowances altogether. At the same time, they should recommend that all the earners in the UK become statutorily obliged to submit an annual tax return with not only their income, but their drawing, their mortgage, and their personal balance sheet in addition to profit and loss account.

Otherwise, there will be a lot of moonlighting, tax fraud, false benefit claims and unfair distribution of wealth between the 50% who are low paid workers and 50% low income pensioners. If it ain't broke, do not fix it. If it is broke, fix it for the long term with minimum cost of collecting tax.

2010
How has NHS evolved over the years

The NHS Act 1946 was enacted on 5th July 1948. Since then it was amended and consolidated into NHS Act 1977; NHS and Community Care Act 1995; Health Authorities Act 1997; Health Act 1999; Health and Social Care Act 2001; NHS Reform and Health Care Professions Act 2002; Health and Social Care (Community Health and Standards) Act 2003 and the latest Health Act 2006 that consolidated all the previous acts.

Health Act 2006 provides a comprehensive health service designed to secure improvement in the physical and mental health of the people and to prevent, diagnose and treat illness.

The next Act in parliament should split the Act into two: National Health Treatment Act and National Health Promotion Act. A new Ministry should be set up for the latter.

Those who are entrusted with health promotion would have a NHP budget to prevent illness. NHT budget should be reduced accordingly. There is an inherent conflict of interest when those who are entrusted to diagnose and treat illness are also given the responsibility to prevent illness.

Once you prevent illness, there is no need to diagnose and treat illness as there would not be any illness to treat.

Nagindas Khajuria FCCA
Simplification Made Simple, Chartered Certified Accountants, London

2010
Is the UK taxation system fair?

According to HMRC tax payer statistics, they collected £157 billion in Income Tax paid by 31,300 million taxpayers on total income of £ 871 billion in 2008/09.

The top 2% that is 651,000 earners who declared £100 K or more shared 33% of the total tax burden, but then earned 18% of the total national income. Their effective rate was 33% (tax) and 35% (tax & NI Employee). The average gross earnings were £2.4 million p.a.

The next 24% that is 7,470,000 earners who declared £30 K or more shared 38% of the tax burden while earning 38% of the national income. Their effective was 19% (tax) and 23% (tax and NI-EE) respectively. The average gross earnings were £44,000 p.a.

The bottom 74% that is 23,150,000 who declared income below £ 30 K or less shared 44% of the tax burden while sharing 44% of the national income. Their effective rate was 11% (tax) and 18% (tax and NI). The average gross earnings were £16,000 p.a.

True, the benefit system distorts the above results. But then why not merge the two systems and legally require all the 31,300 million earners to submit one tax return annually rather than the current 8 million only? There seems to be a lot of cheating going on according to the media and the coalition government in declared income and/or benefits returns.

It is no good to use the public sector as a scapegoat. Tax system needs to be progressive, e.g. 10%, 20%, 30% and so on.

Nagindas Khajuria FCCA
Simplification Made Simple, Chartered Certified Accountants, London

2010
AV Voting System in Action

Ed Miliband won the election to be leader of the Labour Party by a fraction of 1% that took him over the 50% mark in the fourth round count. For Party Members, each had to put in their first, second, third, fourth and fifth preference on the Ballot Paper.

In the May 2010 First Past the Post Election system, while the Tories won 36.1% of the popular votes, they won 47.1% of the Parliamentary seats [voting rights in House of Commons]; Labour 29% [votes] and 39.7% [seats]; Liberals 23% [votes] and 8.8% [seats]; and Others 11.9% [votes] and 4.5% [seats] respectively. This has happened for 100 years.

The AV [Alternative Vote] system is by far more representative than the current FPPS election system and PR [Proportional Representation] system could be even fairer.

Ed Miliband's remarks that he was not going to reject every cut the Coalition proposes; his appeal for a new generation of politics; for unity in their Party; and his plea for humility; and his deep knowledge of issues makes him stand out from the rest.

2010
India needs to pay more attention to agriculture

When I read about the Commonwealth Games Shambles [AV 2 Oct p3], I could not help researching the wider picture how India had "progressed" over the past 60 years.

Its positive share of GDP growth in manufacturing and services was offset by negative share of GDP growth in agriculture in many of those years. Lack of proper planning laws in urban India has meant poor hygiene and overcrowded polluted urban clusters that are allowed to grow in all directions without any designated city/town border limits.

India also needs a Common Agricultural Policy. Its output per hectare is substantially less than that of Europe and even Pakistan. While 75% of the population still live in villages, agriculture now produces 20% of GDP, while manufacturing produces 25% and services 55% of GDP. 60 years ago share of GDP was 55% agriculture; 15% manufacturing; and 30% services.

Hundred years from now a combination of vast areas of beautiful clean country side and production of high quality organic agricultural produce could bring about higher social and economic benefits than manufacturing or services [e.g. manicuring]. CAP in Europe achieved both objectives [countryside and fresh produce].

Nagindas Khajuria FCCA
Simplification Made Simple, Chartered Certified Accountants, London

2010
Cuts–Ready Steady Go–Cart before Horse?

If I were the George Osborne [Go], I would postpone the Comprehensive Spending Review [CSR = Cart] to be announced on Black Wednesday October 20th and replace it by a Comprehensive Productivity Review [CPR = Horse].

The 3-year rolling Departmental Expenditure Limit [DEL] of £387 billion plus the 1-year Annually Managed Expenditure [AME] limit of £266 billion against receipts of £496 billion means a fiscal deficit of £157 billion [13% of GDP].

The Coalition government is right that a good part of public services are over bureaucratic, over-manned and lack fraud free financial control. However, they have not yet fully understood, assessed, consulted or produced empirical evidence exactly why or where this is happening; nor have they come up with detailed costings of the all the hurriedly prepared reforms they are proposing.

Why not publish operational, efficiency, headcount, systems and productivity data [Horse] for consultation this year and agree spending plans [Cart] early next year in the national interest?

Running public services is not a race or a ready, steady, go situation. One does not want a double dip recession.

Nagindas Khajuria FCCA
Simplification Made Simple, Chartered Certified Accountants, London

2010
Quantitative Easing

Federal Reserve Bank in USA and Bank of England continue to support their economies partly by "quantative easing". Effectively it means near zero central bank interest rates and printing money to bolster money supply and supply side growth.

The US Dollar is not only the most widely used currency, it is also the one used for gold, oil and all major commodity market prices as "an industry bench mark price". I believe the next collapse in the world financial system will see the dollar crash to one half of its current value. Money itself 'must' have a correct 'price'.

Growing economies like the BRIC [Brazil, Russia, India and China] need to be wary of the US dollar. Current inflation rate in the UK is about 4% pa. Real cost of borrowing is interest rate less inflation rate. IMF, World Bank, USA and UK continue to confuse and destabilize the entire world financial system by using QE in normal-trading cycles.

The quantity theory of money $MV = PT$ [money supply × velocity of circulation = price level × number of real economic activity transactions] gets muddled up by all the hedging that is done in future interest, exchange, inflation rate and commodity derivative forward contracts from country to country and currency to currency.

Nagindas Khajuria FCCA
Simplification Made Simple, Chartered Certified Accountants, London

2010
Divide and rule policy in Sudan for Oil and Gas scramble

For a few years, Western countries tried to discredit Sudan by fabricating horror stories about genocide in uranium and oil rich Darfur to get a foothold there. The conflicts there were mainly due to famine and poverty. Having failed there, now the regular story being fabricated is that Southern Sudan is predominantly Christian and Northern Sudan is predominantly Muslim.

I was born in the Sudan and grew up there before I came here in 1967. Jews, Christians, Muslims, Hindus, Buddhists and Animists are spread all over the country and live very peacefully together. I did visit the country again in 1982 and 2007. I have lived both in North and South Sudan: All Sudanese are humble, cultured, hospitable and tolerant of other nationalities and races.

Kashmir was created from the divide and rule policy of the West. With the coming of a referendum in Sudan in January 2011 for independent rule in Southern Sudan, I hope both sides look back to their hundreds of years of history of living together and do not make the same mistake that India did in 1947.

2010
"Ostrich among us" by Bhupendra Gandhi on Nagin Letter

Reading Shri Khajuria's letter, "Divide and rule" in last week's AV, I feel we are living on a different planet. It has become fashionable to blame the West, in particular Britain and America. Yet none of us would like to live in Sudan, East Africa or even in India, except to escape for few months from our bitter cold and damp winter. A little bit of gratitude will go a long way in fostering the goodwill that we all need and deserve.

Whether it is Iran, Iraq or Sudan, our one track mind thinks of oil, although the Sudan's oil reserves have already been cornered by China with its vast foreign currency reserves at the expense of West.

The threat will come not from Islam but from China who is the super power of the 21st century, buying up mineral wealth at the expense of sleep-walking West. China has already laid claims of huge part of India, Indo-China, numerous islands in China Sea and vast stretches of Indian Ocean. Yet USA is in no position to challenge China, as it is a bankrupt nation, borrowing $2 billion a day, mainly from China and Japan.

Nagindas Khajuria FCCA
Simplification Made Simple, Chartered Certified Accountants, London

2010
How to Run Hospitals successfully

A study was carried out by McKinsey and the London School of Economics ["Healthcare Management", The Economist, 23rd Oct, p72] of almost 1200 hospital in seven rich countries. [USA, UK, Germany, France, Italy, Sweden and Canada] to find out how the best hospitals always outperform the rest.

The researchers [Steven Dorgan and John Van Reenen] found 5 common characteristics:

1. competition where hospital managers could name more than 10 hospitals they competed with ferociously.
2. those with more than 1500 staff outperformed those that had 500 staff who in turn outperformed those that had 100 staff.
3. private ownership.
4. hospital managers with clinical degrees.
5. hospitals that ranked best on a standardised measure of medical success; death rates among emergency patients experiencing heart attacks.

The score works across countries and cultures.

100 plus NHS hospitals and/or GP led consortiums are likely to be privatised. This will be an excellent investment opportunity.

Happy Diwali and a prosperous New Year to Asian Voice and Gujarat Samachar readers.

Nagindas Khajuria FCCA
Simplification Made Simple, Chartered Certified Accountants, London

2010
World citizen

Shri Gandhi's letter commenting on my letter about Sudan (AV 30th Oct 2010- pg 4) is typical of narrow minded nationalism.

The press is the "Fourth Estate" after the Lords Spiritual [Clergy], the Lords Temporal [Peers] and the House of Commons. I write very responsibly.

AV readers should read "Genocide in Darfur" by S Totten & E Markusen & "Famine that Kills" by Alex de Waal. Research was carried out by 1200 interrogators over six months in 2004 paid by US State Department. Conflict for land and crops with draughts and sand storms were rampant.

Over the past four centuries nations have scrambled for global power, natural resources and international markets. That era is passé. Global cooperation around shared goals of sustainable development should start.

"Our very survival in the long run will be achieved by recognizing that the vast majority of people of Middle East, China, India, and the rest of the world, just as USA, long for their own prosperity and security, not for domination of others ["Economics for a Crowded Planet" and "The End of Poverty" by Jeffrey D Sachs].

Neither China nor USA with their friends and allies should think differently.

Nagindas Khajuria FCCA
Simplification Made Simple, Chartered Certified Accountants, London

2010
Corruption is India's scourge

Your leader article (AV 20 Nov) is right that Government should do more to combat corruption.

Anti-corruption Bills [Lok Ayukta and Lok Pal equivalent for Ombudsman] have been laid before Parliament 8 times over 40 years but have yet to become law. The Judiciary itself has been found to be corrupt. Freedom of Information Bill 2001 has also not yet become law.

Corruption has been of three types. Public-office centred involving bribery, nepotism and misappropriation. Market-centred: maximising personal gain by dispersing public benefits. And Public-interest-centred: filtering public benefit through various powerful social structures, including family, kinship and clan groups and social affiliations.

One study [Vittal 2005] suggested that Rs 50 billion of the Rs 150 billion annual food grain subsidies was lost through corruption representing 31% of food grain and 36% of sugar.

Measures that should be taken are preventive; punitive; transparency and public-private partnership programme similar to Seoul City's Anti-Corruption Programme: Centre for Good Governance 2003: 10–11: deregulation; rotation of duties; zero tolerance; corruption report; online procedures; joint inspection with citizen; elimination of zone jurisdiction system; citizen Ombudsman system; direct dialogue and creation of Transparency Index.

Nagindas Khajuria FCCA
Simplification Made Simple, Chartered Certified Accountants, London

2010
Improving the education system in UK

The White Paper does not go far enough. There are several areas where more could be done:

1. Competition between pupils by setting examinations at end of every term and at year end and awarding marks out of 100 rather than just fail, pass, credit or distinction.
2. Ranking students top of the class, second, third, etc. to encourage completion and recognize talent by producing school term end and year end marks and ranking reports for parents.
3. Key Stage 1 and 2 for 5–11, Stage 3 for 11–14 and Stage 4 for 14–16 year olds idea could be abolished. Those who fail repeat the class.
4. Five Core subjects is too restrictive. Many students may be more suited to Art or vocational subjects.
5. Currently we have famous boarding; academy; free; independent (2,067); Catholic, Jewish, Hindu, Muslim, Anglican, grant maintained community (13,790), voluntary controlled (2,795) and voluntary aided (4,272), foundation (839) and American schools. This is very divisive.
6. One publicly funded and one privately funded LOCAL school should be the future system.

Nagindas Khajuria FCCA
Simplification Made Simple, Chartered Certified Accountants, London

2010
Chickens, drugs and football

When the Indian company that supplied chickens to KFC, etc. and also had interests in pharmaceuticals purchased the English Premier League Club Blackburn Rovers, a journalist asked why? The answer was because "Rovers footballers ran like headless chickens and were into drugs".

That was just a joke. It is promising for future Asian footballers. Thatcher's children did run like headless chickens to Zurich to lobby individual FIFA members for support. That was unsavoury practice by leaders who should have known better.

Bhaichung Bhutia, the captain of the Indian National Football Team, is going to launch his own chain of soccer schools all across India. John Abraham is helping him (http://www.goal.com/enindia/news/136/india/2010/10/28/2185907/specials-bhaichung-bhutia-emulates-david-beckham-as-he-is).

In 2005, BB wrote his life story titled "To Compete on the World Stage, the Hunger to win" was vital. It is a very informative article about what Indian federations, clubs, Sports Authority of India and Indian footballers should do [Page 319 in "India Empowered – Change Agents speak on an idea whose time has come" – Penguin India Books].

2010
Further and Higher Education – England

"Further education" relates to 16–18 year old 900,000 full time [or sandwich] and 2,150,000 part-time students up to A-Level or equivalent vocational courses.

"Higher education" relates to 19–21 year old 1,294,000 full time [or sandwich] and 787,000 part-time students in universities for degree courses.

In 2007/08 Government spent £12.9 billion out of total cost of £16.9 billion. Average cost per under-graduate £10,057. Therefore, number of undergraduates: 1,680,000. Students contributed £4 billion out of £16.9 billion. 9% of non-EU students [513,000] brought in £1.9 billion.

The increase for English students is to pay from £6,000 to £9,000, say £7,000 on average from 2012. Over three years' £21,000 fee debt plus living cost debt of £21,000. Part-time earnings, say £12,000. Total debt of £30,000 × 1,680,000 students = a debt of £50 billion plus interest at 6% pa repayable over 30 years.

Emergency Budget Plan 80/20 ratio between spending cuts and tax increases is flawed. It should be 50/50. Why not make a U-turn?

2010

£160,000,000 to each of 500 GP Consortiums

Andrew Landsley's proposal to abolish 152 Primary Care Trusts and replace them with 500 GP consortiums and give the £160 million each is merely an administration reform rather than a structural reform.

Such administrative reforms were carried out before. They have not worked.

Originally in 1948 it started with 146 Local Health Authorities, 14 Regional Hospital Boards, 36 Boards of Governors and 140 Executive Councils.

In 1974 the above was changed to 14 Regional Health Authorities, 90 Area Health Authorities and 90 Family Practitioner Committees.

In 1997 this was changed to 100 Health Authorities and 400 Primary Care Trusts, 102 Foundation and 139 Non-foundation Hospital Trusts.

NHS is not fit purpose for the 21st century. It has to be broken up into smaller units: some privately owned with a cap on return on capital employed and a cap on earnings before tax, amortisation and depreciation and others publicly owned, supported by a strong medical insurance sector.

Genuine competition, not quasi completion, would drive efficiency. 75% of MPs would agree to such a proposal.

Nagindas Khajuria FCCA
Simplification Made Simple, Chartered Certified Accountants, London

2011
Inequality is unfair

In America, between 1976 and 2007, the top 1 percent of households' share of income grew from 8.9% to 23.5%.

The rich can afford to live in better neighbourhoods, can give their children the healthcare and nutrition that allow them to grow up healthily and can hire tutors and learning aids if their children fall behind.

Poor, less well-educated couples are more likely to break up, and when that happens the economic consequences are more severe than the well off: the cost of maintaining two establishments, shuttling children between two parents, and child care eat up a bigger fraction of poor parents' income, leaving less for other basic necessities, let alone counselling and remedial tuition to help devastated children cope with the breakup. [Fault Lines by Raghuram G Rajan, formerly Chief Economist, IMF].

The same is happening in England. A high price to pay by adopting American ideology.

2011
Forecast increase in both healthcare demand and supply

David Cameron is right about the double whammy on healthcare costs.

His team wants to introduce competition between hospitals so that a GP can compare cost and quality of care to decide to which hospital NHS or non-NHS he wants to refer his patient to.

This can work gradually if there a private and an NHS hospital in each of the 152 conurbations in England.

If he is thinking about competition between one NHS hospital and another NHS hospital, then it will not work as the new costing system in NHS hospitals is just being introduced.

There are 4 stages of sophistication in the system. Some hospitals are currently in Stage 1, others in stage 2, very few in stages 3 and 4.

David Cameron must re-think.

2011
Chillcot Iraq War Inquiry

In the 19th century most oil and gas was in the US. In the 20th century most oil and gas was in the Middle East.

The forecast oil and gas supply security for the 21st century is that half will be in Saudi Arabia, Iran and Iraq and half with the rest of the world.

Mr Blair and Mr Bush [Tom & Gerry] went to war in Iraq in the Dawn of the 21st century to secure oil and gas supplies for the West.

Mahatma Gandhi's autobiography mentions that in the earlier years, he thought God is Truth and later on he changed it to Truth is God.

2011
Understanding the human mind

Dr Iqbal Singh replied to Keith Vaz [AV 5 Feb One to One] that he specialised in psychiatry as he "felt that the real final frontiers in the field of medicine are to understand the human mind".

Broadly speaking, mental illness is divided into two categories: psychosis [madness] and neurosis [hysteria, anxiety and obsessive compulsive disorder or OCD and/or multiple personality disorder]. Hereditary factors have some influence.

Those in the latter category are treated by psychiatrists. One in 10 women and one in 20 men suffer from neurosis. One in 4 suffers from psychosis. However, this categorisation is not fully understood.

Psychosis is further divided into organic psychosis [resulting from physical damage to the brain] and functional psychosis.

Functional psychosis is further divided into schizophrenia [split personality] and manic depressive psychosis [bipolar or two extremes disorder] where hereditary factors conflict with life events for causation.

Theories invoking abnormalities in dopamine [neurotransmitter including adrenalin], the substance responsible for transmission of brain signals, are supported by the fact that some symptoms of schizophrenia can be induced experimentally.

The discovery of Chlorpromazine tranquilliser in the fifties, that lowers the rate at which signals are transmitted by the brain, was of the same significance for mental illness treatment as the discovery of Penicillin was for illness of the body.

Historically, NHS has done well in drug therapy but not in psychotherapy.

Nagindas Khajuria FCCA
Simplification Made Simple, Chartered Certified Accountants, London

2011
Female quotas would target the wrong women

David Cameroon said on Thursday 24 Feb that he wanted all boards of big companies 25% female by 2015. Lucy Kellaway writes in the FT on 28 Feb on page 16 that such a move may be counter productive. She has been a non-executive director in a FTSE 100 company for the past 4 years.

The board there consists of 9 men and 2 women, that is 18.181818% female. The overall average is 12.5%.

She argues that the pleasure of having another woman to accompany her on a 'comfort break' to the loo is a pleasure that should not be underrated.

However, she says, the two of them, by virtue of their sex, have had no tangible effect on shareholder value in their four years in the job.

"The hot debate should not be about executive, or non-executive directors at all, nor should it be about voluntary code of conduct. What matters are the women on the staff, and making sure that the good ones get to the top", she argues.

In her experience, gender is less important than profession: a male journalist and a male accountant probably take more sharply opposing positions on business issues than do, say, a male accountant and a female accountant.

It is the job of the board as a whole to act in the interest of the shareholders. Many boards did not do so during the past 30 years.

That gave a gap in the market that investment banks have now filled by mergers, acquisitions, asset stripping, etc, making billions in bank fees and bonuses that would not have happened in hindsight.

Nagindas Khajuria FCCA
Simplification Made Simple, Chartered Certified Accountants, London

2011
The Female Factor

On 9th March 2011, I attended a lively debate on the 100th anniversary of feminism movement. It was organised by International Herald Tribune, a publisher who's Magazine "The Female Factor" wrote about women's progress in Liberia, India, China, Norway, Afghanistan, Bangladesh, France, Cambodia, USA, Sweden and Egypt.

The future of Arab nations will also very much depend on the role women will play in all Arab countries since they represent 50% of the population. Women are generally freer from corruption compared to men. Saida Sadoumi, a 71-year old Arab revolutionary, camped out in the bitter Tunisian cold for more than two weeks in front of the Prime Minister's house.

Asma Mahfoud, a 26-year old, while surfing the net in 2008, stumbled on calls for a general strike to demand an end to government corruption in Egypt, where networking speeded up the revolution.

The stereotype of the submissive, repressed victim has been shattered by female protestors in Tunis, Egypt and Yemen [The Guardian 12 March 2011 p38: Perceptions of Arab women have been revolutionised]. Arab women of today refuse to be treated with contempt, kept in isolation, etc. They are taking charge of their own destinies, determined to liberate themselves, as they liberate their societies from dictatorship.

Nagindas Khajuria FCCA
Simplification Made Simple, Chartered Certified Accountants, London

2011
Muslims on the Move

The following percentage male and female factors respectively can be the crucial determining factors, whether these countries will get worse or better in the long run, post current gradual evolutions for fairness with freedom.

- Afghanis literacy 51/21 life expectancy 48/46; religion Sunnis 84/Shi'as 15, others 1.
- Bahrainis literacy 92/85; life expectancy 71/76; Shi'as 70/Sunnis.
- Egyptians literacy 68/47; life expectancy 68/73; mostly Sunnis 94/Coptic Christians 6.
- Iranians literacy 86/73; life expectancy 69/71; Shi'as 89/Sunnis 10/Others 1.
- Iraqis literacy 56/24; life expectancy 67/69; Shi'as 63/Sunnis 33%/Others 4%. Omanis literacy 83/67; life expectancy Ibadhi Muslims 75/Others including Shia's, Sunnis and Others 25.
- Jordanians literacy 96/86; life expectancy 75/80; Sunnis 92/Christians 6/Others 2.
- Qataris literacy 81/85; life expectancy 71/76; Muslims 95/Others 5.
- Saudi Arabians literacy 85/71; life expectancy 67/71; Muslims 100%.
- Syrians literacy 90/64; life expectancy 68/71; Sunnis 74/Alawite, Druze and other Muslims 16/Others 10%.
- Tunisians literacy 84/64; life expectancy 73/76; Muslims 98/Christians 1/Jewish and Others 1.
- Algerians literacy 79/61; life expectancy 71/74; Sunnis 99/Christians and Jewish 1.
- Yemenis literacy 70/30; life expectancy 59/63; Muslims including Shaf'i Sunnis, Zaidi Shi'as and small number of Jews, Christians and Hindus.

Nagindas Khajuria FCCA
Simplification Made Simple, Chartered Certified Accountants, London

2011
Family Planning

India's population rose by 181 million persons over the past 10 years from 1 billion to 1.2 billion [AV 9 April p29]. While the rate at which it is growing is less than the previous six decades, there is still an urgent need to continue educating the nation on smaller families.

The forecast by 2045 is 1.4 or 1.6 billion depending on how successfully the Indian Government handles this issue. One key is literacy of women; another is male sterilisation.

The national average in India is now 2.6 children per woman. A national policy adopted in 2000 called for the country to reach the replacement fertility of 2.1 by 2010. That has not happened.

Population growth varies by States. In Kerala, it is 1.7. Whereas in Rajasthan, Madhya Pradesh, Bihar and Uttar Pradesh, where 50% of women are illiterate, and where many marry under the age of 18, fertility rates still hover between 3 to 4 children per woman.

Sterilisation is the dominant form of birth control in India today, but the vast majority of procedures are performed on women. Indian Government is trying to change this. A no-scalpel vasectomy costs far less and is easier on a man than a tubal ligation is on a woman.

Nagindas Khajuria FCCA
Simplification Made Simple, Chartered Certified Accountants, London

2011
NHS—Last family Silver Remaining

Healthcare costs in 2010 were 17.3%, 10.4% and 8.7% of GDP in USA, Canada and UK respectively. US medical insurance cost for family was $13,770 [Employer $9,773; Employee $3,997]. 30 million had no cover. [FT 20 Feb 11 p11 Analysis].

UK's NHS is unique in the entire world: the clinician thinks about treatment first and cost later. Andrew Lansley wants to introduce private competition into the NHS so that it becomes more efficient.

The "consultant" in hospital is as important, if not more, than the GP: yet he is putting all his faith in the GP. 15% of GPs already work in PCTs.

True there are weaknesses in the financial control systems in the 152 NHS Primary Care Trusts and in the 400 NHS hospitals. For example, the combined heading "materials and services" covers 30% of all NHS costs in individual PCT or hospital accounts. Surely, they should be broken down.

Transparency and accountability with improved financial controls is required, not wholesale restructuring of NHS. After all, NIC employee and employer contributions are going up to 13.8% each from 2011–12: that will raise £160 billion a year.

Intellectual property in NHS is invaluable: let us not sell the last family silver remaining.

Nagindas Khajuria FCCA
Simplification Made Simple, Chartered Certified Accountants, London

2011
Strategies and issues of corruption

Two separate but complimentary strategies need to be tackled: the preventive approach-creating a set of rules, systems and processes that provide checks on corrupt actions and encourage conformity to ethical standards; and the enforcement approach-the establishment of anti-corruption laws and institutions.

Most corruption happens at the time of delivery of goods and services by public servants at village, town, region, district, state or central government level.

Potential areas of reform are:

- Business process re-engineering using information technology [e.g. computerisation of the railway passenger system used by 10 million people everyday eliminated corruption there];
- Introduction of Online Citizens' Charters on other key goods and services;
- Procurement reforms: introduction of standardised e-tendering documents for the procurement of goods, services or equipment;
- Each government department or undertaking is supposed to have a full time Chief Vigilance Officer and supporting staff to monitor, investigate and prosecute those involved in corrupt practices under the Civil Vigilance Commission Act 2003-this has not been happening;
- Speeding up the prosecution service: criminal and civil prosecutions are delayed for many years, sometimes until the guilty party has died.

I agree with Hazare's comment: the war on corruption has just begun.

Nagindas Khajuria FCCA
Simplification Made Simple, Chartered Certified Accountants, London

2011
The Alternative Vote Referendum

The results of the last five general elections, i.e. 1992, 1997, 2001, 2005 and 2010 respectively were:

Liberal Democrats - 18%, 17%, 18%, 22.5% and 23% of votes against 3%, 7%, 8%, 10% and 9% of seats.

Conservatives - 42%, 31%, 32%, 33% and 36% of votes against 52%, 25%, 25%, 31% and 47% of seats.

Labour - 34%, 43%, 41%, 36% and 29% of votes against 42%, 64%, 63%, 55% and 40% of seats.

Turnout was 78%, 72%, 59%, 61% and 65% of those eligible to vote. Voting in the UK is not compulsory. Thus 35% to 40% did not vote at all for the past 20 years.

Lord Jenkins had recommended AV+ system where a small top-up list of MPs with no specific constituencies would be elected according to the party's share of votes.

Scottish Parliament and Welsh Assembly use the Additional Member System [AMS] which is essentially FPTP system but with top-up list elected by proportional representation.

Scottish local elections use the Single Transferrable Vote [STV] which is multimember seats elected by proportional representation.

Politicians have not educated the public sufficiently about the pros and cons of the various alternatives. The Alternative Vote System may not be the long term ideal solution but it is definitely a step in the right direction for further refinements based on experience.

2011
Bad Commercial decision by Royal Bank of Scotland

Even without the benefit of hindsight, it is clear that RBS Management's decision to acquire ABN AMRO Holding N.V. on 17th October 2007 was a very poor quality management decision. RBS bit more than what it could chew.

The assets of RBS rose from £871 billion to £1,901 billion and employee numbers rose from 141,800 to 233,600 overnight.

RBS traditional market was UK and USA. RBS Europe and Rest of the World market, of which it knew very little, rose from £74 billion to £446 billion. "Held-for-trading" assets rose from £343 billion to £739 billion. "Loans and receivables" increased from £426 billion to £895 billion.

RBS acquired ABN AMRO equity for £48.6 billion [book value £25.3 billion and goodwill £23.3 billion] of which it £45 billion was paid in cash.

Deloitte & Touche LLP who signed off the audit report of 31st December 2007 accounts on 27 February 2008 stated in note 35 in page 203 that there was not sufficient time to accurately reflect the purchase price of ABN AMRO because of complexity and therefore they had used provisional figures.

Their Audit Opinion on page 119 also stated that audit procedures of internal control for financial reporting for ABN AMRO were excluded by Management [the latter's assets were 40.7% of the total assets of RBS]. Coalition government has yet to put its act together in this area.

Nagindas Khajuria FCCA
Simplification Made Simple, Chartered Certified Accountants, London

2011 Improving NHS

Between 1974 and 2004, the average number of annual GP visits in England had increased from 4.5 to 6.3 for working-age women; 4.8 to 7.4 for elderly women; 4.9 to 6.7 for elderly men; and 3.3 to 3.8 for working-age men, while GP lists sizes have decreased from 2,384 to 1,666 patients per GP according to research by Oxford University in March 2011.

In 2008, there were 37,213 GPs supported by 22,048 practice nurses and 92,436 practice staff, including practice managers, receptionists, IT support and note summarisers, physiotherapists, podiatrists, counsellors, phlebotomists and healthcare assistants [The NHS Handbook].

It appears that many GP practices do not amend their patient list when patient dies or moves on as 1,666 patients multiplied by 37,213 GPs gives a total England population of 62 million. Actual population is 49 million.

In one week, a GP achieves on average 87 surgeries, 15 telephone consultations and 5 home visits. Each GP needs a support staff in the ratio of 3 to 1 to carry out his or her duties.

The appointment system should be abolished. Alternatively GPs could also use the email or text system. £10 charge per surgery visit should also be introduced.

Finally, competing health promotion centres should be set up to educate people on healthy living.

Nagindas Khajuria FCCA
Simplification Made Simple, Chartered Certified Accountants, London

2011
The Global Food System

Like the IMF, the global food system is also run like a monopoly or oligopoly of a few multinational companies or countries.

Commodity trading revenues accounting for 75% to 90% of the world grain trade in 2010 was controlled by two private companies [Cargill and Dreyfus revenues $108b and $34b] and two public companies registered in tax havens [ADM revenues $62b and Bunge $47b].

50% of global seed sales are controlled by four companies [Monsanto, DuPont, Syngenta and Limagrain].

75% of global agrochemicals [e.g. fertilisers, etc.] market is controlled by six companies [Monsanto, DuPont, Syngenta, Dow, Bayer and BASF].

These companies have entered into strategic partnerships, again like the IMF, with each other that may amount to anticompetitive practices. A Global Competition Commission needs to be formed to counter any such practices if they exist. One change over the years has been in feeding animals grain instead of grass that has made meat cheap and plentiful but has encouraged people to eat twice or three times the amount of meat they need to eat nutritionally speaking. That is a very unhealthy way of living.

In addition, what is at stake here is the entire eco-system of the planet as we know it and the culture of food growing and eating habits around the world.

2011
Hidden economy in the UK

The Financial Times article on the hidden economy was interesting [FT 9 June pl4]. It stated that UK had an "estimated" hidden economy of 12% of GDP in 2011.

This appears to be "an exact arithmetical calculation" on known GDP statistics: UK GDP currently is £1,500 billion; UK actual tax burden is 38% or £500 billion. If you gross up £500 billion by the tax burden of 38%, you come up with a white GDP of £1,315 billion. The difference is exactly 12% or £185 billion.

The more accurate estimate is likely to be 20%. In the first year, the coalition government has concentrated too much on ill-conceived Bills, changes and reforms and wasted the nations' valuable time in debating them umpteenth time.

Billions have been wasted by introducing Bills that were not carefully worked out in health, welfare, immigration, university fees, prisons and defence. The Prime Minister is still not learning from his mistakes and is now planning yet another Bill on university course fees auctions and competition.

All that is required is higher calibre efficiency audits of public services provided by both central and local governments that would bring about the right changes to improve productivity and savings gradually.

The hidden economy has a positive effect on the low earners and benefit claimants when their wages or benefits are cut while cost of living is going up and should rightly be ignored.

The same hidden economy has a negative effect on tax evasion by high earners, be they professionals, or large businesses. HM Revenue & Customs need more experienced professionals that could raise billions just from tax inquiries.

Nagindas Khajuria FCCA
Simplification Made Simple, Chartered Certified Accountants, London

2011
Foreign Account Tax Compliance Act [FATCA]

Congress passed this Act in 2010 to be effective 1 January 2013: a significant global development.

Details of accounts containing at least $50,000 belonging to US clients have to be reported to IRS; otherwise Internal Revenue Service will withhold tax of up to 30% from payments to foreing banks [on sale of shares or bonds] deemed to be non-compliant.

US citizens abroad have accounts in Barclays, UBS, Credit Suisse, TD Bank of Canada as well as in Germany, Hong Kong, Singapore, etc. according to Gillian.tett@ft.com [FT 14 Jun p14]. UBS, the Swiss Bank paid $780 billion in 2009 to settle criminal charges that it helped Americans evade tax and handed over client details.

Alternatively there is a voluntary disclosure concession as the best last chance to get into the system and pay a penalty of 25% of the total amount held offshore. IRS has launched this concession on their website http://www.irs.gov/businesses/international/article/0,id = 235690,00.html.

One chemist called Cindy who had left US 30 years ago voluntarily approached IRS last year: no tax was due in the US, yet Tax Return was still due and she had to pay a penalty of US$42,000, 20% of the money held in her account. She gave up the US citizenship.

If successful, I see that other countries [e.g. UK and India] introduce similar legislation. Those who have or plan offshore accounts need to rethink their tax strategies.

Nagindas Khajuria FCCA
Simplification Made Simple, Chartered Certified Accountants, London

2011
Giving bank of England more powers is a bad idea

George Osborne has proposed legislation to abolish the present Financial Service Authority and transfer its functions to the Bank of England. That means that BoE will supervise not only the authorised deposit taking institutions but also all other banks, financial institutions, insurance companies, independent financial advisors, mortgage advisors and thousands of other mutual and pension funds firms.

This is a bad idea and he should rethink. BoE already has too much on its plate: managing the macroeconomic side of the economy: capital account, interest rate, inflation rate, exchange rate, aggregate demand and stabilisation policy, aggregate supply and supply-side intervention, unemployment, non-employment and an eye on global developments.

The FSA formation was approved by Parliament in 1998 and was formed in 2000 to supervise the microeconomic side of the economy. It has functioned fairly well. The only mistake was that it had only one head for whom it was too much to manage.

The different parts can each have a separate Head: Self Regulating Organisations; Investment Management Regulatory Body; Personal Investment Authority; Building Societies Commission; Financial Central Register Helpline; Publications for Consumers and The Financial Services Compensation Scheme. The Self Regulating Organisations include all the accountancy bodies, law societies and Institute of Actuaries; Recognised Investment Exchanges, Recognised Clearing Houses; Designated Investment Exchanges and Ombudsman Schemes.

Nagindas Khajuria FCCA
Simplification Made Simple, Chartered Certified Accountants, London

2011
Indian saris

The Indian sari enhances and gracefully blends with the physique and dusky complexion of Indian women. It is the longest surviving garment style in the world's history of garments. Woven saris are the most celebrated items from handlooms of India.

The handloom sector engages over 6.5 million people, contributes to over 22% of total cloth production, with an average productivity of 5.12 metres per day per loom. The potential for handloom saris has not been fully exploited.

The key is the design. The harmony between the body, the border and the pallav, or the end part is also essential. For long, innovation has not occurred in the area of yarns used in weaving saris.

Fabric weights, handle and transparencies of saris too need some exciting explorations. Motifs-with their forms, details and styles-are perhaps the most important elements in product development and design of saris.

Each woven sari is unique as opposed the mass produced cotton or silk sari. Identifiable distinct traditions still exist in saris known as Andhra, Asavali [Ahmadabad], Patoda, Baluchari, Bengal, Chanderi, Maheshwari, Ikal, Kasavu, Kota doria, Maharashrian shalus, Paithani, Orissa, Tamil Nadu, Varnasi and Tribal.

Some weavers have already adapted to products like stoles, duppattas, dress material, salwar kurtas, etc. Customers have found new ways of putting a sari to use. Decorative borders and pallavs are often used as curtain panels, cushion covers, bolster covers, bags and many more home textile products.

The beauty of an Indian woman is certainly enhanced by the sari. Let us nurture and encourage this tradition, be it in the traditional design, or in its new contemporary design.

Nagindas Khajuria FCCA
Simplification Made Simple, Chartered Certified Accountants, London

2011 Saris and today's women by Jayesh A Patel

The letter by Nagindas Khajuria on the subject of Saris raises a sore point with me. Unfortunately saris are on the way out and are being replaced by black business suits and jeans in women's fashion. Sari for me is beautiful adornment elegant and feminine and are part of Bharat history. Jeans originated as cheap long lasting American farmhand work wear in poor farmhands of 1890s from cut up tent cloth and were fashioned them into jeans. They were made famous by James Dean in the film "A Rebel without a Cause" and this film portrays a culture as far removed from Indian culture as possible, so every time I see Indian people in jeans my heart sinks at what this garment represents.

Jayesh A Patel, Wimbledon

2011 The Metropolitan Police Service and The Metropolitan Authority

TMPS has a staff of 32,000 with 14,500 police officers to cover 600 square miles and 7.2 million population. The remaining staff is divided into other ranks, namely, Commissioner, Deputy C, Assistant C, Deputy Assistant C, Commander, Chief Superintendent, Superintendent, Chief Inspector, Inspector, Sergeant and Constable.

In the last 12 months, just under 1 million crimes among the 7.2 million were reported: 161,000 violence against persons; 100,000 motor vehicle crimes; 95,000 burglaries; 37,000 robberies; 48,000 domestic crimes and 381,000 "others".

With an annual budget of 3.2 billion, it is high time they revert back to single policeman or single policewoman on the street instead of walking in twos. The practice of rushing to the scene of the crime by police cars driving frantically with very loud sirens creates noise pollution and traffic congestion almost every hour throughout Greater London and is not warranted as the norm.

It is best to prevent crime by having police all the time, specially at night, just walking the 600 square miles. The cost of running cars, the security cameras, bureaucracy, hierarchy [too many chiefs and no Indians], gathering statistics [e.g. 8% Indians and 14% Jews in Borough of Barnet] and the practice of paying overtime [when it is a fact that 75% of crimes happen at night] is not a wise way of spending taxpayer money.

Nagindas Khajuria FCCA
Simplification Made Simple, Chartered Certified Accountants, London

2011

The Metropolitan Police

In response to Mr. Nagindas Khajuria's letter regarding his opinions on the Metropolitan Police, I would like to state that reverting back to single man patrols is ridiculous. The police must work in pairs for various safety reasons. For instance, if a police officer is attacked, the second officer can call in for backup and then intervene. Also, a two-man unit provides more authority than single patrols. Secondly, it is absurd to complain about noise pollution with respect to police sirens as they are stopping crimes. I think 10 seconds of noise is a price worth paying for knowing the streets are safer. Regarding the idea of congestion, the police cars rushing may inconvenience you very briefly, however, they are rushing for a reason – namely crime prevention. Hence, to complain about the noise and congestion caused, is simply astounding as it a small externality to allow the police to reach crime scenes rapidly. Thus, perhaps you should look at the bigger picture and compare crime levels to when single patrols and zero police vehicles were used.

Ricky Vachhani, Essex

Nagindas Khajuria FCCA
Simplification Made Simple, Chartered Certified Accountants, London

2011
Time to abandon Britain's CCTV Policing

During England's recent riots, the Police stood by as homes were attacked and businesses destroyed. They relied on CCTV cameras to catch the offenders later on. The footage of flaming buildings and offenders appeared to be more important than use of police batons and tear gas.

Back in the 1970s, many US cities including New York Police Department, abandoned beat policing and took to the car: a philosophy of reactive or passive policing. The policy was a disaster and has now been abandoned in most US cities.

In the UK, the Met went into the opposite direction in the nineties, seizing on closed-circuit television as the primary tool of law enforcement: monitoring trouble spots with cameras and racing to crime scenes in cars. It created a vacuum of authority in public space. Also there was no more any dialogue with the public.

Officers lost any sense that their job was to deter crime by their presence alone, rather than just to react.

In New York, there was also the problem of bureaucracy. They solved it by hiring civilians. In contrast, in London, the Meter hired some 3,000 civilians, gave them six months training, and put them out in the street in place of real police as "community support officers" or "PCSOs".

While Americans are following an updated version of what Sir Robert Peel pioneered in early 19th century, we have lost 200 years of good policing by current practices [FT Aug 11 P11].

Nagindas Khajuria FCCA
Simplification Made Simple, Chartered Certified Accountants, London

2011
Anarchy in the Global Economy

The recent riots in London reminded me of similar behaviour by markets since President Nixon declared on 15th August 1971 that the US Dollar would no longer be convertible into gold following the huge fiscal deficit then caused by the Vietnam War and run on the US Currency.

Since then the management of foreign exchange rates has been similar to riots, looting and stealing as much as you can, hidden under the camouflage of complexity. Give more to those who have has been the ethos. The Police, the Press, the Politicians and the Big Business continue to support this anarchy by scratching each other's back.

Paper money was created, printed and multiplied without any sense of proportion or relevance to the underlying economic strength of the country or countries involved. On powerful computer screens foreign exchange rates move in milliseconds to 4 decimal points in case of major currencies such as the US Dollar, Euro or Yen. Yet these same currencies can go up and down by 25% while Bretton Woods' 1944 idea was that no currency should fluctuate more than 2.5%. Gold was then $35 to the ounce. Now it is $1790 to the ounce. The forecast is $2,500 by end of this year. Surely time has come for the global economy to have one global currency again linked to gold.

International trade is the true wealth creator: it has been hijacked by international finance. The latter has now degenerated in financial engineering and leveraging in the ratio of $260 of paper money for $1 of real money or real GDP.

Nagindas Khajuria FCCA
Simplification Made Simple, Chartered Certified Accountants, London

2011
Scheduled Castes and Scheduled Tribes

Article 334 of the Constitution of India stated that reservation of seats for the Scheduled Castes, the Scheduled Tribes and the Anglo-Indian community in the House of the People and in the Legislative Assemblies of the States shall cease sixty years from the commencement of the Constitution. The words "sixty years" were substituted by Constitution (79th Amendment) Act 1999 to "fifty years" w.e.f. 25th January 2000.

The Constitution was adopted on 26th January 1950 and fifty years elapsed on 25th January 2000. I presume that there has not been any reservation of seats since then. I stand to be corrected by Asian Voice readers on this.

Article 46 called the State to promote with special care the educational and economic interests of the weaker sections of the people; in particular the Scheduled Castes and the Scheduled Tribes who would be protected from social injustice and all forms of exploitation.

Since independence, India's literacy rate and income demographics have improved substantially.

In rural India, the per cent of each income group improved from upper 2.1%, upper middle 3.1%, middle 8.6%, lower middle 29% and lower 57.2% to 8.1%, 6.5%, 22.3%, 42.5% and 20.6% respectively between 1995 and 2000.

In urban India, which is the other 50% of the population, from upper 7.3%, upper middle 9.6%, middle 20.3%, lower middle 34.8% and lower 27.9% to 35.9%, 16.3%, 21.7%, 21.4% and 4.7% respectively between 1995 and 2000.

Therefore, the time is ripe to abolish the reservation system altogether and replace it by bursaries and scholarships on merit to any student in need and means tested welfare benefits to the weaker sections of the community not in kind or currency but by a voucher system.

Nagindas Khajuria FCCA
Simplification Made Simple, Chartered Certified Accountants, London

2011

Is UK serious about economic growth?

Over the past 14 years, my view has not changed that UK should join the Euro currency and abandon the Pound Sterling. In 2000, the Sterling exchange rate was 120 compared to 100 in 2005 and 80 in 2010 when valued against the Euro. 60% of our import export business is with Europe.

Thus in 2000 our export prices were 20% higher than 2005 and import prices 20% lower. In 2010, our export prices were 20% lower and import prices were higher. With such fluctuations in prices both ways, for the past decade we have never figured out in which products and/or services we are "competitive" with European prices and in which ones we are not with our main partner.

Hence we in the UK do not really know in which direction and in what industry sectors we should invest more so that we could export more and in what industry sectors we should disinvest. If there is price transparency on a minute by minute business between UK prices and EU prices, and that is only possible if we had the same currency, we may gradually start producing the right goods and the right services at the right prices and become a major exporter like Germany worldwide.

All the current ideas for economic growth I hear and read about from all the three political parties such as dropping the 50% tax rate, or printing money, or low interest rate, or cracking down on tax evasion, or cutting bureaucracy and waste, or enterprise zones, or lending more to small businesses, or slowing the rate at which public sector spending is being cut, etc. are tinkering on the edges and not taking the bull by its horns.

Nagindas Khajuria FCCA
Simplification Made Simple, Chartered Certified Accountants, London

2011
The known unknown

I am still at the Labour Party Annual Conference in Liverpool. This is my third day and I look forward to hear what Ed Miliband has to say today. Late last night I was watching Andrew Neil interviewing Ed Balls on BBC2 Newsnight and getting Balls' confirmation that yes Labour lost £12 in abandoned NHS IT policy while the Coalition had lost only £2 billion in introducing the new Healthcare Bill.

Civil servants and/or appointed advisors do not sufficiently brief politicians on facts. Labour has not lost £12 billion on NHS project. While only about £4 has been paid to date, the rest of the spending is being revised to drop the national patient database but not many other aspects of the project such as a database for someone like me at least all over London, etc. and that is working very well.

I also met Neil Kinnock and spoke to him while chasing him on the elevator and down for a few minutes. I suggested to him that we should join the Euro. He said had we joined many years ago, UK scene would have been quite different. Now I am not so sure. When I pressed him that even now it is most urgent we consider it, he gave me the impression that he agreed it was a valid argument and needed serious consideration.

Gujarati Asians do not take part as much as they should, especially our young and especially of Hindu and/or Jain background. I know politics is not a perfect science but it is a very important part of daily life. More young people must enter into that career and be passionate about it. Start by being a Local Councillor and work your way upwards.

Nagindas Khajuria FCCA
Simplification Made Simple, Chartered Certified Accountants, London

2011
Dismantling the NHS Programme for IT

Mr Dinesh Sheth states in his letter to Asian Voice [Oct 1, p10] that Labour had lost £12.7 on NHS IT project that had been scrapped. I would like to refer him and readers of AV to the Department Health Press Release that was issued on 22 September 2011 [http://mediacentre.dh.gov.uk/2011/09/22/dismantling-the-nhs-national-programme-for-it].

In this official press release, the Coalition Government state two-thirds of IT infrastructures are well established and so far £6.4 billion has been spent. They now want the private companies to get involved in addition to NHS for any future spending. Thus even they accept that £4.3 billion was wisely spent by Labour. Use of the word "dismantling" is a typical Coalition spin language.

Labour planned total IT spend of £12.65 billion in 2002 over 10 years to 2013/14. The NPfIT [National Programme for IT] represents around 25% of the total spend [The NHS Handbook 2010/11 p234]. The CRS [Care Record Service] is a small part of this project. The other projects are GP2GP; Choose and Book; EPS and its merging with CRS; N3; NHS Choices; NHS Space; PACS; and QMAS to pay GPs [p238]. Most of these are well established and working.

I am registered for access to my Health Space Basic Account on www.healthspace.nhs.uk and plan to register for Health Space Advanced Account by a face to face meeting registration. Then I will be able to see my summary care and prescription record. Everyone can do so.

The National Audit Office did report in 2008 that 'the original vision remains intact and still appears feasible' [p235]. Labour is more competent than Conservatives to reform the NHS in the right way.

Nagindas Khajuria FCCA
Simplification Made Simple, Chartered Certified Accountants, London

2011 Midland Voice by Dee Katwa

I was very pleased to read Dhiren Katawa's page 8 [AV 8 Oct]. The news about Coventry City Football Club [CCFC] is very dear to my passion for football. The Club hopes "to motivate kids to start kicking a football". A book called "The Ball Is Round" by David Goldblatt is the definitive history of how humanity has played, watched and followed football; an epic tale of players, managers, owners, clubs, nations, cultures, money and power [Guardian]. Asian parents need to encourage their children to play this game.

It is a real shame that after seventy years of independence and with over 1 billion people, India still is incapable of producing just eleven world class foot-ballers and fails to qualify to play in World Cup Football games every four years. Partly it was deliberate discrimination against the Indian sub-continent, partly lack of Government and/or business support and partly India's obsession with cricket and/or Bollywood.

"State Bank of India's opening of a new Branch in Wolverhampton" is also Interesting. If SBI opens branches in the UK with a new business model: only individuals or businesses with gross turnover of £250,000 or under can open or stay with them, they could overtake current UK banks. The current account is the key to success in the Banking Industry. Four million self-employed persons have gross turnover under £250,000.

"Challenge to energy giants" is another excellent idea. Councils can go further and lend to local small businesses. Germany's success is partly due to such policy for decades.

Nagindas Khajuria FCCA
Simplification Made Simple, Chartered Certified Accountants, London

2011
The Vision of Europe

European civilisation is 2000 years old compared to the US civilisation that is 300 years old. Europe has been dynamic, vibrant, innovative, diverse, enterprising, fascinating and the most technologically, socially, economically and politically advanced continent.

Its idea of capitalism is less greedy and less selfish than the Anglo-Saxon kind of capitalism. A CEO of Nokia or Michelin or Mercedes gets about 10% of remuneration that a CEO of Motorola, Good Year Tyre Co or General Motors gets.

UK as a member of EU has recently shown that when they see fellow members in difficulty, instead of showing the true spirit of sportsmanship and help fellow members, it wants to rush to get out of membership.

True, many of the 27 members are not as developed as the more advanced economies. That should be in UK's interest, not a disadvantage. As they progress to become more advanced, their population will demand more goods and services.

Splendid isolation is not an option for UK. If they get out of EU, they should urgently form an economic block with US with common language and common ideology of capitalism, values, beliefs and culture.

My forecast is that, if status quo continues, over the next decade or two, it will not be the Euro that will fall, but it will be the Pound Sterling or both the Pound Sterling and the US Dollar that will fall or crash.

Nagindas Khajuria FCCA
Simplification Made Simple, Chartered Certified Accountants, London

2011
The Human Body

The human body is made up of roughly 100 trillion cells. Each cell has three parts: the cell membrane, the nucleus, and the cytoplasm. Nutrients enter the cell via the membrane; the cell converts them into energy that fuels its life functions. Waste gets generated due this metabolic activity that must somehow get out of each cell again via the membrane.

If you do Yoga exercises properly, you should feel a tingling sensation in each of these trillion cells. The cell's membrane must balance containment (stability) with permeability. That is why in Yoga postures you need to be moving as well as be motionless.

Breathing is a movement in two (Tesco) bags: the thoracic bag that contains the heart and lungs; and the abdominal bag that contains the stomach, liver, gall bladder, spleen, pancreas, small and large intestines, kidneys and the bladder. The diaphragm forms the roof of the abdominal bag and the floor of the thoracic bag.

When breathing in and out, both bags change shape but in different ways. The abdominal bag is like a water balloon so that it changes shape but not the total volume. Instead the thoracic bag is like accordion bellows that can change its shape and volume.

The spinal cord is attached to the back of these two bags. In Yoga breathing the diaphragm is the principal muscle that causes three-dimensional shape change in the thoracic and abdominal bags. In inhalation there is spinal extension: in exhalation there is spinal flexion. [Sources: personal experiences and Yoga Anatomy by Leslie Kaminoff – Human Kinetics].

2011
European Union Time Line

1951: France, West Germany, Italy, Netherlands, Belgium and Luxembourg meet in Paris to pool their coal and steel industries under one supranational authority [Treaty of Paris].

1957: The same six nations establish the European Economic Community and the European Atomic Energy Authority [Treaty of Rome]. Aims were to create a customs union; free movement of capital, labour, goods and services; common agricultural and fisheries policies; to coordinate economic policies; harmonise social policies and finally to promote co-operation in nuclear research [Treaty of Rome].

1958: Investment Bank for the EEC was set up.

1960: UK, Switzerland, Sweden, Norway, Denmark and Portugal form the European Free Trade Association.

1961: Finland joins.

1962: Common Agricultural Policy was agreed in EEC.

1967: The coal and steel community, the atomic authority and EEC merge to form the European Commission.

1973: UK, Ireland and Denmark join the EC.

1974: Regular heads of government summits begins.

1975: UK renegotiates its terms of accession.

1979: European Monetary Institute is set up to supervise the EMS foreign exchange rate system.

1981: Greece joins EC.

1986: Single European Act is signed.

1986: Portugal and Spain join EC.

1991: Maastricht Treaty is signed. European Commission becomes European Union.

1994: European Free Trade Association joins European Commission to form European Economic Area.

1995: Austria; Sweden and Finland join EU.

2004: Czech Republic; Hungary; Cyprus; Lithuania; Latvia: Malta; Slovakia; Slovenia; Poland and Estonia join EU.

2007: Bulgaria and Romania join EU.

2011: Application to join: Croatia; Macedonia; Turkey and Iceland. Other potential candidates: Albania; Bosnia; Herzegovina; Kosovo; Montenegro; Serbia.

Nagindas Khajuria FCCA
Simplification Made Simple, Chartered Certified Accountants, London

Does practice of Yoga lead to Hinduism?

Christians who believe that Yoga is evil have not gone deep into the very essence of Yoga. Many Christians still behave like barbarians. Historically the "Europeans" have divided and looted wealth from Muslims Hindus and Buddhists.

Yoga teaches good daily behaviour; moral values; postures; breathing techniques; self control; concentration; meditation and harmony between the spine, a muscles, nerves and ligaments; the activities of the mind and the inner self. Yoga encourages vegetarianism.

Yoga nurtures a sense of non-violence; truth; half-truths; celibacy; non-possession; purity; contentment; study; spirituality; mobility; resilience; suppleness; physical and inner strength.

No.

2011
Banking Regulation

Under the Bank of International Settlements [BIS], based in Switzerland, all banks including offshore banks are regulated where countries have signed up to their Basle I, II and III Accords.

However, transactions in the Eurocurrency market are not subject to the Cash Reserve Ratio [CRR] and the Statutory Liquidity Ratio [SLR] requirements. In 1999, this market was worth US$9.5 trillion. Thus these funds are not legally protected.

Eurocurrency market is a wholesale market in which Eurocurrencies are borrowed and lent in multiples of US$10m. Eurocurrency is not the Euro currency. It can be Dollars, Sterling, Euros, Japanese Yen, etc: known as Eurodollar, Euro Pound, Euro Yen, Euro CAD, etc.

The legal definition of Eurocurrency is a market in which funds are intermediated outside the country of currency in which the funds are denominated. It is not legal tender. It can just be borrowed or lent. One example would be Hindustan Levers deposits US$30 m in an American Bank branch in Germany; another: an American branch in France lends US$30m to British Airways in the UK.

The interest rates paid or charged are naturally lower than domestic bank rates. Rates quoted are usually 1% above LIBOR rate, fixed every six months.

Although City of London is fully regulated, regulators do not have sufficient time or expertise to monitor this complex banking system, esp. the offshore activities of MNCs and tax evasion that follows.

EU is right to propose a transaction tax. David Cameroon was wrong to use the veto in Brussels. He could have said: I have to consult my Parliament for deep reflexion.

Nagindas Khajuria FCCA
Simplification Made Simple, Chartered Certified Accountants, London

2011 Milestones in India's recent history

1885: Indian National Congress was formed.
1893: World Parliament of Religions, Swami Vivekananda: "religions were not meant to spread hatred and discord but to foster love and brotherhood".
1905: Viceroy Lord Curzon partitioned Bengal and Assam into "Eastern Bengal" capital Dacca and "Bengal" capital Calcutta;
1906: All-India Muslim League was formed in Dacca.
1913: Dadasaheb Phalke released the silent feature film "Raja Harishchandra" shot in Dadar; R Tagore was awarded the Nobel Prize for Literature for "Gitanjali" [103 song offerings]; TISCO [The Tata Iron and Steel Company Limited] was formed by J N Tata in Jamshedpur.
1919: M K Gandhi starts non-violent non-cooperation movement. "Strength does not come from physical capacity. It comes from indomitable will".
1931: The first India talkie, "Alam Ara" [Light of the world] was released at Majestic Cinema by A M Irani.
1932: Tata Airlines became India's first commercial airline [renamed Air India International Limited in 1948].
1935: Government of India Act was passed creating the Indian Constitution and elected State governments.
1950: Constitution of India came into force: 395 articles and 9 schedule s.
1953: Madras State split to create Andhra Pradesh.
1954: 3 Academies formed: Sangeet Natak; Lalit Kala and Sahitya.
1960: Mumbai State split into Maharashtra and Gujarat.
1962: Teachers' Day 5 September Dr S Radhakrishnan.
1966: Punjab State split into Punjab and Haryana.
1971: Birth of Bangladesh.
1974: Offshore oil and gas discovered by ONGC 160 km West of Mumbai coast.
1985: India mastered nuclear technology.
1998: India develops its own nuclear weapons.
2000: Chhattisgarh carved out of Madhya Pradesh; Uttaranchal from Uttar Pradesh and Jharkhand from Bihar.

Nagindas Khajuria FCCA
Simplification Made Simple, Chartered Certified Accountants, London

2012
United Nations Organization

Time has come to break up the United Nations Organization into 5 Regional Nations Organizations [RNO]: America, Europe, Asia, Africa and Middle East and 5 regional currencies. BRIC countries have already decided to trade only in their own currencies between themselves. International Monetary Fund and World Bank should also be closed and 5 similar regional bodies formed. British media, politicians and economists view that the entire European Project and the Euro Currency were ill conceived and was all going to fail is Anglo-Saxon wishful thinking.

The 16 EURO countries represent 22% [$12.3 trillion] of world output [$58 trillion] and 29% of world exports with only 5% of world population. Combined Greece, Portugal and Ireland only make up 6% of EURO output. Let due process of democracy there decide Greece's fate. If one or more countries leave the Euro currency, other countries are no fools to give up free flow of goods, services, capital and labour. Also many others are waiting to join. United Nations has not been a success neither in the political sense or nor in the economic sense. Out of 100 biggest economies, 40 are not countries but multinational companies where huge profits are made on purely speculative trading activities. Let them find their own equilibrium without government bailouts.

Nagindas Khajuria FCCA
Simplification Made Simple, Chartered Certified Accountants, London

2012

Marks & Spencer & HSBC link up to open retail banks

Recently I received an annual loan statement from Marks & Spencer Money: opening balance, the 12 repayments and closing balance; no entries for annual interest charged except to state APR 6%.

In this country, it seems anything goes: start selling clothes, then get into groceries; credit cards; lending and now banking. It is becoming like a banking jungle supported by bank bailouts.

What is needed is a new model in retail banking; not more of the same by today's money-hungry financial institutions. Founder Arkadi Kuhlmann and Brand Consultant Bruce Philip found a new model in 1996 by setting up exclusive online banking. Today it is a global enterprise with over 20 million customers in nine countries. It is called ING Direct.

Time is ripe to set up a retail banking model that serves only employees and/or self-employed whose income and/or revenue is up to a maximum of the national average that can move every year. Each country would have their national moving average.

"The reasonable man adapts himself to the world; the unreasonable one persists in trying to adapt the world to himself. Therefore, all progress depends on the unreasonable man" [George Bernard Shaw].

Nagindas Khajuria FCCA
Simplification Made Simple, Chartered Certified Accountants, London

2012
Banks are agents, not principals

The principals are governments, businesses and private individuals. The majority of transactions are carried out by instructions from them to banks.

Daniel Defoe wrote a paper in the 18th century on jobbers and stockbrokers in stocks that it was "a trade in Fraud, born of Deceit and nourished by Trick, Cheat, Wheedle, Forgeries, Falsehoods and all sorts of delusions".

The culture of greed, not just in the banks, but in the wider world, is the cancer that is spreading rapidly.

The joint stock company model of running private enterprise that was introduced in the 16th century has failed.

It is time a new legal structure is conceptualised where investors, employees, customers and suppliers are the joint principals, and management is the agent.

PwC, Deloitte, Ernst & Young and KPMG, auditors of substantial companies, institutions and government accounts have not ensured sufficient discipline.

Banking is an international business: any structural reform and/or legislation solely in the UK will fail. George Osborne should cooperate with the European Union and jointly come up with a Single EU-wide Banking Regulator as well as EU-wide Banking System Structure. Cooperation and competition are not mutually exclusive. Only then London will remain a major financial centre.

Nagindas Khajuria FCCA
Simplification Made Simple, Chartered Certified Accountants, London

2012
International Finance is master and real economy is prisoner

International Finance has become so opaque and leverage so high that it no longer serves the real economy. From one financial instrument, it can create "money" six times over with twelve counterparties. LIBOR [London Interbank Offer Rate] is not calculated in any universal way or at a universally recognized time. Interbank fixing rates are 1, 3, 6, and 12-month deposit rates representing the average of rates collected from sixteen leading banks including Bankers Trust, Bank of Tokyo, Barclays and NatWest at 11 am every trading date.

EURIBOR [European Union Interbank Offer Rate] is collected from 57 prime banks in Germany, France, Italy and Madrid for the Euro currency.

Money available up to one year is known as the Money Market. Money available over one year is known as the Capital Market.

A £100m loan can start life at LIBOR plus 2% rate in Sterling. A SWAP contract can change it to a fixed rate contract. However, the swap can be basic, contingent [when interest rate reaches a pre-specified level; reversible [the loan goes back to floating after a certain period]; puttable [one party has the right, but not the obligation, to cancel the swap after a certain period]; zero for floating [one party, which does not pay interest rate, accepts the other party's payment (in another currency) of a floating rate; extendible [e.g. from two years to three years]. £600m has been created from £100m.

2012 Olympics in World Financial System

MIBOR [The Mumbai Inter-bank Offer Rate] fixing system appears to be more transparent than the LIBOR [London Inter-bank Offer Rate].

MIBOR was developed by The Indian National Stock Exchange and launched as the NSE Mumbai Inter-bank Bid Rate [MIBID] and the NSE Mumbai Inter-Bank Offer Rate [MIBOR] for overnight markets on 15 June 1998.

These two rates were based on rates pooled by the NSE from a representative panel of 31 banks/institutions/primary dealers. Currently, quotes are pooled and processed daily by the Exchange at 9:40 [IST] for the overnight rate; and at 11:30 [IST] for the 14 day, 1 month, and 24 month rates.

The rates pooled are then processed using the boost trap method to arrive at an efficient estimate of the reference rates. It is used as a benchmark rate for majority of deals struck for floating rate debentures and term deposits. The benchmark is the rate at which money is raised in the financial markets.

Call Rate is different and that is highly volatile.

That is called "Reuters MIBOR" [Mumbai Inter-Bank Overnight Rate]. That is arrived at by obtaining a weighted average of call money transactions of 22 banks and other players overnight. Whereas "MIBOR" is the official benchmark rate for interest rate swaps [IRS] and forward rate agreements [FRA]. MIBOR is transparent, market-determined, and mutually acceptable to counter-parties as a reference.

In early seventies, as a treasurer in a major oil company, I used to call daily three or four major London banks and "walk over" several million pounds Sterling daily in the money market.

2012
Olympics in Politics

The average turnout in the last five general elections was 67%. The popular votes average was Labour 37%; Conservatives 35%; Liberals 20%; and Others 8%. The parliamentary seats average was Labour 53%; Conservatives 36%; Liberals 7%; and Others 4%. If there are no boundary changes during this parliament, the next general election result is likely to be similar.

The past two years have clearly proved that it is not in the culture of any British political party to work harmoniously with one or the other of the two parties.

In the long term national interest, all the three political parties should be abolished.

We cannot have gold, silver and bronze medal in the race to run the country.

In true democracy all members of Parliament would belong to the National Party and MPs would vote on a bill by bill basis.

After all, forcing or coercing back benchers to follow the party line is antitheses to democratic representation through 600 or so parliamentary constituencies.

The ideologies of private enterprise, trade unions, public services, taxation, economic growth and social justice are so muddled up in the psyche of the three current political parties that none of them are able to lead the country in one clear long term direction.

2012
Official records

Let us collect 100,000 UK signatures and/or 1 million EU signatures from 7 EU countries.

Last week I registered with a new GP practice. One of the questions I had to answer after being in this country for 45 years and having become a naturalised citizen for 40 years was about my ethnic origin. Let us ask UK Parliament and the European Parliament to propose a law and make it illegal for public authorities to ask for ethnic origin in all the 27 EU countries. After all, we are contributing on equal footing with the white majority in the welfare of all these countries and making them richer; and we are equally as loyal. It is discriminatory and degrading. It reminds ethnic minorities to remember their ethnic origin in-everyday life and every day activity.

Public authorities should ask 3 questions: UK national; EU national; or foreign national.

The above practice falls foul of the racial discrimination clause in Human Rights Act. The United Kingdom first signed and ratified the European Convention on Human Rights [ECHR] in 1950. Since coming into force on 2 October 2000, the Human Rights Act has made the rights under ECHR (Convention Rights) enforceable in our own courts. Our children are born here. Our grand children are born here. They can be proud of their ethnic origin, follow their customs and religion etc. but they should not be categorised in official records as such as all human beings are individuals in many respects.

Nagindas Khajuria FCCA
Simplification Made Simple, Chartered Certified Accountants, London

2012
Cable's war on 'shady' tax havens

So read the Sunday Times headline on 23 September 2012.

If one reflects back on the history of taxation and the history of Tax Returns in the UK, one can see that UK tax law encourages tax evasion and breakdown of marriages.

When I began filling in Tax Returns in 1970, the Return had two columns: one for wife and one for husband. In 1991, "independent taxation" destroyed all that EXCEPT when you claim welfare benefits: Then suddenly the income of spouse or partner becomes relevant.

Then, the tax return also asked if the couple had a mortgage, with whom and for how much, what car(s) they drove and what their total annual living expenses were.

Now the Liberal Party is going completely the other way: those who earn under £10,000 need not fill in a Tax Return because personal allowance will soon be £10,000.

Tax evasion is something that is practiced by the very poor, the middle class and the filthy rich in equal measure.

If Cable or any other politician in the land is serious about tax evasion, or Marriage, or welfare benefit fraud, or redistribution of wealth, then the only long term way is to go back to the old system.

Even if one earns £1 per year, one should be required to fill in a Tax Return. Personal allowance should be abolished. Tax rates of 5%, 10%, 15%, 20%, 25%, 30%, 40%, 50% and 60% should be introduced to kill four birds with one stone. A millionaire one year can be a pauper the following year: thus mansion tax is wrong medicine.

Nagindas Khajuria FCCA
Simplification Made Simple, Chartered Certified Accountants, London

2012
Ganga now a deadly source of cancer

Your article [AV p25 27 Oct] refers to industries along the river which have been releasing harmful effluents into the river over decades. It also states that the disposal of waste has been arbitrary and unscientific. And how it is causing more cases of cancer than in other parts of India. The Industrial Revolution began about two centuries ago. I believe it has now reached a saturation point with mass production of mobile phones, cars, computers and thousands of other products that are discarded every time a new model comes up and perfectly good products are abandoned to pile up in huge industrial recycling plants. It is madness. In 2008, for the time in world history, the urban world population crossed the 50% of the world population mark. Mega cities with 10 million plus conurbations are cropping up everywhere.

India needs to reverse this trend of this harmful industrial relentless mass production and get back to basics: encourage and improve villages, small towns and cities and have strict planning laws where the bigger city conurbations have legally defined boundaries and are not allowed to grow in all directions.

50 years from now the countries that have developed more in organic agriculture, not in industrial mass production, will enjoy a happier cleaner and healthier way of life. These countries will also be able to make best use of all natural resources and become economically more successful. The above is the long term solution for Ganga and many other great rivers of India that have sustained India for two thousand years.

Nagindas Khajuria FCCA
Simplification Made Simple, Chartered Certified Accountants, London

2013
Special relationship with USA

In both, first and second World Wars, USA had to intervene to bring about world peace.

Winston Churchill delivered a speech at Westminster College in Fulton, Missouri on 5 March 1946. The US President had travelled 1000 miles to listen to him. Parts of this speech follow.

"The United States stands at this time at the pinnacle of world power.......Opportunity is here and now, clear and shining, for our both countries.......I have strong admiration and regard for valiant Russian people.......Nobody knows what Soviet Russia intends to do.......

An Iron Curtain has descended across the Continent. The capitals of Europe: Warsaw, Berlin, Prague, Vienna, Budapest, Belgrade, Bucharest and Sofia—all these famous cities and the populations around them lie in what I might call the Soviet sphere.

It is necessary that constancy of mind, persistency of purpose and the grand simplicity of decision shall rule and guide the conduct of the English- speaking peoples in peace as they did in war."

The above circumstances no longer exist. USA now wants to have a special relationship with EU. Both are economic blocs of $16 trillion each. The entire rest of the world is just another $16 trillion GDP annually.

Mr Cameron will soon give his most important speech, probably on 22 January 2013, on our relationship with the EU and a referendum on the EU if 32 important areas could not be renegotiated. Neither renegotiation nor referendum is in the national interest.

It is time for Labour to have the above constancy, persistency and simplicity and decide in their 2015 Manifesto that if elected, they will recommend joining the Euro currency in the national interest: Real One Nation Labour.

2013

German central bank's gold reserves and Africa?

Bundesbank has announced publicly that it plans to physically move back all their 374 tonnes of gold from Banque de France and 300 tonnes out of their 1500 tonnes of gold from New York to Frankfurt between now and 2020 (FT Jan 17, 2013).

Germany's official gold reserves are 3,391 tonnes and represent 11% of total world official gold reserves.

When I compare such wealth with Mali, I feel very sad for Malians. After the Portuguese discovered Africa in 1488 (Bartolommeo Diaz) and in 1497 (Vasco da Gama), two thirds of Europe's gold came from mines between the southern fringes of the Sahara and the shores of the Gulf of Guinea.

Present-day Ghana was called Gold Coast. In 2002, Mali's exports were $915 million (cotton, gold, livestock). Population below poverty line: 64% (2001 est.). Life expectancy: 45 years (2004 est.).

Mali was ruled by France for most part of the last century, it's government is still under its protection for its commercial interests there.

If Europeans are not able to uplift the lives of Africans while benefiting from their mineral resources, they should get out of Africa.

Civil wars are going on in 25 of the 50 African countries. Let them sort themselves out. To lump them all Islamists or Jihadis or terrorists is too simplistic. The motive may be commercial interests in many cases.

Nagindas Khajuria FCCA
Simplification Made Simple, Chartered Certified Accountants, London

2013
Animal spirit of capitalism

India's progress after independence does not match its past glory. American writer and humorist, Mark Twain, once said, "India is the cradle of the human race, the birthplace of human speech, the mother of history, the grandmother of legend and the great grandmother of tradition".

In terms of quality of life, the gap between the rich, middle class and the poor, between different states and among sub-regions have continued to widen.

There are 50 elite industrial families that give 300 million Indians a decent quality of life. However, they have not done enough to uplift the other 900 million; upon whose consumption and expenditure they rely to increase their personal and corporate wealth [with helipads and yachts].

Your article "India needs greater financial supervision, liberalisation: IMF" [AV 26 Jan p20] advises India to gradually reduce mandatory holdings of government securities by financial institutions and allow greater access to private domestic and foreign capital. It also recommends RBI directors do not sit on the board of PS Banks. I believe their advice is misplaced.

Private enterprises are still not sufficiently transparent and accountable, nor are they free from corruption, tax evasion, greed, profiteering from speculative short term investments and exploitation, to be given a bigger role.

On the contrary, well-run public enterprises, such as State Bank of India, should emulate private businesses like Tata Group and acquire foreign businesses. SBI could start with a stake in say Santander [10th largest bank in the world], now in need of new direction.

Non-Violence versus Military Interventions on Valentine's Day

Tributes to Mahatma Gandhi (1869–1948) on his 65th Death Anniversary, (AV 2 Feb pl4–17), were very well written. My memory of Mahatma Gandhi goes back to 1947. I was four. My mama was carrying me on his shoulders to Lakhajiraj School in Rajkot, Gujarat. He told me "See there, Gandhi ji is leading a procession march".

By his amazing strength and endurance to accept the harsh physical punishment meted out to him and his followers, he succeeded in arousing the conscience of the aggressor.

Reflecting on the past 65 years truthfully, G8 countries used military interventions as the modus operandi for maintaining world peace and harmony among diverse nations, cultures, values and beliefs.

I am a Hindu brought up in a Muslim country from birth to age 25 except for 3 years. (1946–1949) in India as a child. I found during those 22 years that the Muslims there were no more or less violent than other races I came across.

Gandhiji's second message was that all Indians, both Muslims and Hindus, should live together in harmony and India should not be split into two countries.

On Valentine's Day, leaders of the Indian sub-continent and leaders of the G8 countries should commence a dialogue of understanding through love and respect towards diverse cultures, through economic and technical collaboration rather than military interventions.

An Asian Union [AU] similar to European Union [EU] should gradually evolve with SAR (South Asian Rupee) similar to the Euro as the next step; India, Pakistan, Bangladesh and Sri Lanka would become the Germany, France, Italy and Spain of the AU, Bhutan, Myanmar, Sikkim and Nepal could join later on.

Nagindas Khajuria FCCA
Simplification Made Simple, Chartered Certified Accountants, London

UK India Special Relationship

Part of the two day trade delegation was spent on discussing sale of helicopters contract in 2010 with bribery allegations and selection of 126 Raphael military aircrafts from France to be ditched in favour of British made aircrafts.

I believe this was waste of time and money. Such large projects take many years to come to fruition. A two-day delegation is not the time or place to discuss such commercially sensitive and militarily confidential negotiations.

Britain is very good in many sports: men's football, women's football, rugby, swimming, snooker, tennis, etc. Not only in terms of enthusiasm, interest and media coverage, but also in arranging clubs, matches, training, coaching, etc.

Britain is also good in the quality of construction and design of sports facilities, setting sports standards in schools, manufacturing of relevant equipment and sportswear, etc.

There is a trade gap in India in the encouragement of sports in India; there is also a trade gap in the quality of labelling and packaging manufactured products compared to China; trade gap exists in the quality of Museums for arts [painting, sculpture and ceramics] and sciences, in bookshops, etc.

Why not trade in the technical knowhow in all above areas in return for the immense economic contribution the Indian Diaspora has been making for decades in the UK?

Recent article in the Times [Feb 20 p1] stated that 75% of 3 million new jobs created in the previous 15 years were taken up by immigrants, failing to mention that most of these immigrants were British citizens. Such coverage in mainstream media continues to create disharmony among British citizens and stifles better UK-Indian relations.

Nagindas Khajuria FCCA
Simplification Made Simple, Chartered Certified Accountants, London

2013 – My 40th anniversary to have become a UK citizen

I became a naturalised citizen in 1973, thanks to my oil company employer who wrote to Home Office as my student visa granted in 1967 had finished.

On Mothers' day I was listening to LBC while having breakfast. The discussion was about who would win in the next general election. I telephoned LBC and was pleased to given two minutes before the 11 am news.

I said to Ian Dale that we needed a 15-year plan so that everything is stable. The Coal and Steel Community preceding European Union had a 25-year plan.

The seat of government, the financial centre, architecture, theatres, museums, and all that is best is in London and South East representing 15 million people.

Over the past 50 years all political parties have given less attention, relatively speaking, to the other 45 million living in the middle or north.

May be the financial centre or the seat of parliament should be moved to middle or North.

My published forecast before the last General Election was within two seats of actual seats won and I had also forecast a pact between Conservatives and Liberals. This time my forecast is approx 23% each including UKIP in 2015 and 8% independents. It is time for a National Government with a 15-year plan.

Nagindas Khajuria FCCA
Simplification Made Simple, Chartered Certified Accountants, London

2013 The British Budget

Samuel Brittan has written an excellent article on the history of The British Budget since the 19th century (FT 13 Mar p13).

Where will the money come from? How will it be spent? How much are we likely to borrow? Two months ago the Chancellor sent his chief economic advisor to USA and Canada to seek expert advice on what economic strategy he could consider to stimulate growth in the UK. The Bank Base Rate was 5% on 10 April 2008. By 5 March 2009 it was to 0.5%: a very temporary measure due to a very temporary global financial crash.

On 31 March 2008, £1 = $1.99; on 31 March 2012 it fell to £1 = $1.60.

In March 2008, the UK Retail Price Index was 212.1. In March 2012 it rose to 240.8.

If I were the Chancellor, I would abolish Personal Allowance altogether and require all earners to fill in an Annual Tax Return. There is a lot of debate about strivers and scroungers but no evidence of the extent of either.

I would introduce a 5%, 10%, 15%, 25% and a 35% Income Tax Rate in addition to the current 20% and 40% rates.

I came across a client whose turnover was £100,000. He was declaring a turnover of £50,000. He employed two persons paying them £15,000 each in cash, No PAYE, no NIC. These two employees were claiming unemployment benefits.

In another case, £1 million dividend was extracted from a liquidated company that was implicated in the famous mobile phone Vat carousel fraud of £652 million.

Nagindas Khajuria FCCA
Simplification Made Simple, Chartered Certified Accountants, London

2013
Public mood is changing

The key issues on which the 2015 elections will be lost or won are welfare benefits, NHS, halfway house EU membership and Immigration. They are all irrelevant. We have always muddled through them. We do not know any better.

Three years ago, I remember Harriet Harmen coming to my table at a Labour Party dinner after I had responded to a question that was raised on the floor. Chuck Umunna was sitting at the next table. I did speak at length with him also.

I was discussing with her the chronic UK trade deficit problem for decades. She said my ideas made sense and she would ask the Labour Party Economic Policy Unit to contact me. That never happened.

The Tory Party has dramatised EU working time directive of 48 hours per week, patient treatment short comings in 10 out of 400 NHS hospitals and the case were six children were murdered to sway public mood in their favour re welfare, NHS and EU membership reforms. Tory reforms are all dog's breakfast.

Labour Party can turn the table and beat the Tories at their own game by fighting the next general election on one issue, repeat, one issue only.

"If we are elected, we shall recommend joining Euro currency. We have no comments on any other issue".

They could lose the next general election but would win the following five general elections. Only 18 countries working as a team using a single currency would create genuine economic growth.

2013
Poverty in the UK

Average national wage is discussed often enough; however, "average wealth" hardly crops up in the nation's debate.

A Treasury Report, published in 1999, concluded that 12 million people in the UK were in poverty.

In various ways figures for income alone under-estimate the degree of inequality in British society.

Income can be "original"; "disposable"; and "final".

Distribution of original, disposable and final household income, 1998–99 [As a percentage of the average income of all households) was as follows respectively:

Original Income: Bottom Fifth 14%, Next Fifth 35%; Middle Fifth 79%; Next Fifth 128%; and Top Fifth 245% of average income.

Disposable Income: Bottom Fifth 36%; Next Fifth 56%; Middle Fifth 85%; Next Fifth 119% and Top Fifth 206% of average income.

Final Income: Bottom Fifth 48%; Next Fifth 62%; Middle Fifth 86%; Next Fifth 111%; and Top Fifth 193% of average income.

The wealthiest top 1% owned 23%; the top 10% secured 56% of wealth; and the top 50% owned 94% of total wealth.

Thus the remaining 50% of households, or 12 million households, owned 6% of the nation's total wealth.

England extended its territory by military conquest of Wales and Ireland and unification with Scotland. The English State became Great Britain in 1707 and United Kingdom in 1801.

The Act of Union in 1707 united the two Parliaments. It allowed the Scots to run many of their own institutions, including their legal system, their church and their schools.

Nagindas Khajuria FCCA
Simplification Made Simple, Chartered Certified Accountants, London

2013

Monarchy Parliament Civil Society Landed Gentry and Working Class

Let us turn the clock back 798 years.

June 1215 Runnymede: rebellious barons imposed Magna Carta [The "Great Charter"] on King John of England, designed to prohibit arbitrary royal acts by declaring a body of defined law and custom comprising 63 clauses.

1649: Charles I, reigned 23 years, executed, aged 48.

December 1688: James II, reigned 3 years: reign ended with flight from kingdom. Parliament's powers rising: Monarch's powers waning.

17th century: British white settlement and conquest in North America and the Caribbean.

1757–1857: extensive conquest of India; acquisition of islands, trading posts and strategic positions from Aden to Hong Kong; white settlement in Canada, Australia, New Zealand and the Cape in South Africa.

19th century: Britain becomes greatest industrial and commercial power—territories that Britain did not rule but fell under her influence: dependant territories in Africa; parts of South America, the Middle East, the Persian Gulf and China. After WWI, Britain could not control such an extensive empire. For 300 years, Britain had enjoyed world sea power, kept France and Germany at bay; however, it gave way to USA to become the new world power.

Britain was at its best when it was closely linked to its Empire and in the last century as a junior partner with USA.

2013: Britain is 23rd in U.N. human index classification. Its long term future is to be a key member of the Euro currency block of 17 advanced nations.

Nagindas Khajuria FCCA
Simplification Made Simple, Chartered Certified Accountants, London

2013 London needs a more visionary town planner

Shree Navinbhai Shah's article "Future Growth of London" [AV 11 May p3] was timely.

The Mayor has invited several experts to advise him as how best to plan additional housing, schooling, medical care, child care, etc for further increases in the population of London. Namely Roger Tym & Partners, Catriona Riddell Associates, Martin Simons, Martin Crookston, Dr Nicholas Falk and John Hollis.

The Inner London population has been around 3 million since 1961. The Outer London has been around 4.8 million if one includes 0.3 illegal immigrants. Total 7.8 million.

According to the 2011 census, total London population shot up to Inner London 3.2 million and Outer London 5.3 million. Total 8.5 million.

My view as a Londoner (1967–2013) is that we should formulate a long term plan to reduce London population back to 7.8 million by 2036. The city has reached it's optimum capacity.

Economic laws of diminishing returns and tail end developments will set in.

Half of London's commercial and residential properties are ugly, dilapidated, discoloured and in need of internal and external redecorating, double glazing, roof and gutters repairs, etc. The Mayor should plan to uplift all these properties rather than build new even if it means government grants and/or long term soft loans. Millions of cars parked in narrow streets and roads are jamming free flow of vital traffic.

We could move the seat of Parliament to Birmingham and the City of London Financial Centre to Manchester respectively or build two new cities up North. Both these groups would then be spurred into new ways of thinking.

Nagindas Khajuria FCCA
Simplification Made Simple, Chartered Certified Accountants, London

2013
The New Tory Party

David Cameroon, if he wins the 2015 General Election, has decided to pass legislation to hold an in or out referendum in 2017 as regards European Union Membership depending on his renegotiation of terms as if was like making instant coffee.

Rome was not built in a day. Nor was the European Union. Neither was the Tory Party.

The name Tory was taken from 17th century Irish outlaws who plundered and killed English settlers (Irish 'toraidhe' outlaw, highwayman). Lord Liverpool adopted the title 'Tory' when he became Prime Minister in early 19th century.

Toryism developed into Conservatism under Sir Robert Peel, Prime Minister (1834–35 and 1841–46).

Then the Conservatives were in power for long periods 1886–1905, and 1922–45. More recently out of the last 63 years, they have been in power for 40 years 1951–64, 1970–74 (under Heath), 1979–1997 (under Thatcher and Major).

In his Emergency Budget, George Osbourne, decided in June 2010 that as they were not going to join the Euro currency during their 5-year term, he was closing down that research department within Treasury.

UK joined what is now the European Union in 1973. Neither the Tory Party, nor the public who are also Tories have been able to figure out whether membership benefits exceed costs, or vice versa, for 40 years. How is it possible to get this done in 4 years?

Both decisions were selfish.

2013
Significant developments of the 20th century

The two most significant developments of the 20th century were the Internet and the Euro (1).

The European Union evolved through the signing of various treaties. The dictionary defines "treaty" as a formal agreement between states. If the UK opts out of the common market in 2017, it will end up as a Turkish corner shop.

Treaties were negotiated and signed by the representatives of the Member States, ratified by the national parliaments and approved by the European Parliament.

Ministers from Belgium, Luxembourg, Italy, France, Germany and Netherlands met in Paris on 18 April 1951 and signed the Treaty of Paris to form a common market in coal and steel.

Six years later ministers met in Rome on 25 March 1957 to sign the Treaty of Rome to form the European Economic Community - EEC.

UK, Ireland and Denmark joined in 1973; Greece in 1981; Spain and Portugal in 1986.

The European Single Act was signed in the Netherlands on 17 and 28 February 1986 to define qualified majority voting; legal relationship between the Council and the European Parliament; and foreign policy cooperation.

Six years on, The Maastricht Treaty or the Treaty of European Union was signed on 7 February 1992 in Maastricht, Netherlands, to form the European Union; the Economic and Monetary Union; Police and judicial cooperation in criminal matters [JHA]; the concept of European citizenship being superior to national citizenship; and EEC became EC.

The Treaty of Amsterdam (1997); Treaty of Nice (2001) and the Lisbon Treaty (2007) followed.

2013

The Good Maharaja: a tale of compassion and humanity

Your editorial about some 5 000 Polish children arriving in Jamnagar in 1942 as refugees reminded me of the exhibition of Stephan Norblin, a Polish artist's works, at the National Gallery of Modern Art in Mumbai.

Stephan Norblin, a Polish artist and his wife were welcomed as refugees in India. He was an eminent painter, illustrator and designer. A master of many arts: drawings and illustrations; posters; portraits; stage and costume design.

In 1941, the Norblins arrived in India where until 1943 the artist created portraits and murals for the New Palace of Maharaja of Morvi. The portraits faithfully reproduced the visages of the subjects, emphasizing their exalted status and depicting the richness of national costumes festooned with jewels. He also painted large murals in the Palace, inspired by Hindu mythology, but also incorporating genre, zoomorphic and floral themes, skilfully combined characteristics of local Indian art newly discovered by the artist—colourfulness, horror vacui, density of motifs, flatness and linearity—with the style of European Art Deco—synthesis, geometric rhythm, monumentalism, decoration and a refined-eroticism which unified the two styles.

His most famous creation followed: the huge murals, paintings on canvas and interior designs, and furniture commissioned by the Maharaja Umaid Singh for his monumental Umaid Bhawan Palace in Jodhpur, Rajasthan.

I am currently attending arts classes at The Institute Arts Centre. My subjects are drawing, painting, life drawing, sculpture, ceramics, digital art, history of modern art and calligraphy.

Nagindas Khajuria FCCA
Simplification Made Simple, Chartered Certified Accountants, London

2013
Asian food

Last Friday afternoon I called my GP and 1 asked her to send me to RFH as I was very poorly.

The treatment at the hospital has improved tremendously. Even though it was weekend, various tests were done promptly and there was full coverage of doctors and consultants both on Saturday and Sunday.

Thus my clinical treatment and management has been excellent.

However the so called Asian vegetarian food is included here under the banner of Asian Halal. The meals I am served are frozen and expire on 18 May 2014, They are full of preservatives, tasteless and with zero nutritional value.

I ask readers to campaign for better hospital food for British Asians. This has been the case for ten years.

Nagindas Khajuria FCCA
Simplification Made Simple, Chartered Certified Accountants, London

2013 Fiscal Budget

The Fiscal Budget is likely to be £745 billion in 2015.

To continue to now play the world policeman role, spending billions on futile wars, profiting from export of armaments, having journalists and informers in virtually every country while its own population's sixty percent need welfare top ups to survive implies delusion for grandeur. Charity begins at home. New thinking is urgently required.

Cut out the above unnecessary meddling rather than destroy the quality of life of millions of own citizens.

Low interest rates from 4 December 2008 of 2%; 1.5% from 8 January 2009; 1% from 5 February 2009 and 0.5% from 5 March 2009 have not created any additional economic growth whatsoever.

Money is a commodity like any other. It has an annual value. Historically for decades it has been about 5% per annum base rate. Quantitative easing and printing money is deceiving the world's financial system.

It is high time base rates are gradually increased to reflect the real fundamentals. We continue to have unsustainable fiscal deficits, weak growth and negative real returns.

QE has increased pension funds deficits; lowered annuity rates; reduced current and expected future incomes and redistributed income and wealth towards the wealthiest and most indebted groups.

The hype and hoo-hah about the welfare budget being £220 billion is also misleading. £110 billion are paid by 25 million PAYE employees in National Insurance Contributions that entitle them to return of their own savings in State Pension, Jobseekers Allowance, SSP, Maternity Pay, NHS medical treatment, etc.

Nagindas Khajuria FCCA
Simplification Made Simple, Chartered Certified Accountants, London

2013

Does BPJ need to rethink its policy on Andhra Pradesh?

Andhra Pradesh can be neatly divided into three zones: 9 districts forming the coastal region (Andhra Pradesh region); 4 districts forming the interior region (Rayalseema region); and 9 districts adjoining Hyderabad forming the Telengana region.

Barring Hyderabad, Rayalseema and Telengana regions have inferior social and physical infrastructure.

The "Telengana region" has uplifted the state as a cyber hi-tech state. Firms registered as Software Technology Parks at 1,345 is second only to Maharashtra. It has the largest number of arts, science, commerce, engineering, technical and architecture colleges. It is definitely a Knowledge State, a growing haven for students from around the world.

"Andhra Pradesh" has a thriving port infrastructure—13 major and minor ports with Vishakapatnam being the second biggest port, handling the largest tonnage in India. This region has the third largest power generation and the highest hydel power generation in the country.

The State remains predominantly agrarian with more than 60% of population dependant on this sector. Fertile land and water have assured a surplus good grain production with high yields, and ground nuts, tobacco, cotton, castor and sugar cane are major crops.

Major industries are IT, auto components, horticulture, poultry, pharmaceuticals and textiles.

However, drawbacks are too many to list [www.phdcci.in].

United the strong parts would uplift the weaker parts; divided could create lower GDP growth overall long-term.

Finally, united the State would have an interdependent economy of industry, IT, agriculture and exports.

Nagindas Khajuria FCCA
Simplification Made Simple, Chartered Certified Accountants, London

2013
Secularism & Politics

The Congress Party and its allies as well as foreign countries who support their coalition to win in the next General Election in India have began to use the "Secularism Card" to discredit the BJP and its allies as Hindu-centric and not secular.

The Pears' Cyclopaedia 2010–11 and 2001–2002 editions described Hinduism under paragraphs J26 as below: "A militant political Hinduism is threatening the cohesion of India, fanned by Bhartiya Janata Group (BJP), which extols Hindu fundamentalism."

Hindus are by far more liberal and tolerant towards Christians and Muslims than the other way round.

I hope Indians will not fall into this trap of the secular card when they vote in the next General Election.

Narendra Modi does strike me as someone who is clean from corruption, economically more competent than his rivals, highly disciplined and even somewhat authoritarian. But India does need someone who is determined, visionary, practical, pragmatic and sufficiently autocratic to drive through change in Judiciary, Governance, Police, Black Economy, Inequality, etc.

The Economic Times of India as well as Amartya Sen recently showed less confidence in Narendra Modi. I believe they both have been mislead by the wrong propaganda rather than substance of Narendra Modi, or Hindus or Hinduism.

Authors of such publications as above should be sued for blasphemy and malicious labelling of Hindus (about 800,000 worldwide) and/or the BPJ Party as a party of fundamentalists. If Hindus are fundamentalists, then I could say Muslims are fanatics and Christians bigots.

Nagindas Khajuria FCCA
Simplification Made Simple, Chartered Certified Accountants, London

2013
Britain is no longer a country of choice for immigrants

Of the 6 billion world population, only about 200 million people across the world live in a different country than the one they were born in, be it for economic reasons, personal reasons, moving for love or family—or to flee war or prosecution. It is a mere 3.33%.

The top emigrant countries are China 8.3 million [.6%]; India 11.4 million [1%]; Mexico 11.9 million [10.5%]; Russian Federation 11 million [8%] and Ukraine 6.6 million [14.4%].

The top migrant destinations are Canada 7.2 million [21.3%]; Germany 10.8 million [13.2%]; Russian Federation 12 3 million [8.8%]; Saudi Arabia 7.3 million [28.3%] and USA 42.8 million [13 8%].

The percentages relate to the relevant country's own population. Britain has 6.9 million foreign born residents [11.5%].

Labour's idea of three types of ID cards was very practical: national, EU national and non-EU national. They had already spent £1 billion designing and piloting that project. The Coalition dropped that idea. ID cards are ideal.

There are 100 countries round the world which have a compulsory ID card system including Germany, Belgium and Spain. India, with its population of 1.3 billion, is planning to introduce cyber-age biometric ID cards.

Stamping the Passports of the six countries subject to £3,000 bond upon arrival and upon departure is another better way to monitor immigration.

Conservative's actions to target illegal immigrants more aggressively is to win the next Election. NHS scare stories are again designed to win the next Election.

Nagindas Khajuria FCCA
Simplification Made Simple. Chartered Certified Accountants, London

2013
Help to Buy or Help to Cry?

I am writing about Help to Cry. I am sorry to give your predecessor Chancellor's H.T.B. stimulus plan H.T.C.

In 2013, house prices were nearly five times average earnings. By 2016, it was clear that housing was less affordable as prices had increased to six times average earnings. The state then was too scared of voters to scrap the program. You asked me when the Financial Policy Committee would recommend that we bury the H.T.B. The short answer is: we can't.

The rise in prices has created such an affordability gulf that withdrawing subsidised mortgages would lock a large chunk of the population out of the market. It would have been better back in 2013 to encourage borrowers to use low interest rates to keep paying off their debt, as they were doing until H.T.B. arrived. Now, the economy is perilously over indebted. Any interest shock could force the government to prop up the banks. The markets will turn on us. The only solutions would be a vast money printing exercise—again.

What Britain needs is the 1970s' plan to build 300,000 to 400,000 houses every year.

(Adapted from International Herald Tribune, 19 August 13 pl6 by Charlotte Hogg, Governor of Bank of England)

Nagindas Khajuria FCCA
Simplification Made Simple, Chartered Certified Accountants, London

2013
German traditions compared to British

Two-third of Germany's industry is owned by small and medium sized family businesses. In the UK, it is one third. Two third is owned by multinationals in the UK encouraging employee culture.

German mothers stay at home at least three years after every child is born so that right from birth, the child is brought up with more love, kindness and attention compared to childminder; in the UK mothers go to work after six months because of tax incentives and/or mentality that demeans housework.

Germans start work on average 20 minutes earlier than the British. All routine chores, personal hygiene, studies and paid work are all timed in a 24-hour day.

Manufacturing is regarded very highly. 50% of German students join apprentice training in industry. In the UK, it is less than 25%. Many of the others follow wishy washy university degrees and become unemployable after graduating.

Two third of Germans live in rented accommodation during life time. In Britain, it is one third. Average German owes £30,000. Average Briton £68,000.

German Company Law requires a workers' representative in the executive management of the firm. Employees are valued far more than in the UK.

No matter what party comes to power in 2015, unless there is a cultural reversal of British traditions, the UK economy will remain in doldrums.

2013

Should use of chemical weapons be a game change?

Chemical and biological weapons were used in World War I, World War II and Vietnam War in recent history.

The fundamentals have not changed in Syria. There is a coercive dictatorial regime in Syria that has been suppressing several substantial groups which may not be united but are all opposed to the current regime. But so are many other Arab countries. At least they are stable with less killings than otherwise.

The West should not invade in any manner or form without Russia and China agreeing to their plan of action in the UN Security Council.

Unless the intention is to continue to get practical experience of modem warfare with modern weapons on real live people. No other end game would be achievable.

The West invaded Iraq and 65,000 innocent Iraqis were killed. It invaded Afghanistan and tens of thousands died there including Talibans they wanted to cleanse ethnically. Now it is recommending reconciliation with Talibans.

In Lybia, oil production is down to less than half and the country is no longer stable. There is a blood bath in Egypt also. But that is ignored because it is not close to the Middle East oil fields.

United Nations Resolutions and International Laws are two sides of the same coin. The more advanced a nation is, the more respect it should have for both.

2013 Accountancy news

Last Friday I had the honour and pleasure of meeting two of the most prominent Gujarati accountants and learn about their future plans: Sri D Desai and Sri Shailesh Haribhakti. They had come for a few days to EU and UK for meetings with current and potential MNC clients.

Kolkota's Dilip B. Desai Group and Mumbai's Haribhakti Group entered into a strategic alliance on 13 May 2013. It was a historic moment of coming together of two reputed Chartered Accountancy firms in the field of Indian Auditing, Taxation, Corporate Advisory and Accountancy. Their merged group is now called Desai Haribhakti Consultants India. The Group has a team of more than 1300 professionals with 80 partners and directors in 17 offices, with pan India and cross border presence with the best of the corporate houses as their clients.

DHC was appointed by the Government of India as Statutory Auditors to the Reserve Bank of India. It is now the biggest domestic accountancy firm. Both Sri Desai and Sri Haribhakti senior were gold medallists in their CA final exams. Their two books: Taxation of non-residents Indians and Bank Audits may be of interest to readers. So may be this news to those young British Indian students who may want to train under them. Their industry sector knowledge makes them surpass The Big Four when it comes to Indian Businesses who want to expand in India and/or overseas.

Nagindas Khajuria FCCA
Simplification Made Simple, Chartered Certified Accountants, London

2013
Syria reminds me of King Asoka and Kautalya

In the 3rd century BC King Asoka argued against intolerance and in favour of understanding that even when one social or religious sect of people find themselves opposed to other ones, 'other sects should be duly honoured in every way on all occasions'.

He went on to say: 'he who does reverence to his own sect while disparaging the sects of others wholly from attachment to his own sect, in reality, inflicts, by such conduct, the severest injury to his own sect'.

Asoka strongly believed in promoting voluntary good behaviour without the use of force and promoted such ideas through inscriptions throughout India.

On the other hand, Kautilya, who was the principal advisor to Asoka's grandfather Chandragupta (the Mauryan emperor who established the dynasty and was the first king to rule over nearly all of India) and author of the celebrated 4th century BC treatise Arthashastra (broadly translatable as 'Politics and Economies'), put his emphasis on building up and making use of institutions, rules, restrictions and prohibitions as major contributors to good behaviour.

Modern Western philosophy on fairness and justice is broadly the latter while for a better definition of justice it is important to give more emphasis as to how people behave in real life.

The aim should not just be to prevent injustice, it should also be to enhance justice. Here US and France's proposal to fire surface to air ballistic (SAM) missiles and air to surface guided (ASM) missiles fails totally.

Nagindas Khajuria FCCA
Simplification Made Simple, Chartered Certified Accountants, London

2013
Evolution of the British Legal System (part one)

It is highly respected in the UK as well as in many parts of the world. It is enshrined in the British Constitution which has two constitutional functions: a description of how we are governed and a prescriptive account of how we ought to be governed.

It started with the Magna Carta, now coming up for its 800th anniversary and due for another appraisal. The 1689 Bill of Rights established the Crown-in-Parliament as the supreme authority of the state.

On the other hand, the 1653 Instrument of Government installed the Crown as the lord protector or head of state who could not however alter, suspend, abrogate or repeal laws or introduce or raise taxes without the approval if parliament.

The Crown was supposed to delegate his judicial authority to the judges and devolve his administrative authority to parliamentary ministers, subordinate to parliament. In return, the state undertook all the three core functions in the monarch's name.

Blackstone in the 18th century assured three institutions: Parliament for the redress of grievances; jury trial for the protection of the innocent; and habeas corpus for the restriction of state power.

Dicey in the 19th century encapsulated the entire system as "rule of law", derived from the rights of individuals, guaranteeing those rights by equal application of the same law to everyone from the Prime Minister to the postman.

By the end of the 20th century, the tripartite system of powers: legislature, judiciary and executive was not working well.

Nagindas Khajuria FCCA
Simplification Made Simple, Chartered Certified Accountants, London

2013

Evolution of the British Legal System (part two)

The independence of the judiciary (courts) from the executive (ministers) and the legislature (parliament) was compromised when a politician was appointed with both hats: The Lord Chancellor and Minister of Justice in 2012. This is the first time a non-lawyer has been appointed since mid-17th century.

This new Minister published a consultation paper in April 2013 to drastically reform the Legal Aid system. The responses will be published this autumn.

The reforms will starve claimants of legal aid on several fronts: lawful residence' or 'strong connection test'; access to justice for prisoners; and much more widely for judicial review claims (in which much of the cost is incurred in early stages), unless and until the judge gives a go ahead.

Access to justice remains a pillar of our constitutional law. The reforms will mean only those who can afford legal fees would have access to justice. 40% of cases brought in 2011 under Legal aid were successful (144 out of 356).

Indeed by contrast to the Minister's Legal Aid reform consultation paper, 145 barristers who are members of the attorney-general's panels and who argue cases on behalf of the central state have written to the Minister: 'We consider that the LA reforms will undermine the accountability of public bodies to the detriment of society as a whole and the vulnerable in particular'.

What fails in UK Courts can succeed in Strasbourg under the European Convention on Human Rights as happened in a phone-tapping case where UK law was silent either way. (The British Constitution by Martin Loughlin).

2013 Buying a house

Apart from paying the deposit of 40% say on a residential property of £200,000, one has to make a monthly mortgage payment of say £700 on an interest and capital repayment basis.

In poor households (about 6 million), one spouse earns £18,000 a year with effective tax NI burden of 24.25% and net monthly pay of £1,254.81; and the other spouse part time, earns £9,000 per year (tax burden 3.67%) and net monthly pay of £737.48. Combined say £2,000.

In lower middle class families (a further 6 million) one spouse £27,000, tax & NI burden 31.43%, net monthly pay £1,764.81; the other £18,000 per year, net monthly pay £1,254.81. Combined say £3,000.

There is no way these two groups (50% of population) can afford to pay the monthly mortgage repayment even on the cheapest low specifications new built or old residential property. They simply would not have savings for the other 20% deposit, nor a monthly surplus to repay the mortgage. If the salary were £36,000, tax & NI burden is 35.02%; £72,000 37.80%, £144,000 38.73% and £288,000 39.19% respectively. Net monthly pay £2,275; £4,470; £8,920 and £17,820 respectively. These two groups probably also own several buy to let properties. They will take advantage of the housing subsidy.

Mr Cameron should scrap the entire housing subsidy project urgently. He should also introduce a progressive system of taxation prevailing in other countries: 5, 10, 15, 20, 25, 30, 35 and 40% in income bands; not just 20 and 40% which is a regressive system.

Nagindas Khajuria FCCA
Simplification Made Simple, Chartered Certified Accountants, London

2013
Narendra Modi as a manager rather than a leader

In politics, as well in big business, there is a culture of glorifying the influence of the Prime Minister, or PM designate, or CEO of a multinational business, as the sole or prime motivator behind success or failure of a country or a company.

UK prime ministers have up to 40 personally appointed advisors from tax payer's money on top of 14 cabinet ministers and 14 civil service first secretaries behind the scenes.

India is a vast country with diverse demographics and 1.27 billion people to manage, Narendra Modi should from now begin the process of selecting and nominating his key team of 23 cabinet ministers with 23 portfolios. It is best not to appoint advisors at all and waste tax payer's money. They generally conflict with civil servants and/or cabmet ministers. It is better to lead, inspire, manage, train and empower the latter two groups only.

It should be his official team, rather than just himself, that he should present to the Indian nation, to manage this complex country with huge problems in so many areas as no one individual can manage them all on his own.

Such a move will also put brakes on the harmful envy that may be created all round if Narendra Modi becomes too popular as a single individual to his own detriment.

A leader has to show from now that not only he is a good leader nationally, but also a good manager/delegator with inter-personal and human resource skills who can pick up a corruption free team that would work harmoniously, effectively and fast if the people of India gave the team the mandate to do so in 2014.

Nagindas Khajuria FCCA
Simplification Made Simple, Chartered Certified Accountants, London

2013
John Fitzgerald Kennedy's legacy

On Thursday, 22 November 1963, I was on the third floor of the seven storey American Embassy building in Khartoum, Sudan. I was an employee there from 1960 to 1967.

I was told of the assassination of the 35th President within minutes.

He graduated from Harvard in 1940 and same year he published "Why England Slept", a best selling analysis of Great Britain's unpreparedness for war. He then served as a torpedo boat commander in the Pacific and was decorated for his courageous conduct when the boat was hit and sunk.

In 1946 he was elected as a Democrat in the House of Representatives. In 1952 he won a Senate seat. He married in 1953.

In 1960, he defeated Richard Nixon by a narrow margin in the popular vote, and became the first Catholic, and at 43 the youngest person to be elected president.

His aim was to introduce civil rights, medical care for the elderly and space program by legislation. He supported desegregation in schools and universities.

He faced a series of foreign policy crisis: unsuccessful invasion of Cuba, building of Berlin Wall, the Cuban Missile crisis and Vietnam War.

In the Vietnam war, ground troops increased to 16,000; but he was skeptical about that and wanted to find an alternative to ground troops. That may have been contrary to what the military wanted. Lyndon Baines Johnson who took over increased ground troops to 400,000.

Of the many conspiracy theories, the Vietnam War stands out as history tells us that some Generals regularly exceeded their powers during those dreadful 12 years of warfare in Vietnam.

Nagindas Khajuria FCCA
Simplification Made Simple, Chartered Certified Accountants, London

2013
Boris Johnson's speech by Kevin Khajuria

The title of the speech was "What would Maggie do today?" when he gave this speech at the Centre for Policy Studies on 28 November 2013.

He went on to praise her for many of her achievements. However, there were mistakes too. Utility companies should not have been privatised. Boris says if she were alive today, she would bring back 75,000 assisted places.

Education results in reading, maths and science among 65 advanced nations to be announced next Tuesday will show that UK has gone down even further in the past four years. For 100 years private schools have enjoyed lion's share of all education funding and charitable donations.

Many public owned companies were privatised at below true value, losing the public purse billions. Burma Oil should not have been sold. Today, it would have been a major source of lower cost energy. Travelling by car is much cheaper than travelling by tube or train now. Off shoring of manufacturing plants should not have happened.

Boris speaks about 16% having IQ below 85. IQ stands for Intelligence Quotient. The score of an IQ test equals mental age divided by biological age. Intelligence is mental flexibility, whereas knowledge and skills can be acquired by life experience, through parents, teachers, employers, etc. and accumulated over life course. Sub-categories of ability are verbal and non-verbal intelligence.

Psychometric test measures intelligence, abilities, personality and mood states.

Boris's way of judging people was very crude and contentious. His ideology that greed is good is not what we want to teach our children. Education can and should uplift those below IQ of 85, may be in other fields such as sports, arts, vocational qualifications, etc.

It should also be in a what you know society, not a who you know society.

2013
A tribute to Nelson Mandela

We witnessed two opposing ideologies in the twentieth century: nationalism and internationalism.

The founding fathers of the European Union believed in internationalism and over 65 years have developed a strong supra-national semi-political semi-economic unit. UK on the other hand has remained more nationalistic and isolationist. India split up from one nation to three nations.

South Africans moved from being dependent to independent and now to interdependent. What I found most hypocritical is that while Western countries boasted about their belief in liberty, equality and freedom over the entire century, they accepted the laws of Apartheid in one of their colonies up to and as recent as 1994. Yes 1994.

"The South African Nationalist Party won the South African General Election in 1948. Voting excluded 80% of the population, and this continued until 1994. They won on a blatant racist card—they promised to keep 'the Natives', black persons, in their place. And they meant it" (Archbishop Desmond Tutu in Tribute from D.T. in "Mandela": a book by Peter Hain, senior Labour politician).

These Western nations are pouring in verbal praise of the highest degree. But the same people are also violating international law in other countries. Just study around the mess in which Libya, Iraq, Egypt, Syria, Afghanistan, the three Congo countries, and many other countries are.

Deeds are stronger than words. Only if Mandela's death changes the Western nations' foreign policy of frequent military interventions more for their own national interests will his legacy have a lasting influence.

Just visit any public toilet at airport, museum, five star hotel, etc, in any Western advanced country, you will see a black person cleaning it.

Nagindas Khajuria FCCA
Simplification Made Simple, Chartered Certified Accountants, London

2013

PM Cameroon, cap in hand, in China

CB's article (as I see it, 7 Dec 2013, p8) rightly makes the point that Mr Cameron insisted on human rights redress in Sri Lanka, but ignored the issue in China despite the fact that there were human rights issues in China in general and Tibet in particular.

Money has become the new Christ in many human endeavours. So one is not surprised. India, they say is the most spiritual of all countries. However, while they are praying in their temples, etc., China is forging ahead at full speed.

60 years ago, five Indian industrialists went cap in hand to General Electric in USA. The result today is that India has become a world leader in IT and Communications. Now it is time to go to 100+ countries with a cap in hand and ask them to teach us how to manufacture electronic goods such as computers, mobile phones, cameras, TVs, DVDs, tablets, etc., how to package them with leaflets in 10+ languages etc. in the most professional and attractive manner; and start manufacturing those as well other simple goods, but packaged professionally.

Yesterday day I saw a high value Philips DVD in Tesco manufactured in Turkey and three BIC biro pens in a superb gift package licensed by BIC in France and manufactured in Estonia.

There has been a world wide technology transfer between North and South American continents, Far East, China, Europe, Russia and former USSR countries in electronic goods manufacturing over 50 year. The Indian subcontinent, Africa and Middle East have been left out. By hook or crook, the latter three groups will have to break that mould.

Nagindas Khajuria FCCA
Simplification Made Simple, Chartered Certified Accountants, London

2014
Tax evasion: Sounds familiar?

Since the pro-business Tory party won the general election in May 2010, they have concentrated on benefit cheats and welfare benefits cuts like a blood hound; but they have not shown the zeal of even a watch dog as far as tax avoidance, tax evasion and tax fraud is concerned.

The benefit cheats evade tax but so do many small businesses and several medium and large businesses who use dubious ways, non-domicile rules, off shore accounts, transfer pricing, money laundering, fraud, deliberate under declaration of income, etc to pay no tax or little tax. When a pro-business political party becomes the party of government, their loyalties should change from pro-business to being neutral to business and anti-business when it is obvious that a vast number of businesses and another substantial percentage of high net worth individuals pay far less tax than the correct amount of tax due on the correct amount of income earned.

I believe the £10,000 personal allowance should be abolished and even the poorest should pay some tax, say 1% on the first £1 to £10,000 income band. So there is an accurate picture of every one of the 22 million households cumulative earnings and wealth accumulation during their life time.

My Xmas message is that there is an urgent need for taxation policies that redistribute accumulated wealth and a more progressive taxation system to ensure that one full time wage and one part wage is sufficient to maintain a decent standard of living, supplemented by welfare benefits where needed. A work life balance is fundamental to keep the mind and body happy in a warm home.

Keeping people employed is more important than keeping triple A credit rating.

Nagindas Khajuria FCCA
Simplification Made Simple, Chartered Certified Accountants, London

2014
India taxes reform debate

Sunday evening's debate on NDTV was about proposals for taxation reform by BJP and now more generally by experts and other parties in India.

As a percentage of total tax receipts in 2011–12, Corporation Tax accounted for 34%; Income Tax 18%; Import Duties 15%; Excise Duties 13%; Service Tax 11%; Education Cess 2% and other taxes 7% of total INR 90bn tax revenue. Total tax burden is very low at 8% of GDP (UK is 38% of GDP).

Abolishing or reducing taxes may not be a good idea. A simpler more progressive system of taxation is desirable. AAP is already arguing for this.

I believe the black economy is a very large part of the Indian economy. The "cake" is not distributed equitably. Basically there is an India of haves and another of have-nots.

There is now a momentum to combat corruption. Surely combating tax evasion should be a part of this reform. One idea could be inclusion of private drawings and personal profit and loss and balance sheet in Tax Returns. A mismatch between declared income and private drawings often implies tax evasion.

I was told in Mumbai that when a new model of Mercedes comes in town, Senior Tax Inspector telephones a client: "new Model of Mercedes has come". Next day the Mercedes would be delivered at his home. So Tax Inspectors need to make returns of private drawing as well.

Tax reform could improve education, healthcare and life of the have-nots.

Nagindas Khajuria FCCA
Simplification Made Simple, Chartered Certified Accountants, London

2014
Sugar produces salt in the body

High blood pressure, diabetes, kidney disease and heart failures are far more common in BME communities than white people. American Society of Nephrology recently presented their findings at the annual meeting that "high fructose corn syrup causes salt to be reabsorbed in the body and that can lead to high blood pressure. High corn syrup is a sweetener which is common in almost every product including fizzy drinks. It can raise the risk of proteinuria – a medical term used when the kidney filters begin to fail and allow high amount of protein to be excreted in the urine.

Fizzy drinks have no nutritional value. They also cause obesity, type 2 diabetes, osteoporosis and more. High blood pressure and kidney disease are linked in a vicious circle. Eliminating acidic foods, meat and wheat flour products and replacing them with plenty of fruit and vegetable have a profound effect on kidney health caused by high blood pressure. Eating alkaline foods could help slow down the progression of kidney disease (summarised from Kidney Patient Newsletter article at Royal Free Hospital waiting room January 2014). The same hospital sell fizzy drinks!

World Health Organization is considering recommending 5% of daily energy intake in the form of sugar instead 10%. In UK the recommended intake is 11%. The head of sugar intake government advisor is also a paid advisor to Coca Cola and Mars corporations. Ironic? Yes. Unethical? Yes.

Nagindas Khajuria FCCA
Simplification Made Simple, Chartered Certified Accountants, London

2014

Blaming the Moguls or the British

Mr Ramesh Jhalla writes in his letter of 18 January that "later British ended Mogul dynastic rule and helped Hinduism to enter 20th century with dignity that was trampled by Moguls. Mr Burjor Avari disproves this statement by his letter of 25 January claiming that Indian share of world GDP remained the same during the Mogul era between 1500 and 1700 at 24.4%.

Here I agree with Mr B Avari. However, when Indian share of world GDP is compared with Western Europe, I am not convinced that comparing the whole of Western Europe is synonymous with comparing Britain with India. Thus here Mr B Avari's presentation of statistical data is misleading.

Taking these statistics between 1820 and 1950 further, while India's share decreased from 16.0 percent to 4.2 percent or 11.8 percentage points, China's share went down from 32.9 percent to 4.6 percent or 28.3 percentage points. China was not ruled by the British then.

During the same period, Western Europe's world share went up by only 3.2 percentage points and North America's by a staggering 28.7 percentage points. So "our good old British friends could not have trampled India's dignity" (Mr Avari's statement).

Finally, to present statistics that do not add up to 100% is also misleading.

To my mind, both the Moguls and the British have enriched India's cultural heritage, religious diversity, dynamism and the links India now has with the entire world including the British and the Christian and Muslim world.

Nagindas Khajuria FCCA
Simplification Made Simple, Chartered Certified Accountants, London

2014 Darfur crisis

I blame super powers to have split Sudan into two countries and for the recent bloodshed. I attended the independence celebrations in the Prime Minister Ismail Azahari's home in 1956. I visited Wau in South Sudan in 1958 during my summer holidays. The Dinka and other tribes in the town did not wear any clothes. The West has been wrongly accusing the Arab North of ill treating the Christian South.

There were tribal wars in the South since 1956. The West did not bother until oil was produced in 1979. Division has made both North and South poorer. The Darfur crisis that preceded the separation was a West sponsored fabrication of facts for access to oil.

2014 The heart of the matter

I read the article on pages 74 and 75 of the Accounting and Business, March 2014 ACCA Monthly Magazine on NHS finance called "The heart of the matter".

The government has appointed six directors, one each, from NHS England; Department of Health; Healthcare Financial Management Association; NHS Monitor; NHS Trust Development Authority and Health Education, England. This new Council will work with clinicians to tackle a possible funding gap of £30 billion by 2020/21 based upon current model of care. The article writer states that this Council will work with value as well as cost.

Page 93 of HMRC 2008–09 Annual Accounts, paragraph 4.1 states that revenue from National Insurance Contributions was £98 billion. Cash paid to National Insurance Fund was £73.6 billion and to NHS £22.5 billion. [NIF funds State Pension]. Therefore the bulk of NHS funding comes from general taxation, NOT National Insurance Contributions. Consequently impossible to forecast.

Finance professionals are not competent to assess value. They need to concentrate on cost, cost and cost. Every patient that comes out of a GP appointment should be given a debit and credit real time invoice suggesting to him or her how much her consultation had cost NHS for that single event. Until that is implemented, all above initiatives are muddled, very costly and very bureaucratic quango attempts that do NOT go to "The heart of the matter".

Nagindas Khajuria FCCA
Simplification Made Simple, Chartered Certified Accountants, London

2014
Ukraine and the Crimean Region

The Times Leading article "Turning off the Gas" (8 March 2014 page 24) recommends that US increases it gas production from the shale (fracking) revolution there and all EU countries must speed up exploiting gas from fracking to turn off gas from Russia.

Gas is part of a very complex energy mix worldwide. About quarter each of gas is produced in North America, EU including Russia, Middle East and Asia respectively. Gas demand has doubled in the past ten years.

In Europe gas is traded at wholesale prices on virtual online platforms in London, Netherlands and Brussels. Natural Gas Front Monthly Average Prices were €31 to €23 megawatts per hour in the two years ending 2012 quoted in these platforms.

Platforms were: NBP (UK) [National Balancing Point]; TTF Netherlands [Title Transfer Facility] and EEX Brussels. [Source: page 28, Eon 2012 Annual Report].

Governments plan energy mix production policy on a long term basis. For example, Germany has banned nuclear production; France has banned fracking. Fracking will produce very little gas in densely populated countries which is most of Europe and may damage the substrata permanently.

Shale gas is very expensive compared to fossil fuels and has already damaged water reservoirs and habitat in the US even though US is not densely populated.

Crude oil, gas, coal and electricity are bought at wholesale prices in a truly live daily market.

Such ideas will damage US and EU more than Russia as Russia would sell their gas elsewhere.

2014 Pension planning

The age of 40 is when one needs to look back and look forward to plan for adequate pension income during retirement. The Pension Bill 2013 with major changes has been amended by the House of Lords and sent back to the House of Commons for final approval on 12 March 2014.

Currently 58% of the population have no private pension provision. Two thirds of the employed population earn below both the mean and the median average income. True, some of them and their employers are contributing towards their occupational pension schemes. The latter will not do badly forty years from now [Source: The Open University].

But for the rest, may be half the population, it will be hard to survive from State Pension only of £144 per week rising every year.

Those having high income can contribute towards pension provision and save 20% or 40% tax on these contributions up to £50,000 every year. However, two thirds of the population do not have these levels of income.

For redistribution of wealth, one idea that current and future Chancellors could consider is to gradually reduce over say ten years the tax relief on pension contributions over £3,600 a year, starting from the coming Budget on Wednesday.

Recently Office of Fair Trading raised concerns that more than £160 billion worth of savings may be held in poor value trust-based schemes. Also huge management charges are eroding the value of thousands of pension plans [Source: The FT].

2014
Multiculturalism and "The Euro Debate"

In the forthcoming debate between Nick Clegg and Nigel Farrage, they are going to "debate" about the need to replace multicultural identity with a British identity. The idea is to borrow from USA the concept of fusing various cultures and think of oneself as "British".

That cannot happen even if British citizens are given the first chance to fill a vacancy. Also being British means priority in many other areas. Generally non-citizen Europeans get more opportunities then even white as well as black and brown British citizens when the latter do not have the right "looks".

Unless the attitude of employers, both public sector and private sector is changed, the debate's idea will not work. Citizenship does not mean what it should like in the USA where all cultures get more opportunity provided they are citizens. Here, the concept is citizenship is not all that powerful.

In addition, when one takes the history of the Longbridge car manufacturing plant in the UK, the Rover Brand (British 1948-1978) collaborated with Honda (1979-1988) and was owned by BMW (1994-2000). There were cultural clashes and productivity went down.

Cultural clash between the British and Indians have worked better than Japanese, Chinese and German cultures. Making sense of multiculturalism can become making nonsense of multiculturalism.

Nagindas Khajuria FCCA
Simplification Made Simple, Chartered Certified Accountants, London

British Business is truly international

National Freight Corporation, British Gas, British Telecom, British Airways, British Rail, British Steel, ICI, Rolls Royce, P&O, Cadbury, Selfridges, Harrods, Gross-Rail, Bombardier, Tetley Tea, Rover, Jaguar, Li Ken Sheng, Autonomy, Sigma, Ford, Nissan, Toyota, Tata Steel, Tata Motors and many others are 40% to 100% owned by Americans, Canadians, Europeans, Japanese, Chinese, Indian, Qatari and many other nationals. Many Investment banks, Insurance companies, retail chains, etc. operating here are 40% of more owned by Americans, Europeans and others.

Many British companies like Unilever, Vodafone, Tesco, WWP, British Petroleum and others own and successfully operate hundreds of subsidiaries in over 70 countries.

Inward manufacturing industry not only creates jobs in that industry but further five jobs in the supply chain and logistics. Inward services industry investment again creates British jobs in those services plus further three jobs in the supply chain and logistics.

Britain Research and Development sector has some of the best British brains and benefits from technological advances developed elsewhere and brought into Britain. The British give their best to other countries.

Importing apples from New Zealand costs 50 times in CO_2 emissions than growing them here according to research published recently. Why not produce, import or export close to home?

Sterling has lost world trade transaction share from 30% to 4% now. Euro now has 30% share. Most exports from UK are quoted in US Dollars or Euro. Why not adopt US Dollar or Euro NOW?

My minority third view for Britain is to become price transparent by adopting the Euro as its currency.

Nagindas Khajuria FCCA
Simplification Made Simple, Chartered Certified Accountants, London

2014

Parties will soon publish their 2015 election manifestos

In 1949, the Conservative Party election manifesto was called "The Right Road for Britain".

It stated that services constituted a cooperative system of self-help provided by the whole nation and designated to give all the basic security of housing, of opportunity, of employment and of living standards below which our duty to one another forbids us to permit anyone to fail.

This Sunday, I was returning from a wedding reception venue in Bath Road, Hounslow. Apparently the owner had other 400 or so properties. Many landlords own anywhere between 100 and 200 residential properties while we daily debate in the media about the need to build more houses.

There is now a debate about inflated house prices and the next housing bubble to be bigger than the last one.

Equality in opportunity often does not result in equality in outcome. Many can only find part time employment. Million young people are unemployable.

Living standards are not all that great for many. Future governments need to work harder to ensure that growth and prosperity reaches a much bigger proportion of the nation as a whole.

The modern ideology is supremacy of the individual who is encouraged to look after himself only. It is time to think about others we have permitted to fail.

Nagindas Khajuria FCCA
Simplification Made Simple, Chartered Certified Accountants, London

2014
High speed 2 project

The High Speed 2 rail project bill is being proposed in Parliament and if approved, work on the London-Birmingham route will commence in 2017.

The next elected government in 2015 should seriously rethink the project. HS2 will save journey time to Birmingham by 33 minutes from the present 82 minutes. Contrast journey time from 300 km per hour to 30 km per hour within the city. One could easily waste these 33 minutes in traffic jams within the city.

The whole project is very costly environmentally and economically. HS2 will mostly be used by those in the 50% tax bracket. HS2 will only connect to 6% of the total number of 525 pair cities in the UK. It will be a motorway route, not a network.

The current high speed trains travelling at 125 km per hour and the new ones called Pendoleno are giving an excellent service. They are only being used at 50% capacity. The price structure is very confusing and/or very expensive at peak times. Why not spend money instead on improving the existing network operationally and subsidising fares so that they are used to full capacity?

HS2 benefits' inclusion of £36.96 per hour of costs saved by a railway passenger has been described as voodoo economics by 2016 London Mayoral hopeful Christian Wolmar in his article "What is the point of HS2?" [London Review of Books, p3, 17 April 2014].

Nagindas Khajuria FCCA
Simplification Made Simple, Chartered Certified Accountants, London

2014
Being Indian

The timing is right for a new beginning for India. The Muslims of India are different from the Muslims in other parts of the world. If you study carefully all the terrorism activities around the world over the past 50 years, you will come to a factual conclusion that Indian Muslims were not involved in most of them.

The Muslims invaded India in the 11th century. The British in the 17th century. Hindus remained a majority before then, during their rule and now. When the same people invaded Africa or other Asian nations, they managed to convert them to Islam or Christianity. Not in India.

Communal harmony in India has been the norm throughout centuries. It is not going to change now.

All Indians pursue the desire to work hard and progress in a true democracy that you are experiencing right now: 15% increase in turnout in the democratic elections compared to the last General Election.

It is expected that India will be the third largest economy in the world by 2028 after USA and China [Accounting and Business UK 02/2014, page 8, Trends].

Current widely publicized attempts to arouse communal disharmony will not work in India.

The factual history of relations between Hindus and Muslims is more fully described in "Being Indian – Inside the Real India" by Pavan K. Varma [pages 161–173] and "India – A Portrait" by Patrick French [pages 340–48].

Banias are interested in doing business with each other rather than killing each other.

2014
Nandan Nilekani of Infosys joins the race

Outsiders are joining long established insiders and are getting into politics. Nandan Nilekani is campaigning for Congress in Bangalore South. Meera Sanyal, former head of Royal Bank of Scotland's Indian operations is now a candidate for the AAP in Mumbai. Jayant Sinha, a Harvard Business School degree holder, a partner at McKinsey and now running Indian arm of a technology investment fund set up by eBay founder is running in Hazaribag, Jharkhand. He is also the son of Yashwant Sinha, former finance minister. So not an outsider. [FT Magazine, April 26/27, p14–17].

Roll back to April–May 2004 elections. 5,398 candidates from 220 political parties contested the same 543 parliamentary constituencies. Sonia Gandhi confounded political pundits by leading Congress Party to victory. 380 million people, representing about 56% of the 675 million registered, voters, exercised their preference using 1.25 million electronic voting machines in 700,000 polling booths across the country, the highest in Ladakh at an altitude of 5,180 metres. [Being Indian, Pavan Varma, p55, 2005].

One word to describe Narendra Modi is development. He could confound political pundits, by leading BJP to victory in April–May 2014 elections.

2014

High Speed 2
By Lord Dolar Popat Govt Spokesman for Transport House of Lords

Nagin Khajuria's letter [High Speed 2 project, 19th April 2014] suggested that the investment in HS2 could be better spend elsewhere. May I kindly suggest that he reconsider? Demand for rail travel had doubled in the last 20 years to 1.5 billion journeys a year. In addition, more and more freight is now being transported by rail. This means that parts of the West Coast Main Line–our nation's most important rail artery-are now effectively full in terms of the number of trains it can carry during peak times. Those who use the line regularly will already know that these trains are very busy at peak times, and this will only get worse without more rail capacity.

The construction of the M25, the Jubilee Line and High Speed 1 faced similar opposition at the time of their constructions, but it is inconceivable to think how we would survive without these infrastructure assets today. Essentially we rely on a Victorian railway and infrastructure investment is long overdue. The Government have looked at the alternatives; investment in electrification, extending platforms and lengthening trains is already happening. But these will not provide the massive increase in North-South rail capacity that our country desperately needs.

HS2 will link 8 out of Britain's 10 largest cities and deliver improved rail services to more than 100 cities and towns. This isn't just about London and Birmingham, but about delivering growth, jobs, connectivity and capacity across the country. Only HS2 can treble the number of seats leaving Euston at peak times. Yes it is an ambitious project, but it is also necessary to ensure we have a transport system suitable for the 21st century.

Nagindas Khajuria FCCA
Simplification Made Simple, Chartered Certified Accountants, London

2014

Arjuna's Chariot

After 40 years of almost uninterrupted rule by the Congress Party, India was ruled by BJP-led coalition from 1998. In 1990, L K Advani, atop a chariot, made his way through the crowds lined on both sides of the street; they cheered him wildly and covered him in garlands of white and yellow flowers.

In retrospect, his journey in an air-conditioned Toyota truck, decorated every inch as Arjuna's Chariot, explains what Hindus are. Mahabharata is much more than a legend or myth; it is a source of true knowledge and wisdom. History for Indians is not like history for Westerners, long gone and dead.

Hindutva is an all-embracing conception of India, which includes religion, nationalism and culture" [The Genius of India by Guy Sorman, MacMillan India Ltd 2001]. Time may be near for L K Advani to ride on such a chariot in 2014, 24 years later. "India is a nation of billion people. A nation's progress depends on how it's people think. It is thoughts which are transformed into actions" [India 2020 – A Vision for the New Millennium by A P J Abdul Kalam with Y S Rajan]. Thus India has to think now as a one nation of 1.3 billion people.

2014
Indian business acumen

Amul dairies: 173 milk producers' cooperatives and 22 federations supply pasteurised, packaged and branded milk to more than 1000 cities across the country. 11 million farmers earn more from what they produce (page 76).

Lijjat papadums, with 6 branches, employ 40,000 women and have over $60 million turnover.

Rag packers, hawkers, construction workers and slum-dwelling weavers were helped by Ela Bhatt to form Self-Employed Women's Association (SEWA). It has 71 cooperatives and 70,000 members. Among their many activities, it runs a very successful micro-finance bank.

Subhash Chandra who set up the first Hindi language satellite channel is now worth $2.5 billion dollars.

Karsanbhai Patel started making detergents in his back yard and made Nirma one of the world's largest-selling detergent powders. Karsanbhai inspired C K Ranganathan to sell shampoo in sachets at 1 Rupee per piece. It now has a turnover of $40 million. Naresh Goyal was an employee of Lebanon International Airlines, Jordanian, and Philippine national Airlines. Now his creation Jet Airways increased its gross revenue from $43 million to $500 million in less than a decade. 5,000 dabawallas deliver 150,000 lunch boxes to offices in Mumbai. Only one mistake occurs in 8 million transactions. Turnover is $ 20 million, earning them $100 each. (Being Indian by Pavan K Varma pages 75–90).

There are hundreds more. Most started from humble background. If elected with a firm majority, the BJP party must nurture thousands of small scale industries (SSI) by international standards. If it falls prey to takeovers by multinationals, it will destroy the creativity, enthusiasm and entrepreneur spirit of millions of Indians.

2014
Lost opportunity

The recent victory of BJP made me wonder about events in my adopted country. It has been governed by 5 British Prime Ministers. Margaret Thatcher (11 years); John Major (6 years); Tony Blair (9 years); Gordon Brown (2 years) and David Cameroon (4 years). This is a total of 32 years.

The decade started by privatisation of many publicly owned utility, transportation and other monopoly enterprises to promote competition in the belief that it would result in better quality services at lower costs. In the second decade, liberalisation was followed by further deregulation. One example is deregulation of financial services such as banking, insurance, mortgages, loans and pensions. In the last decades, deregulation was followed by re-regulation and stricter supervision by public sector watchdogs including the financial sector.

BJP should plan 30 years ahead and take the losing parties in confidence in a 30-year plan. Five year plans are no longer relevant. That would ensure that egos, rivalries and political squabbling over ideologies do not make any political party not see the wood for the tree.

Nagindas Khajuria FCCA
Simplification Made Simple. Chartered Certified Accountants, London

2014
SAARC invite

SAARC, or South Asian Association of Regional Cooperation can start now. Culturally the 8 countries have a lot in common.

Two vital areas of comparative advantage and transfer of technical know how include imports and infant industries: Imports from far away countries can be substituted by imports from those closer. Infant industries could be gradually mentored and funded to become mature industries and substitute imports. Same goes for exports.

Each country has its own strengths and skills. Even within each country, the internal provinces or states again have unique human skills. It is time to open up and share knowledge instead of keeping them secret.

Some countries in the EU, even now, use their own currencies such as Florin domestically as well as the Euro for bigger transactions. I witnessed that in Budapest while on holidays there last year. The exchange rate differential between buying and selling rates in relatively small economies within SAARC can take up a big chunk in transaction costs.

May God bless our new Prime Minister to have started this new initiative. I did try to meet Mr Modi about five years ago. I waited on the second floor of their party headquarters. His right hand man saw us. I had come with my first cousin whose father had founded Virani High School in Rajkot 70 years ago. We discussed ID cards. May be we can have biometric SAARC ID cards for a start.

Nagindas Khajuria FCCA
Simplification Made Simple, Chartered Certified Accountants, London

2014

Europe

A Belgian, a Frenchman, a German and a Luxembourg person are now competing for the post of the job of the President of 28-country EU. Four more countries, Turkey, Serbia, Ukraine and one other waiting to join.

The EU has a very rich heritage of diverse cultures, languages, and much more. It is a continent that makes up only 7% of the world's land surface. Its population of 506 million people is also 7% of world population. Yet it has a GDP of $17 trillion: 33% of world GDP.

Romania was admitted to the EU in 2007. For years, people from France, Britain, Germany, Switzerland, Australia and Spain have been buying huge parcels of agricultural land in Romania. This has resulted in a green revolution there.

True there is some begging, some organised crime and gangs across Europe. However, most Romanians are hard working. They enjoy good life. There is reverse migration, 15,000 Italians live in Timisoara alone. They have created 3,000 companies in a city of 400,000 inhabitants.

The US alone has a GDP of $17 trillion. That is why the UK continues to remain it's staunch ally at the expense of its own political freedom. USA is in the process forming an economic pact with Europe.

The third dimension to the UK EU referendum debate is not just in or out, but rather with joining the Euro also if it is in especially if UK does not want to continue as US poodle.

2014

School education

In the 1960s and 1970s, most grammar schools and secondary schools were replaced by comprehensive schools. In total there are 20,000 schools.

The concept of "academies" was introduced very recently. In 2010 there were only 200 academies. By March 2012 the number rose to 1,635 academies. Another concept is "free schools". These were introduced as an extension of the Academies Programme and are still funded by the government but not controlled by the local authority and may be set up by parents, teachers, charities and businesses.

A series of reports by the schools inspectorate into 21 Birmingham schools found an atmosphere of intimidation, a narrow faith based ideology, manipulation of staff appointments and inappropriate use of school funds.

Academies elsewhere also had problems. Aldhelm's Academy was conned out of more than £1 million in a simple email fraud.

E-ACT runs 31 state-funded free-schools and academies around England that have opted out of local authority control.

The Education Funding Agency report highlighted a culture of "extravagant" expenses, "prestige" venues and first class travel at the E-ACT group.

The OECD report on school performance league tables among 65 most advanced countries found that UK had fallen from 4th to 14th in Science, 7th to 17th in Literacy and 8th to 24th in Mathematics between 2000 and 2006. By 2010, it had fallen further in Maths to 26th and in Literacy to 25th.

Academies and free schools concept is flawed and not an answer to incompetence in teaching and learning methodologies.

Football in India
2014

I read with great interest in the Asian Voice on Modi being invited to watch the World Cup final in Brazil. For 70 years, just under 2 billion people in the Indian sub-continent have either played cricket or watched cricket.

Football is a much faster moving game than cricket where all the 22 players are fully energized for ninety minutes. Each player has to run like an athlete in splendid coordination and teamwork with great stamina. It is very sad that the SAARC countries have not encouraged football for the past 70 years.

I would urge Mr Modi to attend this event to give football the boost it needs in India. The final is two days before the BRIC summit in Brazil. It is time to begin to teach football to Indian children from age 6 in every city and ever village. They will also benefit from physical exercise.

The Purchasing Power Parity GDP, that takes differences in living costs in account, in the four BRIC countries in billions of US Dollars is: India: 5,000; China 13,400; Russia 2,600 and Brazil 2,400 billion US Dollars. A combined BRIC PPP GDP of US$ 23,400 billion. World PPP GDP is US$ 86,000. So BRIC's share of world PPP GDP is just over 25%.

With such economic clout, one urgent matter the BRIC countries could discuss is an exchange rate snake system similar to the pre-Euro system in Europe where exchange rates between member countries were not allowed to fluctuate more the 2.5 percent.

Nagindas Khajuria FCCA
Simplification Made Simple, Chartered Certified Accountants, London

2014

D-Day 70th Anniversary: Rejoice or Regret?

It was 6th June 1944 when Allied Forces landed on the beaches of Normandy, France. General Dwight D Eisenhower was selected as the Supreme Commander. In the Far East, Japan had invaded China in 1937. The US had declared war against Japan to protect their interests in that region. Japan's allies' Germany and Italy had declared war on the US. This bitter fighting carried on until 1945.

The US dropped two atomic bombs on Hiroshima and Nagasaki on 6 and 9 August 1945. In World War I [1914–18], there were 6 million casualties and 12 million injured, leaving 3 million widows and millions of children living without fathers or with injured fathers. In World War II [1939–1945] altogether there were 30 million casualties. That would have probably resulted in another 15 million injured and left 15 million widows and 30 million children growing up without fathers.

Historically, over the almost 50 years I have lived in London, I continuously see coverage of sacrifices and heroism to save the world from oppressors by legal and illegal invasions of other countries. When soldiers, some with severe injuries come home or their bodies or injured bodies are flown back, there is praise for the sacrifices and heroism. Apart from the soldiers, the bravery also comes from sophisticated weaponry and safety gear worn in land, sea and air attacks and recently by use of drones. It is time to forget the past and live in the present.

Nagindas Khajuria FCCA
Simplification Made Simple, Chartered Certified Accountants, London

2014
Doing things mindfully

While eating, if we chew slowly and concentrate on what we are eating rather than allowing our mind to let other thoughts coming in, we would enjoy that food more and digest it better.

Jon Kabat-Zinn, a MIT- educated scientist has developed a curriculum called Mindful Based Stress Reduction. There are now 1000 certified MBSR instructors in every US State and 30 countries.

He maintains how hard it has become to think about just one thing at a time. Busy mind is multi-tasking with technology gadgets.

There is constant struggle between distraction and mindfulness. The MBSR class meets every Monday evening for eight weeks and costs $350 per person. 477 scientific journal articles were published in 2012.

Source: The Mindful Revolution – the science of finding focus in a stressed out, multitasking culture by Kate Pickert. (Time magazine, 3 Feb 2014, p38–41).

I have practiced Yoga and Meditation for 35 years. MBSR is mostly same. Credit goes to my wife and daughter, both BW of Yoga qualified teachers (www.yogawithsejel.co.uk).

The great sage Patanjali (c 300 BC) composed a book called Yoga Sutras from ancient traditions going back 6000 years before him. It described eight levels of attainment: Yama; Niyama; Asana; Pranayana; Pralyahara; Dharana (think of one thing at a time); Dhyana (meditation); and Samadhi. No credit given to him and Hinduism.

There is no thought on this planet that has not passed through an Indian mind. Sadly those minds are not given credit in history in the making now.

Nagindas Khajuria FCCA
Simplification Made Simple, Chartered Certified Accountants, London

2014
ISIS

According to the Penguin India Reference Book 2005, page 321, Shia Muslims in Iraq were 60%–65% and Sunni Muslims were 32%–37%. Christians and others were 3%, while Muslims were 97%.

Bryan Walsh writes in Time magazine double issue July 7/July 14, 2014 on page 23 his viewpoint "Blood for Oil— If the violence in Iraq spins out of control, global crude prices could skyrocket....if Washington can't help Baghdad stop ISIS now, oil will be a casualty.

Mr Walsh also states that nearly all of Iraq's oil fields and infrastructure are in the predominantly Shi'ite south, far from the fighting.

It is quite conceivable that Shia Muslim controlled government have not given sufficient attention to the Sunni minority population in the past. The civilized countries in the world appear to worry more about price of crude oil rather than the researching into the demographics of a sovereign state.

In Sudan, as the oil was mainly in the South, the West helped to split the country in two: North Sudan and South Sudan. These two separate nations are worse off now than when they were as one nation.

Just because oil in Iraq is in the South and the Shias live mostly in the South, the West should not ignore the rights of the Sunnis who (by deduction) must mainly be in the North. After all, they are almost 40% of the population.

Nagindas Khajuria FCCA
Simplification Made Simple, Chartered Certified Accountants, London

2014
'Life'–a project for the not-so-fortunate

Your article (AV 5 July p25) on 'Life' a charity with headquarters in Rajkot was very interesting.

The photo of the six-storey HQ building shown in your magazine is structurally and architecturally truly a state-of-the-art construction and the view from its roof terrace of the Race Course in Rajkot is stunning.

Your article quotes statistics over the past 30 years: Life's has distributed 59,000 units of blood or blood components; carried out 624,000 screenings for thalassaemia; assisted in building 2,200 homes for the homeless in Mumbai; donated sewing machines and given IT training to 4,500 widows; planted 243,000 trees from seedlings and donated them when they reach 10 feet; built 65 modern primary schools and 5 health centres in 70 villages in Gujarat.

During my trips to Rajkot over 15 years, the officials took me to several villages to see the schools; experience yoga; visit the Blood Bank building; visit the trees plantation project and critically review their audited accounts. Their modus operandi is to involve the villagers themselves; the donors; the State government; and the Central Government. That way not only larger pools of funds are generated, but also there is expertise, coordination and understanding at entire country level.

I would encourage parents to send their children during summer holidays to visit an NGO such as 'Life' in Rajkot or 'Anarde' in Mumbai that have been running with total dedication and professionalism. The trustees would make their stay and visit most enjoyable and educational.

Nagindas Khajuria FCCA
Simplification Made Simple, Chartered Certified Accountants, London

2014
Footpaths, pedestrian crossings, bicycle lanes and public toilets

I visit cities in India often. People going about their business, young and old, hardly walk. They travel in motor cycles, cars or three wheelers. Traffic flows in complete chaos and costs the country in poor physical health, in Co_2 emissions costs and unaffordable oil imports costs.

The latest Union Budget has rightly allocated funds and/or changed rules to attract privatisation, public private partnerships, facilitated foreign companies and governments FDI and FII investments to improve the country's infrastructure in railways, roads and air travel.

However, urban planning also urgently requires better footpaths, pedestrian crossings, bicycle lanes and public toilets to improve the quality of life in every city.

Technology is likely to develop further in the field of communications by video conferencing so that travel will be less necessary.

Births per thousand in India is 22 compared to 13 in China. The population is more or less the same now at 1.3bn and 1.14bn. The density of population in India per square kilometre is far higher than China. Even though life expectancy in India is 65 compared to 74 in China, population is likely to grow faster in India. Cities will become even more congested.

Slow and steady progress, step by step, in wider aspects of daily life could be the long term answer rather than faster progress in some areas and neglect in others equally important.

Bring back the bicycle to India for much wider short term travel rather than the scooter [with bicycle lanes].

Nagindas Khajuria FCCA
Simplification Made Simple, Chartered Certified Accountants, London

About the Author

I have known Nagindas for more than 32 years. When I first met him in the early 1980's I was a newly qualified accountant, and Nagindas had already been in practice for more than 15 years. At the time he had just returned from a stint of work in the Middle East, and since I was contemplating going to the Middle East for work also, he was a source of much advice and guidance, and indeed, he was a kind of role model to me—he inspired me to achieve his level of attainment.

Since I returned to the UK in the early 2000's, Nagindas has acted as my accountant (as I have moved away from the world of accounting and auditing). The last 15 years has been the time when I have come to know Nagindas at a much closer, professional and personal, level. Professionally, I would say that he is a competent and thorough accountant with integrity and always has the best interests of his clients at heart. I have found that he does not panic in crisis situations—his approach to crisis management is to always act in a cool and calm manner. On any particular aspect involving accounting, auditing or taxation matter, he first develops deep understanding of the subject matter—he does not comment until he has all the facts—and when he does, he goes to the "crux of the matter"—this is reflected in one of the companies he has set up.

At a personal level—Nagindas is approachable and jovial—and humorous at times—many a times I can think of examples where his particular take on a matter was accompanied by humorous anecdotes which made a lot of sense and captured the essence of the subject or idea being discussed. I personally think this is reflected in some of the 'Letters to the Editor' that he has written to newspapers over the last decade and a half.

S. K.
Markets and International Banking
Royal Bank of Scotland

Index

Accountancy

All Greek to me	49
All the same under the skin [Six Accountancy Bodies in UK]	4
Branching into quality	7
Conflict Zone	38
Rethink merger approval	86
Separate Ways [The Big Five Accountancy Firms]	16
Shaken but not stirred: Mrs Doyle's substitute - James Bond - etc	15
Stretching a point [Extend public funds audit to private co recipients]	16
The all new FRSSE [Financial Reporting Standards for SMEs]	27
The end of Chinese Walls	3
The real objective	51
The shorter and simpler the better	71
Time for a rethink	18
Too many hats: accountancy firms should wear fewer hats	42

British Politics

2013 - My 40th anniversary to have become a UK citizen	198
A tribute to Nelson Mandela	223
A Woolf in Sheep's Clothing?	129
Are politicians opportunists?	130

AV Voting System in Action	142
Blaming the Moguls or the British	228
Britain is no longer a country of choice for immigrants	211
British Afro-Asian Party Independents [BAAPI]	127
Ditch the US link	41
Elections: an unbiased view	138
Evolution of the British Legal System (part one)	217
Evolution of the British Legal System (part two)	218
Gordon Brown - is he a Charlie?	79
How do you solve a problem like this?	125
Michael Martin: a persona non-grata?	126
Monarchy Parliament Civil Society Landed Gentry and Working Class	202
MP Pay Reform	125
Obama cites Mahatma Gandhi to back his call for change	103
Official records	190
Olympics in Politics	189
Parties will soon publish their 2015 election manifestos	234
The Alternative Vote Referendum	161
The Metropolitan Police Service and The Metropolitan Authority	169
The Metropolitan Police	170
The New Tory Party	204
The Political Conference "Question Time"	136
Time to abandon Britain's CCTV Policing	171
Tories need to concentrate on substance	40
Where do we stand? Thinking Aloud	105
Yes (Prime) Minister	128

Economics

Anarchy in the Global Economy	172
Cuts - Ready Steady Go - Cart before Horse?	143
Female quotas would target the wrong women	155
Great idea	26
If it ain't broke…	140
International Finance is master and real economy is prisoner	187
Jawaharlal Nehru and his contributions [I met him in 1957]	131
Living beyond ones means	139
Lost opportunity	241
Mortgage debt could be tied to maintenance	35
Quantitative Easing	144
Strategies and issues of corruption	160
Tackling Naxalite Violence	135
The Female Factor	156
The Global Financial Crisis [1971 Nixon abandoned Gold Standard]	111
The Global Food System	164
The System and Systemic Failure [no drinking water in supermarkets]	123

Education

Asian school governors underrepresented	124
Educating Britain	50
Education	36
Further and Higher Education—England	151
Improving the education system in UK	149

Mind the gap on universities' tuition fees [16–24 year olds]	23
School education	244
Value of degrees in today's workplace [sometimes zero]	24

Enterprise

A powerful message	54
Animal spirit of capitalism	195
Are the right checks and balances in place?	55
Bad Commercial decision by Royal Bank of Scotland	162
Banking	42
Banks are agents, not principals	186
Boris Johnson's speech by Kevin Khajuria	222
Bradford & Bingley Bank nationalisation confirmed	101
Caveat emptor [Let buyer be ware]	47
Competence of non-executive directors & planned review	23
Enterprise is held back [taxation of personal service cos.]	7
Fingers in too many pies [Executive & Non-Exec Directors]	22
General Motors decline	129
German traditions compared to British	213
Keep cool for best results by Dr Rajesh Khajuria	9
Look at the bigger picture [BMW bought Rover for £800m]	4
New Labour does get IT right most time	45
Nothing right [Big Brother and the art of EU double speak]	43
Pensions dilemma [Mark to market valuation flawed]	24
PM Cameroon, cap in hand, in China	224
Rover was not about numbers	46

Environment and Climate Change

Breakthrough in global warming	64
Ganga gets a tag	109
Ganga now a deadly source of cancer	192
Hindu Forum needs to rethink appeal to save Shambo [cow]	59
Rest periods for cows	126

European Union

Accentuate the positive aspects of the euro	25
"Alice in euro land" by M Fitzpatrick. Tenon Group, E C 1	26
Airbus wins	43
Back Chat	31
Banking Regulation	182
Britain and the euro - leaders of the pack or out in the cold?	10
British Business is truly international	233
Euro issue cannot be forced	29
Europe	243
European Union Time Line	180
High price of euro [1-5 para by Cliff Redman, Worthng] [6th para by David Ball, Newham]	32
Is UK serious about economic growth?	174
Multiculturalism and "The Euro Debate"	232
Put an end to jingoism [Brits are over-nationalistic]	12
"Rose-tinted view of EU" by John Broughton, Ruthun	30
Significant developments of the 20th century	205
Special relationship with USA	193

Staying in control	13
The known unknown	175
The Vision of Europe	178
Tongue firmly in his cheek by J E Francis, Loxley	13
We need full euro debate by Geoff Wood, Marlow	11

Fiscal Policy

Are we too stubborn to move forward?	8
Beyond our means [Japan, Germany, France lower deficit]	28
Cable's war on 'shady' tax havens	191
Can higher taxes solve the budget deficit?	138
Fiscal Budget	208
Foreign Account Tax Compliance Act [FATCA]	166
Hidden economy in the UK	165
Keep it simple	37
No government should play tax or race card	17
Not the time for tax rises [Ken Clarke's debut Budget 1993]	21
Pension planning	231
Shaken but not stirred [HMRC lost billions in IT contracts]	15
Statistics rethink [Chain weighting to measure output/growth]	22
The British Budget	199
What a Waste [Anne Redston at Ernst & Young article]	39

Indian Business

Accountancy news	215
Angry India moves to patent yoga poses	121

Corruption is India's scourge	148
Does BPJ need to rethink its policy on Andhra Pradesh?	209
Does practice of Yoga lead to Hinduism?	181
Doing things mindfully	247
Economic downturn an invitation to innovate [Indian households]	118
Gujarat ranks 5th or 6th overall [compared to Punjab, Kerala, etc]	120
India taxes reform debate	226
India to host International Accounting meet in mid-Jan 2009	118
Indian business acumen	240
Indian saris	168
Is steam Yoga substantial enough to warrant a patent?	63
Jawaharlal Nehru and his contributions	131
Life'—a project for the not-so-fortunate	249
Men inflicting violence is old story	56
Narendra Modi as a manager rather than a leader	220
Nehru and Hindi	132
Non-Violence versus Military Interventions on Valentine's Day	196
Olympics in World Financial System	188
Saris and today's women by Jayesh A Patel	169
Secularism & Politics	210
Supreme Court asks Vodafone to respond to Tax Authorities	119
UK India Special Relationship	197
Young Asians lack experience	58

Indian Politics

Ambani brothers at war again	81
Arjuna's Chariot	239

Being Indian	236
Common thread of violent deeds and instigations	97
Deal Wins [Indo-American Nuclear Accord ratified by Parliament]	93
Does money talk in elections?	122
Experience speaks for itself	54
Facts about ethnic minorities	60
Family Planning	158
G20 Finance Ministers Summit	122
Immigration red herring	53
India needs to pay more attention to agriculture	142
India-Pakistan: Hope springs eternal	113
Indo-American nuclear accord a landmark deal	66
Industrial Output in India dips for the first time in 15 years	117
Israel at 60 [India should foster stronger ties with Israel]	75
Land of Amarnath Yatries triggers political tremors	87
Milestones in India's recent history	183
Nandan Nilekani of Infosys joins the race	237
President Medvedev comes calling	115
SAARC invite	242
Scheduled Castes and Scheduled Tribes	173
Secularism & Politics	210
Tackling Naxalite Violence	135
The 15th General Election in India	120
The Rape of Tibet	71
Vote of confidence to decide UPA's fate	91
What is Britishness?	124
World markets on roller coaster—India sits pretty	99

Inequality

£1 billion package for UK housing industry	95
Africa's real problem	48
Bias towards India in the Western media	107
Buying a house	219
German central bank's gold reserves and Africa?	194
Inequality is unfair	153
Is the UK taxation system fair?	141
Marks & Spencer & HSBC link up to open retail banks	185
Pension planning	231
Poverty in the UK	201
Tax evasion: Sounds familiar?	225
Tax targets	40
Work-life balance	44

Monetary Policy

Bank of England, Treasury and Financial Services Authority	123
Encouraging savings	3
Exchange Rate–Business Letter [Geoffrey Dicks article]	14
Get Real [MPC's dilemma interest rate higher than inflation]	18
Give Mervyn growth and unemployment too	33
Giving Bank of England more powers is a bad idea	167
Help to Buy or Help to Cry?	212
Inflation, unemployment, interest rate and Sterling	127
Interest dilemma–MEP Member against rate increase	20
Public mood is changing	200
Scary Pound [Commenting on David Smith's Economic Outlook]	19

National Health Service

£160,000,000 to each of 500 GP Consortiums	152
60 years of NHS	89
American invasion leads to a less productive workforce	9
Asian food	207
"Astonishing Read" by James Percival	36
Dismantling the NHS programme for IT	176
Forecast increase in both healthcare demand and supply	153
GP Visits	137
How has NHS evolved over the years	140
How to Run Hospitals successfully	146
"In it ain't broke, don't fix it"	68
Improving NHS	163
National Insurance Planned Increase in 2011	137
NHS–Last Family Silver Remaining	159
"Paying for GP is not practical" by Kevin Olney, Coventry	34
Sharing the care for mentally ill patients	52
Sugar produces salt in the body	227
The heart of the matter	229
The Human Body	179
Trying to book an appointment with your doctor?	33
Understanding the human mind	154
Vegetarianism, protein and climate change	134
Why is our NHS such a mess?	119

Sports

Chickens, drugs and football	150
Football in India	245

Midland Voice by Dee Katwa	177
The Good Maharaja: a tale of compassion and humanity	206
The Raisôn d'être of Bollywood [Observer article]	62
World Cup 2010 in South Africa	136

Transport

Footpaths, pedestrian crossings, bicycle lanes and public toilets	250
Get London Moving [motor traffic congestion is getting worse]	5
Hidden costs by Simon Eakin, London N1	15
High Speed 2 By Lord Dolar Popat Govt Spokesman for Transport House of Lords	238
High Speed 2 project	235
Indian Railways under Lalu Prasad	121
London needs a more visionary town planner	203
MP Pay Reform	125
Off the rails [Privatisation of British Rail]	14
Poor Management of London Underground Upgrading	128
Train spotters know best [British Rail was undervalued when privatised]	6

Wars

Afghanistan elections	130
All too easy to feed anti-American mood	27
Anarchy in the Global Economy	172
Blind terror [How to fight the new terrorism]	41
Chillcot Iraq War Inquiry	154
Darfur crisis	229
D-Day 70th Anniversary: Rejoice or Regret?	246
Divide and rule policy in Sudan for oil and gas scrample	145

High petrol prices	76
ISIS	248
Israel continues strikes on Gaza	117
John Fitzgerald Kennedy's legacy	221
Military invasions	135
Multiculturalism among Afghanistan and its borders	133
Muslims on the Move	157
Nuke Deal Jitters	83
"Ostrich among us" by Bhupendra Gandhi on Nagin Letter	145
Should use of chemical weapons be a game change?	214
Special relationship with USA	183
Syria reminds me of King Asoka and Kautalya	216
Tension in Darfur and its relevance to oil supplies	70
UK India Special Relationship	197
Ukraine and the Crimean Region	230
United Nations Organization	184
Why do people resort to violence?	65
Will oil result in strife?	57
World citizen	147